ADVICE,
A HIGH PROFIT
BUSINESS

ADVICE, A HIGH PROFIT BUSINESS:

A guide for consultants and other entrepreneurs

HERMAN HOLTZ

PRENTICE-HALL
Englewood Cliffs, New Jersey 07632

Library of Congress Cataloging-in-Publication Data

Holtz, Herman.
    Advice, a high profit business.

    Includes index.
    1. Consultants—Marketing. 2. Information
services—Marketing. I. Title.
HD69.C6H618 1986   658.4′6′0688   85-24405
ISBN 0-13-011958-X

Editorial/production supervision
    and interior design: Allison DeFren
Cover design: Wanda Lubelska Design
Cover photos: Courtesy of BASF Systems Corp.,
    Micro DataBase Systems, Inc., and Western Electric
Manufacturing buyer: Ed O'Dougherty

© 1986 by Herman Holtz

Printed in the United States of America

10 9 8 7 6 5 4 3 2 1

ISBN 0-13-011958-X 01

Prentice-Hall International (UK) Limited, *London*
Prentice-Hall of Australia Pty. Limited, *Sydney*
Prentice-Hall Canada Inc., *Toronto*
Prentice-Hall Hispanoamericana, S.A., *Mexico*
Prentice-Hall of India Private Limited, *New Delhi*
Prentice-Hall of Japan, Inc., *Tokyo*
Prentice-Hall of Southeast Asia Pte. Ltd., *Singapore*
Editora Prentice-Hall do Brasil, Ltda., *Rio de Janeiro*
Whitehall Books Limited, *Wellington, New Zealand*

2285735

CONTENTS

Preface

A former neighbor of mine, who drove a truck for a supermarket chain, was given to describing himself as being "in food distribution." In so doing, he joined the ranks of undertakers called *morticians,* garbage collectors called *sanitation specialists,* and janitors called *custodians* or *sanitary engineers.* The urge to find euphemisms to describe one's job is not limited to blue-collar workers, as technical writers called *documentation specialists* and "job shoppers" (free-lancers), who sell themselves as *consultants,* will tell you.

Dignifying one's occupation by changing its nomenclature is not all vanity or face saving. To at least some degree, it is an attempt at dealing with today's prejudice that everyone should be a specialist. Much of the specialization mania of this era is the result of advancing technology and the complexities created by it.

Living in society has, in general, become more complicated. Before World War II, a relative handful of Americans were required to make out income tax returns every year. Today, only a relative handful are exempt from the requirement. At that time, only a handful of executives and professionals needed to have something called a *resumé* when they were out job-seeking. Today, there are few jobs that do not require one. At that time, household products were more simple and less expensive. If a 39-cent potato parer broke, you could afford to throw it away. Today, you can hardly do that with your $90 food processor. If it proves defective, you must go back to the dealer you bought it from, hoping to find him or her still in business. Even if the dealership still exists, you might have trouble getting satisfaction. Sometimes you can't even discover the address of the manufacturer because it's a company owned by another company, and you don't know how to research the matter.

Government agencies have been established because of these and other problems of modern living. The Consumer Product Safety Commission warns the public against toys and other products considered unsafe for one reason or another. The Pension Benefit Guaranty Corporation tries to protect the worker against loss of pensions resulting from bankruptcies and other business disasters. The Federal Trade Commission, the Federal Communications Commission, the Federal Aviation Administration, the Securities and Exchange Commission, and many other federal, state, and local government agencies and bureaus are involved in some manner with furnishing services and protection to the public. However, even finding the right agency can be confusing.

Small wonder that the average individual gets a headache when he or she is faced with some of our modern problems—making investments, deciding on a major appliance purchase, trying to get a complaint adjusted, trying to find the right government office or coping with ever-expanding bureaucracy in general, writing a good resume, deciding whether or not to buy a microcomputer and, if so, which one is best, and literally hundreds of other modern problems. *Modern* because many—perhaps even most—of these problems did not exist a half-century ago.

How do we cope? We cope sometimes by enduring the problem and simply throwing up our hands. For example, we simply throw out an expensive appliance or pay an exorbitant price to have it repaired, after trying, in vain, to find the dealer or manufacturer and get the guarantee made good. Or we don't pursue the tax refund we believe is due.

Some of us cope by reading such books as Ralph Charrell's *How I Turn Ordinary Complaints into Thousands of Dollars,* in which the author furnishes instructions on how to cope successfully with some of our modern frustrations. Or we read books on investment by such best-selling authors as Douglas Casey, author of *Crisis Investing*. (Of the 40,000 new books published annually, more than one-half are non-fiction, and some considerable proportion of those are of the "how to" and advice-giving categories.)

Some of us cope by subscribing to one or more of the estimated 30,000 newsletters published in the United States, of which quite a large percentage are unabashedly of the advice-giving genre, on marketing, investing, collecting antiques, numismatics, and hordes of other topics.

Many turn to radio and TV call-in talk shows, where they can get advice from the broadcaster. For example, one TV broadcaster, Paul Berry (ABC Channel 7, WJLA, Washington, DC), pursues problems for his viewers and reports them over the air, after they have been solved. He gets people refunds that are due, helps them get their complaints adjusted, finds bureaus for them, and does many things that they cannot manage for themselves.

And, finally, many cope by hiring a specialist, usually on a fee basis, to help them write resumes, plan stock portfolios, organize an office, design a plant, figure out a tax return, and otherwise apply some special expertise as an investment counselor, writer, procedures specialist, or other type of consultant.

Where once the bulk of advice-giving for fees was the province of lawyers, physicians, and a few other professional specialists, today there are many kinds of specialists who sell advice. There are newsletter publishers, columnists, broadcasters, consultants, and service specialists of many other kinds and categories whose fields are, generally, selling advice. In some cases, the advice is totally general, offered to a whole class of people; in other cases, it is specific, directed at individuals on an individual basis. And there are some advice-sellers who do both.

It has been observed, especially by some recent forecasters of overall social and economic trends, that American industry is likely to change drastically in the soon-to-arrive future, from one dominant in heavy industries to one dominant in information industries. There is, of course, close linkage between the information business and the advice business. In fact, in some respects it is difficult to distinguish one from the other, since the seller of advice bases that advice on the possession of specialized information and includes at least some of that information in the advice given.

Advice, A High Profit Business is geared to people who wish to profit from the ever-expanding pool of opportunities to satisfy the constantly growing hunger for information. In the pages to come we will discuss not only how to package advice, but also how to market it. Marketing means doing whatever is necessary to find the right prospects and persuading them to buy. And that is what any enterprise is all about, is it not?

Herman Holtz
Silver Spring, Maryland

Chapter 1

What Is "The Advice Business?"

A fool sometimes gives weighty advice. —Nicholas Boileau

LIKE QUICKSILVER, THE DEFINITION
IS HARD TO CAPTURE

Selling advice is not a business per se. Just imagine hanging out a shingle that says ADVICE: ONE FLIGHT UP. Or running a Yellow Pages advertisement that says: *Dr. Smith's Advice Service, Hours 9 to 5. Reasonable Rates.* Or fighting competitors by claiming that your advice is better than anyone else's.

Yet advice is a salable item, and it is the essence of a great many successful enterprises. It is among the most valuable commodities sold by doctors and lawyers, by consultants, and by many others. It is sold by direct personal contact, by the printed word, on radio and TV, to individuals on an individual basis and to individuals on a group basis.

The term *advice business* is a general designator that puts a finger on the *sine qua non* of various enterprises, on what the enterprises are all about, on what is a common denominator among them. This is not unprecedented: Druggists, physicians, dentists, and manufacturers and vendors of prosthetic appliances and a vast variety of related goods and services can all be said to be in the *health* field. (It is somehow unacceptable to call the maintenance of health a business, so most professionals prefer to refer to it as a *field* or *profession,* to avoid the stigma of associating anything as crass as profit with people's health.) Whatever you choose to call it, it encompasses many enterprises and professions, and a great many of these depend to at least some extent on the furnishing of advice.

Of course, this is not confined to the health field, but is true for a great many general fields of trade and commerce which can be characterized by a single, catch-all term, such as these few examples:

Transportation	Construction
Publishing	Entertainment
Clothing	Leisure
Food	Distribution

As in the health field, each of these terms suggests many individual enterprises. *Transportation,* for example, includes trucking companies (from the largest to the individual owner-operator), railroads, airlines, bus lines, and sundry other modes of physical transport. But it also covers a variety of publications devoted to transportation activities and enterprises. It also includes a variety of other functions and enterprises —for example, brokers and agents, who are specialists in transportation and advice, and who make specific arrangements for transport and travel services, taking their profits as middlemen. Advice is very much a part of the service offered by such agents, but there are also travel and transport consultants whose service to clients is primarily the furnishing of guidance (i.e., advice).

In most fields today there are similar situations, wherein many of the enterprises within those fields include the furnishing of advice or guidance, and some consist almost entirely of advisory services. As complex as our world and society are today, it is difficult to find any field in which there are not many specialists whose occupations are based on guiding those less knowledgeable about that field. Some of these are older, long-established fields, such as entertainment and advertising; others are newer, such as those that deal with computers and data processing. And in some cases the field is a hybrid, such as computers *and* entertainment—video games, special effects on TV and in moviemaking, and sundry other such applications of computers to entertainment projects. In short, it is not only high-technology enterprises that entail the selling of advice, but also the older industries. However, quite often it is an older industry to which new technology is being applied that requires the services of specialists.

So the term *advice business* applies to a wide variety of enterprises that incorporate advice giving or some type of advisory service as a basis of the enterprise. Some of those enterprises were suggested in the Preface and included newsletter publishing, consulting, counseling, résumé writing, and several other specialized services. Advice is offered in lectures and seminars, over the airwaves, in personal consultation, and by other means and media. Specialists are known by a variety of names, some linked closely to the specific field of advice, others more general: investment counselor, management consultant, educational specialist, training technologist, information systems analyst, software developer, computer designer, traffic analyst, and on and on. Some do not identify themselves but only the services they offer, which are based solely or in part on advice. They offer to do such things as manage your portfolio, guide you in your job hunt and résumé writing (and may write your résumé for you, but even that is done by working quite closely with you), show you how to organize your doctoral dissertation, help you select the right computer for your needs, organize your office force and procedures, and otherwise guide you in doing things that require expert knowledge.

It may have occurred to you that selling advice is not an enterprise existing in isolation from others. That is, advice giving is not akin to an isolated spot in the midst of a larger field, but is often simply a subset of that field. There are, for example, periodicals, agents, brokers, consultants, and other information- and advice-oriented undertakings in and about almost every field known—restaurants, energy, jewelry, mining, export-import, farming, office supplies, government, and whatever else keeps human beings occupied. There are seminars, newsletters, magazines, news tabloids, conferences, conventions, trade shows, exhibits, displays, and other methods of offering information and advice.

But the lines of demarcation are often blurred and frequently do not exist at all. Drugstores sell food items, and food stores sell drug items, department stores sell automobile tires, and gasoline service stations have coin-operated copying machines, while bookstores sell gift items, and gift shops sell virtually anything.

So it is not at all easy to define the advice business. Yet it exists; it is very much a reality. It exists all about us, in almost everything we do. We can identify it easily even if we cannot readily define it.

ADVICE IS NOT A REGULATED BUSINESS

For the most part, advice is not regulated or licensed as a business or profession, although some sellers of advice, such as physicians, lawyers, professional engineers, and plumbers and electricians, are licensed and regulated. But the selling of advice itself is not a profession, and hence requires neither licensing nor regulation. Anyone is free to sell advice in any form, with the exception of advice in some regulated and licensed professions. And even in these fields one is free to sell *general* advice to the public at large (rather than to individuals), because it is then *information.*

That is a point that must be clearly understood. Any layperson is free to write, lecture, and otherwise render advice in general for fees as long as the advice or information is general and not offered to an individual as an individual. For example, you may write and lecture on what you believe to be the merits of a vitamin as long as you are speaking in general terms and are not offering diagnostic or remedial medical advice to a particular person for a fee. Or you may write and lecture about contracts, torts, and sundry other legal matters in the abstract, but unless you are a licensed attorney, you may not counsel a person in legal matters for a fee.

Therefore, even the licensed and regulated professions are, to some extent, open to everyone as advice-based enterprises. (Witness, for example, all the successful diet books by authors who are not physicians and could not lawfully prescribe their diets for individual people and accept fees for the service.)

This is not to say, of course, that you must not comply with any local ordinances in your jurisdiction that require you to register your enterprise as a for-profit or nonprofit business and/or to purchase mercantile or other licenses required in your local community and state. For example, if you operate under your own name as, say, John G. Petrofsky, Publisher, you may or may not need a mercantile license of some sort in your community. But if you operate as JGP Enterprises or Excelsior Publishing Company, you will probably be required to register in your state and possibly in your county as well under laws that exist in most jurisdictions requiring you to register your assumed company name. Such laws are designed to protect the public against unscrupulous operators who might do business fraudulently and vanish in the night or otherwise evade responsibility for the obligations of the enterprise.

Except for these types of requirements, you are free to sell advice to everyone on any subject if you sell it on a general basis; and to individuals for specific fees as long as the advice is not in a licensed or regulated field (unless, of course, you are licensed in that field). That means that you have quite a broad vista of possible enterprises open to you, limited only by your own knowledge, skills, resourcefulness, and energy. Let's have a look at just a few examples of how others have taken advantage of the many opportunities that are thus available.

CAREERS AND EMPLOYMENT

Although employment agencies and similar enterprises have been with us for a long time, recent rises in unemployment statistics have swelled the numbers of such enterprises and have inspired imaginative entrepreneurs to conceive of new ways to aid those in need of help in finding employment. Unfortunately, some of the services have been of little value. However, other people who have entered the field have provided useful and worthwhile services. Here is one such example.

In the Washington, D.C., area the federal government is, of course, the major employer, and a great many job hunters pursue job opportunities with the civil service. The office responsible administratively for federal service is the Office of Personnel Management or OPM, which operates a large suite of offices in a federal building in downtown Washington. Naturally, one presumes that in that office one can find listed all the federal job openings in Washington, at least, if not in the United States.

To your horror you learn, if you pursue this, that the OPM's own office is one of the poorest sources for such information; several of the other agencies' own personnel offices offer much more information. But even then, none approach the degree of completeness you would expect to find. You discover, if you pursue the matter long enough, that there is no single source of complete information. You must assemble and compile the entire list of available job openings by visiting several offices regularly and by reading several publications that list openings, such as the *Federal Times* and the other *Times* newspapers published in Washington (*Army, Navy,* and *Air Force Times*).

Recognizing this situation for what it was, an enterprising person in the Washington area devised a new service: a biweekly publication that listed all or nearly all of the federal job openings in the area, with other helpful information, such as how to make out application forms (Form 171), how to handle interviews, and other such tips. Soon the service was expanded from written information and advice to more formal seminar training in how to pursue and win a government job. (Of course, there are now several such services in the area, and all are prospering, as they offer a truly useful service.)

There are, of course, also a number of résumé services, both firms and individuals who moonlight at night in their own homes, who advise clients on how to prepare the most effective résumé or government Form 171 (the job application form, which serves as a résumé for federal jobs). Even when what is being sold is primarily the service of writing the résumé, the seller must consult with the client as to what is probably the most useful and most important information to include.

In one case a career-counseling firm included among its services a weekly half-day session for all clients as a seminar session in how to prepare an effective résumé (under the not-unreasonable premise that clients are in the best position to write a résumé and need only counseling to do so), how to handle various problems, how to conduct themselves in interviews, and generally offering useful advice for job seekers. This was not the entire service the firm offered, but was probably the most valuable of its services.

SELLING INFORMATION ON HOW
TO FIND INFORMATION

As foreign competition, especially that of the industrious Japanese, has made broad inroads into what was once American dominance of many heavy industries, the notion has begun to gain currency that the United States will soon assume a new role in the world's economy as one based on being a leader in what is being referred to as the *information industries*. Whether or not we reach a dominant position, there is little doubt that the United States already plays a major role in this field. For example, despite the strong position that Japan has in microcomputers and microelectronics generally, their strength lies mainly in the manufacturing aspects of the industry. Both the R&D (research and development) elements of microelectronics and the software end of the computer business are still dominated by American entrepreneurs.

America is in a powerful position in the "information business" in still another sense—in the richness of universities, libraries, and archives. Washington, D.C., is possibly the richest store anywhere of records and information. The city is host to a great many energetic researchers, digging out facts for books, for commercial and industrial applications, and for a variety of other uses. Here are stored historical data, scientific facts (including many of the latest discoveries revealed in space explorations), political information, and sundry other records.

Unfortunately, the federal government is both the best and the poorest source of information in many ways: best in terms of its potential, the actual volume and variety of information, but poorest in terms of guidance to information seekers. Despite the many individuals and offices established to provide information and help American citizens seeking information, getting help from federal offices can be and often is a totally frustrating experience. (In my own case, for example, despite my long experience in dealing with federal agencies, it was only by chance that I finally learned of a federal publication entitled "Catalog of Federal Domestic Assistance," in which is recorded most of what anyone would want to know about federal grants and other assistance programs designed to benefit Americans and American organizations.)

An enterprising person named Matthew Lesko came to this realization when, for a client, he tracked down in the Department of Agriculture the world's leading expert on potatoes. He was thus inspired to launch a successful firm, Washington Researchers, in Washington, D.C. The chief business of the firm is to help others learn how to find what they are looking for in this bureaucratic capital city. Initially, his services included actually doing searches for clients, for fees, but he later turned this aspect of his work over to another organization, as he learned that simply advising others on how to find information would keep him more than busy conducting training seminars and publishing manuals and newsletters. (Later he began to write books dealing with related subjects for publication by commercial book publishers.)

INFORMATION ON WINNING BUSINESS

There is a wealth of activity centering on advising others on how to win business—on selling, on marketing, and on innumerable specialized areas and aspects of sales and marketing. There is an almost continuous out-pouring of advice on these subjects in the form of books, magazines, newsletters, conventions, conferences, seminars, meetings, audiotapes, videotapes, and other specialized packages of sales and marketing advice.

In my own case, in most of my lecturing and consulting activities, I sell advice on how to win federal government business. I advise my readers, listeners, and clients on how and where to learn of government sales opportunities, how to write effective proposals, how to negotiate contracts, and on whatever else I have had experience with in regard to doing business with government agencies.

There are organizations and publications devoted to advising others how to apply for and win grants from government agencies and from various foundations. Those who prove especially successful at sell-ing and, especially, at writing or lecturing effectively on the subject de-velop national reputations. Such people include the late Elmer Wheeler, who became best known for his famous advice, "Sell the sizzle, not the steak"; the late salesman-author Frank Bettger; and author Joe Girard.

ADVICE ON BEING HAPPY AND SUCCESSFUL

There have been many advisors on happiness, wealth, and success who became almost household names as a result of their advice. One of the best known is Norman Vincent Peale; however, Dale Carnegie, Napo-leon Hill, W. Clement Stone, and Earl Nightingale have also been highly successful. In more recent years, Zig Ziglar has become more and more well known for similar advice.

A few years ago the late Joe Karbo began to run full-page adver-tising for a paperback book of less than 100 pages, entitled *The Lazy*

Man's Way to Riches, which sold for $10. He sold hundreds of thousands of copies—some reports have put the total at well over 600,000—and his successors continue to offer the volume, using the same advertising appeal. Although this little book included factual information, it was based mainly on advice centered on Karbo's own version of "positive thinking," which he called "dynapsych."

MICROCOMPUTERS

When the first computers became available commercially, they were an almost instant success, despite numerous technical problems and astronomical prices. Soon enough it became obligatory for the larger organizations to own one, and even those companies of insufficient size to justify the expense of owning one did the next best thing and bought time and services on other people's computers.

The microcomputer has changed all that. Today, because microcomputers can be bought as cheaply as TV receivers (even more cheaply for certain types of micros), even the smallest enterprise can afford to own a computer, and most do, unless they truly have not even an occasional need for computer capabilities. Microcomputers are not only rivaling TV receivers in price, but they are rivaling TV receivers in popularity and universality of existence.

Unlike the TV receiver, however, the microcomputer is not a passive device—a device that the user simply turns on and then observes. The computer is what the industry calls *interactive*: the user and the machine react to each other. The user of a computer must *do* things with the computer to get useful results. And those things are somewhat more complicated than simply pushing buttons or even than pressing keys, as with a typewriter. In short, the user of a computer must learn how to use the computer, to become educated in or be advised in the use of the computer.

This has opened a vast new field of activity in the advice business. The technological breakthrough of the microcomputer has produced a flood of information and advice: seminars, books, booklets, lectures, demonstrations in retail outlets, articles and even regular columns in newspapers and magazines, and computer programs designed to teach—*tutorials*—some of which teach the user how to use the program which is itself presenting the tutorial information. And, of course, many newsletters have been born as a result of the microcomputer revolution.

AGAIN, WHAT IS THE ADVICE BUSINESS?

We have looked here at just a tiny sampling of activities and enterprises included in what I refer to generally as the advice business. That was purely to get a small cross section and to illustrate not only the many opportunities that exist to base an enterprise on advice and information, but also to illustrate the difficulties in articulating a clear-cut definition. Note that rarely is the commodity traded purely advice in the strict definition of that word—as counsel. Nor is it always advice in a freer definition of that word—in its extended meaning as news or information reported. Quite the contrary; quite often it is something else that is the apparent primary commodity—a service, perhaps—with the information or advice component an apparent secondary or additional element.

For example, in my own advice-selling activities, I am often called upon to actually write part or all of a client's proposal, which is obviously a service based on my own skills as a writer and as a government-marketing specialist. Still, despite the fact that my function is focused on specific writing activity, that writing is in truth a reflection of my advice to the client: I am writing for the client what I advise the client is in my opinion the best way to present the case to the customer. It is really for that judgment of mine, based on my special knowledge, that the client is paying, rather than for my writing skills per se.

It is not always easy for a client to perceive this, and on at least one occasion I failed to make a prospective client understand this. The prospective client insisted on protesting that as a writer I was too high-priced, and I somehow failed to make that prospect understand that my writing was incidental, that it was for knowing *what* to write—advice, in fact—that I commanded my fees.

But it is not only the client who sometimes has difficulty in perceiving what he or she is really being asked to pay for; frequently, the seller has some trouble in understanding this, too, and that becomes a serious problem for the seller. Let's analyze this, for it is an important consideration in the entire matter.

DEFINING YOUR BUSINESS

Later in this book we are going to reach a chapter in which the primary objective will be to explore the subjects of marketing and sales and to apply the information we derive to the selling of advice in its various forms and phases. When we do, a major point we will have to make clear is that you, as the seller of information or advice, must know what business you are in. Although that may appear to be an absurdly simple thing to know, you will discover that it is not quite as simple as it appears to be. Quite a few large and successful businesses—even entire industries—have perished or all but perished as a result of their failures to determine what businesses they were in.

The classic case is that of the railroads, which lost much of their freight business to the trucking companies because the trucking companies provided much better services, and much of their passenger business to the airlines because the airlines provided much more rapid transportation. As an entire industry the railroads failed to identify those market segments for whom speed of transportation was not as important as other factors, such as cost and perhaps convenience (airports are generally inaccessible and laborious to reach). In any case, they insisted on being in the "railroad" business, rather than analyzing that they were or should have been in the "convenience" business or the low-cost-freight-forwarding business, or in whatever business definition identified where they could look for patronage that rivals could not take from them. In short, they failed—refused—to analyze the situation from the *customers'* viewpoint, and so never did discover that they were not really in the "railroad" business at all.

By this same token, you are in the advice business only if your customers wish to pay for advice specifically. Perhaps in some cases that is exactly what they wish to buy. But in other cases—probably in *most* other cases—customers wish to buy something else. The customer who subscribes to your investment advisory newsletter may be paying for your advice, and you are selling advice, but the subscriber is actually trying to buy good investments—profits—so advice is the means, not the end, and it is always the end, not the means, that customers want.

That is the essential difference between what you sell and what the customer buys: It is largely a matter of viewpoint, yet it is critically important to your success that you master this principle and not only understand it but know how to put it to work for you. The business you are in is whatever the customer or prospect perceives your business to be, as well as what you perceive it to be, for customers rarely buy what you sell. You may sell perfume, but customers buy sex appeal—admiration and glamour. You sell automobiles, but customers buy comfort, ease, prestige, the admiration and envy of friends, a feeling of success, a sense of security, or whatever owning a specific automobile means to that buyer.

So do sell advice, certainly, but be aware that the customer is not, as a rule, buying advice. The customer is probably buying whatever he or she thinks will be the benefits of good advice. For example:

- If you are a hair stylist, patrons certainly pay for having you "do" their hair, but your advice as to what hair style is most attractive, most suitable, or "the latest thing" is of supreme importance, and whether the patron thinks so or not, it is often that consideration of being counseled and guided in hair styling that leads the patron to you, far more than your skill as a hairdresser. And it is not truly even your advice as an experienced hairdresser that the patron is buying. The patron is buying a result: being made attractive.

- You can have your stationery printed up in thousands of readily accessible places, and for approximately the same price, but you are likely to go back to the printer who counsels and guides you as to what is most prestigious and attractive for your need. If you have faith in the printer's advice, you have no trouble believing that your stationery speaks well for you, and that is what you are buying.

- All those diplomas and certificates the physician displays on the walls of his or her office play some part in your sense of security and satisfaction with the treatment and medical advice, but what you really wish to buy is being made to feel better, and that includes both physical and mental comfort—a sense of security, an allaying of fear.

This helps to explain why it is difficult to sell advice, in one way: The customer does not really wish to buy the advice per se but wants the results—the benefits—of good advice. When selling advice is your business or a major element of your business, you must arrive at a second definition of your business by considering what your advice will do for the customer and why that is a good thing for the customer—what/how the customer can recognize and acknowledge that beneficial result. Later, we will explore how you can and must use this information in your sales and marketing activities, but for now it is important that you understand it in principle only as a means of understanding your customers.

HOW MUCH IS ADVICE WORTH?

Pundits have observed often that advice is cheap. One (Robert Burton, in *Anatomy of Melancholy*) remarked: "Who cannot give good counsel? 'Tis cheap, it costs them nothing."

That is hardly true today. Advice, given professionally, is costly, and sometimes bad advice is far more costly even than good advice (in its consequences, that is). That is why one specialist can charge several times more than another, if he or she has a sufficiently large reputation, for in general the "market" for advice or information has nothing to do with the intrinsic value of the form or medium in which the advice is delivered. A 500-page novel may retail for $15 or $20, while a 100-page special report may fetch $25 or even $50 if the content of the report is considered valuable enough. One man in Washington wrote a thin volume on the subject of consulting, hardly an exhaustive or even an authoritative work on the subject, but because there was so little published on the subject, he had no difficulty in selling many thousands of copies at $20 each. (He is still selling the book at a most satisfying rate.)

It was for this reason that Joe Karbo had no great difficulty in selling hundreds of thousands of copies of his *Lazy Man's Way to Riches* paperback book at $10 each; his advertising copy persuaded the prospects that the content of this little publication was worth many times more than the cover price. Whether this was so or not—*is* so or not, for the book is still being sold at the same price—depends almost entirely on the buyer's perceptions. It is really not the seller who determines what something is worth, but the buyer. The seller can and does have an asking price, but that is a meaningless figure if the buyer refuses to pay that price. The market value of anything is set by what buyers will pay. That is the market for the item, whether it is goods or service, tangible or intangible.

The job of marketing is therefore not only to persuade prospects that they need and want whatever is being offered, but also that the value is a fair one, that it is worth what the seller asks. Marketing must determine what the value of the item is—what buyers will pay for it, that is.

There are, of course, many factors that influence buyers and therefore determine the market price of the advice or information you sell. We discuss this in greater depth later, but be aware that value is not an absolute of any kind. There are several kinds of values, and they fluctuate also. There are, for example, at least three:

Intrinsic value, that value which supposedly inheres in an item, such as the gold in a gold ring. For example, a gold ring may be worth many thousands of dollars as an heirloom, as a famous piece of jewelry with a romantic history, or as an ornamental piece, and yet be worth little if melted down and sold as gold per se. The value of the gold is the ring's intrinsic value; the other is its *esteem* value.

Of course, esteem value may fluctuate and does. Take a famous painting, for example. It has great esteem value. But suppose that it is a counterfeit, a high-quality copy painted by an accomplished art forger. The value of the painting drops to nearly zero the minute it is revealed as a forgery, despite the fact that it is a skilled piece of work, perhaps every bit as good a piece of work as the original of which it is a forgery.

There is also the concept of *added value.* A rough diamond does not look like much when it is picked up, but it has a certain value as a gemstone. However, once cut and polished, its value increases considerably, and set in a ring or other setting its value increases still more.

The concepts apply to advice also. Some advice or information may be considered to have an intrinsic value—a physician charges by the visit, generally, and most lawyers charge by the hour for consultation and advice, and that might reasonably be called the intrinsic value of the advice. But some physicians charge far more than the average physician, as some lawyers charge far more than the average lawyer, usually because the person has "a reputation"—has somehow come to be considered far better than average at his or her profession—and thus, his or her advice has esteem value. But value can be added, too: A newspaper publisher, for example, may select certain information from the public press and then do something with it—combine several pieces of related information and present an analysis, which would add value to the original information, for example. Or a consultant might select general information and construct it to apply to an individual's special circumstances, thereby adding value to the original information.

These several kinds of values are not totally independent of one another. Added value and esteem value may, in fact, be the same thing in many cases. That is, the fact that the data come from a person "with a reputation" itself adds value—it adds esteem value. Or the mode of packaging the information may add value, either because it lends esteem value or because it lends convenience value. Information packaged as audiocassettes will generally bring several times the price it would in the form of words printed on paper. And a set of audiocassettes packaged in a specially designed case will fetch a better price than it would shrink-wrapped and handed over in a brown paper bag.

Probably in no other area of trade and commerce is customer perception quite as important in establishing value as it is in the advice business. And that is because for the most part, advice has relatively little intrinsic value—at least, as compared with its final market value. The market value is made up almost entirely of esteem value, and that is, in turn, mostly added value or what the seller has done to make the raw data more valuable to the buyer.

THE INFORMATION INDUSTRY

In these few pages we have established that advice and information are so intertwined today that they are virtually the same thing, at least as far as our discussions in this book are concerned—as far as marketing advice/information is concerned. But that does not consider the enormous impact of computers generally, and of microcomputers more recently. It is, in fact, to computer functions and data processing that the term *information industry* refers most specifically.

Although the digital computer had earlier origins, it is generally seen as being born in the form of the ENIAC (Electronic Numerical Integrator and Computer), built during World War II to calculate artillery firing tables. It was soon apparent that calculations and arithmetic or mathematical operations in general were among its less noteworthy capabilities, impressive though they were, and that the digital computer was rapidly emerging as the embodiment of what an early experimenter, Charles Babbage, sought—an "analytical engine." The computer turned out to be misnamed, for its ability to make mathematical computations is eclipsed by its almost fantastic capabilities to accept, store, manipulate, process, and present information in general. The computer has had a great effect on our society and has given rise to what we now consider to be an industry—information—but the microcomputer has had an even greater effect because it has placed the digital computer within the reach of almost anyone who wants one, and the advice business will never be the same again. Although the earlier digital computers the "big" computers—revolutionized business and industry in many respects, by and large they affected only the larger business organizations. The microcomputer has changed that; it has made ownership of computers available to even the tiniest enterprises and has entered the private lives of millions of individuals as well. And the latter will almost surely have the greater impact overall. Already it has created thousands upon thousands of new jobs, new small and not-so-small business enterprises, and what may be fairly considered to be an entirely new industry.

In fact, what has come about is probably more correctly stated as several new industries. There is the manufacture and marketing of computers, for one thing. It is really not an extension of earlier computer manufacturing. By far the majority of those manufacturing micros are not the manufacturers or former manufacturers of big computers but are new entrants in the field. (However, many manufacturers of allied equipment—calculators, typewriters, and cash registers, among other things—have chosen to expand into the manufacture of micros.)

Distribution of micros is another new industry. Big computers were generally marketed by the manufacturer directly to the user, via the manufacturer's own marketing and sales forces. To some extent, micros are sold this way. However, "computer stores" and mail-order sellers of micros and allied equipment and supplies dot the landscape already, and their numbers are growing rapidly. The Radio Shack stores sell their own TRS-80 and other models, and they have sold many of them, but it is a rare city today that does not boast a number of computer stores selling scores of other models and makes.

Software development is still another industry. As in the case of computer manufacturing, it is mostly a different breed of software developers that have sprung up to write programs for the microcomputer.

Relatively few microcomputer owners write their own programs, and the packaged programs have proliferated to an even larger degree than have the makes and models of machines, including a great many tiny developers—even one-person or free-lance developers.

Finally, there is the other information revolution: the revolution in information *about* computers, computer applications, computer software, and a great assortment of other topics related to microcomputers. Before it finally slowed, the outpouring took the shape of hundreds of books; literally dozens of slick-paper magazines, some of them quite thick every month, with almost every other page given over to advertising; a number of newsletters; teaching programs about computers, some on paper and some on disks and tape, to be run on a machine and presented on a screen; many special reports; and a few highly specialized publications, such as reference data, glossaries, and reminders printed on heavy cardboard stock for durability.

This was, of course, a reflection of the hunger for information and advice about micros and their many applications. There was and is a market for all of this, or it wouldn't—couldn't—be produced. The computer is not only here to stay, and it has not only produced several revolutions in several fields, but it has demonstrated again and again our incapacity for realistic appraisal and forecasting. Even those of us deemed to have great imagination and vision have consistently underestimated the impact of the computer. For example, in the Stone Age of computer technology, when ENIAC was still the model for new computers, a number of scientists predicted that seven computers the size of ENIAC would be sufficient to handle all the calculations the world would ever need! (But then most scientists of that day thought the sole function of a computer was to compute.)

Computers, then, and especially microcomputers and all the activity centering on microcomputers, are major focal points in the advice business, in that much of the advice business is about computers and computer activities, and computers are a major instrumentality in the gathering, generation, and delivery/distribution of advice. And if the quality of our earlier forecasting about the future of computers is any reliable barometer, the ultimate impact of the computer is yet to materialize, and will almost certainly be far, far greater than anyone can now envision.

THE KNOWLEDGE INDUSTRY

Still another modern euphemism is the "knowledge" industry, which refers, once again, to information. However, if the word *information* has been appropriated by those in the computer field, who try earnestly to persuade us all that the word is synonymous with *data* and *data processing,* the term *knowledge* has been appropriated by those in the education and training field, who would like us all to consider the term definitive of their field.

The advice business is, then, all of these. And whether we refer to advice, information, knowledge, or a similar term, as we proceed to explore the field further in these pages, we are still referring to the same thing. The difference is almost entirely in the packaging, and nothing else. In a large sense that is what the rest of this book is about: how to package that information or knowledge, referred to here as "advice," to make it useful to buyers.

Chapter 2

Opportunities for the Enterprising Individual

One phenomenon of the past few decades has been something called an "information explosion," but it might justifiably be called an opportunities explosion.

AN AVALANCHE OF INFORMATION

Milestones in the development of civilization have been keypoints in the evolution of man's ability to record and communicate—in fact, to disseminate information. The historical milestones were the development of an alphabet, of writing, of printing, and of movable type. But the latest and probably the greatest milestone has been the modern digital computer, with its manifold increase in our abilities to record, communicate, and disseminate.

One of the consequences of post–World War II activity in developing Buck Rogers technology—rockets, radar, missiles, satellites, space platforms, TV, microcomputers, microelectronics generally, and almost countless other examples of science fiction come to pass—has been what some called an "information explosion." Suddenly the demand for scholars of every kind, especially scientists and engineers, was so great that universities were churning them out in droves. Suddenly dozens of new professions or at least new professional specialties were created. One could not be merely an electrical engineer, a mechanical engineer, or an aeronautical engineer. Now one had to be a radar engineer, a stress analyst, an aerodynamics specialist, a test equipment scientist, a nuclear fuels professional, a celestial mechanics physicist. Many went on to specialize even further as the technology leaped forward, and some devoted their efforts to becoming information specialists, perhaps actually designing computers and data systems, perhaps actually analyzing problems and writing computer programs, or perhaps working on the abstract level of "information theory." A rocket or missile project required the skills of mechanical, electronic, aerodynamic, and even chemical engineers, and suddenly we found ourselves faced with the problem of "interdisciplinary" projects, trying to determine which of all of these scientific professionals could best lead this team of scientists. There was more, however. We needed to support these specialists with other specialists—technical writers, illustrators, draftspeople, logistics professionals, purchasing agents, administrators, project planners, meteorologists, technicians, maintenance specialists, troubleshooters, and others.

Without computers and several other modern aids, such as microfilming and, later, microfiche and microforms, many of these projects would not have been possible; the sheer volume of information and required records would have sunk the effort. Not only was the volume of information spewing out at an ever-increasing rate, but the volume of information required to control—to manage and administer—these many vast projects was also mounting steadily. Manual control would have been simply impossible.

Which is cause and which is effect? It is impossible to say. Without these many vast projects undertaken by the government (not all military projects, either, although they began that way, but later there were NASA space programs, environmental and pollution control programs, and others which were large and scientific also) it is not likely that computer technology and other breakthrough achievements, such as microfilming, would have been even attempted on a grand scale, much less carried through at such vast cost. On the other hand, without these technological breakthroughs the projects could not have been carried out. So it proves almost impossible to determine which is the chicken and which the egg, much less which preceded which. But that is not of any great importance. The point is that in the process of their symbiotic development and coexistence, the technologies and the technological achievements spawned a vast new population of professionals and others, who have been called *paraprofessionals, subprofessionals,* and *quasiprofessionals* (take your pick). These include all those technicians, technical writers, designers, and others mentioned before as representative of our new class of *specialist.*

Chicken or egg, the proliferation goes on; the array of specialists continues to broaden, and with it the opportunities for ventures into advice-based entrepreneurship. In the microcomputer, for example, we see a phenomenon that we have seen before. In fact, it has happened so often as to be predictable (hence probably not meriting the epithet *phenomenon*). The professional economist probably has articulated a principle which notes and perhaps attempts to explain, or at least rationalize, this effect so often observed: When a new product or service is created and offered, and the public accepts it without hesitation—when, that is, a market is exhibited—swarms of entrepreneurs venture quickly into that market, some on a relatively large scale, some on a relatively small scale.

Examples of this are readily available. In the lifetimes of many who are still with us today there were over 50 different automobile models, each manufactured by a different entrepreneur. There were as many TV models in the early days of that consumer item. There are still a large number of airlines, as there were once a large number of railroads, and there are a great number of trucking companies. (The ultimate shakedown to a relative few survivors is of no significance to this discussion, valid economic effect though it is.)

THE NEWEST SET OF OPPORTUNITIES

The microcomputer is only the latest item to bring about such an economic result, and like the others has produced in its wake waves of supporting needs that represent entrepreneurial opportunities linked to advice. Those who wish to buy a microcomputer are bewildered by the vast array of makes and models, as well as by the even greater jungles of peripherals and software programs. They are for the most part unable to proceed without help. And it is not one-time help, either; they need help at every step, as they progress from a simple micro to a complete system.

This applies both to individuals buying what are termed "personal" and "home" computers, and to small business owners trying to select a microcomputer for their businesses. For the home user, computer video games often tend to be a main concern; for the small business owner, the principal concerns tend to be accounting and word processing functions. In both cases, the person tends to feel totally insecure in proceeding without the help of someone who can offer expert guidance.

A visit to any well-stocked bookstore will soon show the market for advice related to microcomputers. Most bookstores maintain a complete set of shelves, sometimes both sides of an "island," to stock and display books related to computers. Virtually all are linked to microcomputers and software used in micros. Not even TV was faster to catch on and expand its retinue of admirers than was the microcomputer. It is a poor newsstand that does not display at least a few of the many microcomputer magazines that have sprung into existence. And most are thick with advertising, as well as with news and advice—mostly advice.

A FEW FOR-INSTANCES

A newsletter named by its publisher *Micro Moonlighter* tells readers how to "moonlight" with their micros to earn money. The newsletter is growing rapidly and even appears on some newsstands, which is rather unusual for a newsletter. (And there are other newsletters of this type and a few small books, as well.)

A couple in California has been conducting successful seminars along the same lines—how to earn money with a microcomputer—and with seminars on related subjects, such as how to select a microcomputer to buy, where to make the best purchase, how/where to select software, and similar subjects.

Many people write articles for magazines, counseling readers on microcomputer subjects and on both hardware and software. Others publish newsletters dealing with related subjects, and more than a few conduct lectures, seminars, and workshops, as the California couple does.

Many of these people do not think of themselves as computer specialists, nor do they think of themselves as sellers of advice. Rather, they tend to regard themselves as specialists in whatever medium they use to sell their advice, so that they see themselves as lecturers, seminar producers, publishers, writers, teachers, consultants, engineers, analysts, technicians, or however they visualize the work or service they sell. Most people are inclined to view transactions from their own viewpoint —defining the transactions by what they do, without any effort to perceive the transaction from the other party's viewpoint. The seminar presenter is therefore *lecturing* or presenting, while the attendee is *learning* or getting information. Neither thinks of the information as advice because advice is not a salable item: The seller does not expect to be able to sell advice, and the buyer expects advice to be offered free of charge. Therefore, advice must be packaged properly.

For example, one man who presents seminars regularly advertises them and solicits attendance by mailing out large quantities of a type of mailing piece known as a *broadside,* a large brochure that opens up to a piece at least 11 by 17 inches, but often 17 by 23 inches or even larger. This person promises to teach attendees at his seminars how to develop and use mail advertising successfully. He promises, in fact, to teach attendees many things, such as how to "create powerhouse promotions" and how to persuade even the most reluctant prospects.

The broadside is a "busy" one. (That's a term that means it has little white space, but is heavily loaded with text, blurbs, headlines, and illustrations.) Obviously, this direct-mail expert believes in busy copy. (Some hold the opposite view.) The copy is loaded with promises and representations intended to prove that the promises are valid and will be made good. These include testimonials from previous seminar attendees who have kind and laudatory things to say about the seminar and information about how expert the presenter is. The latter evidence includes accounts of the presenter's activities as a writer of magazine articles on the subject and his honors as an expert in his field. And to prove his expertise as a copywriter, he reports that he wrote the broadside in less than seven hours. (The broadside is approximately 11 by 20 inches in size.)

Nowhere does this man promise "advice." His main promises include one to deliver 150 valuable ideas in three hours—virtually one idea a minute—and information on how to get profitable results. He uses the words *learn, discover, teaches,* and promises free subscriptions to two newsletters he publishes. But he focuses on benefits—on what attendees will gain in direct results, primarily the ability to turn out highly successful direct-mail advertising, advertising that produces profitable results (results at a profitable rate, that is). This demonstrates his understanding of the most basic principle of marketing and sales— selling to the prospect's interest, focusing the message primarily on what the prospect will gain by becoming a customer.

That Washington, D.C., consultant who wrote and marketed his volume on the consulting profession went on to write a second and a third volume on the subject. Meeting with continuing success in this enterprise, he solicited others to write volumes for him on various aspects of the profession, and soon found himself in the publishing business, with over a dozen thin books, all selling successfully. His Consultant's Library sells only books of potential usefulness to consultants and would-be consultants. But he obviously understands quite well what it is that people buy—what business he is in. Because he obviously understands the principle of selling results, not means, to prospects, the titles of his books carry the promise of desired results, offering such terms as *success, win, guide, compete,* and others, usually in direct association with *success, successful,* and *successfully.* His concept of advising the advisors on how to be successful has proved its merit by leading to its own success as an independent publishing venture.

SOME SPECIFIC OPPORTUNITIES

There are, of course, many large enterprises that are based wholly or in part on rendering advice. These include publishers of books, magazines, and other periodicals; organizations developing, selling, and/or presenting training programs (including many schools, colleges, and universities, of course); radio and TV broadcasters; and many others. However, with only a few exceptions, most advice-based enterprises can be launched on a small budget and on a small scale. Yet many have grown to very substantial size in a few years, despite the most modest of beginnings. One man, for example, built up a newsletter publishing venture to a point where he published seven such periodicals. He sold out to a larger newsletter-publishing firm for quite a lot of money, and went on to continue serving as editor of those publications for the new owner.

Newsletters are a particularly easy publishing venture in which to get started, although perhaps not quite as easy as it may appear. Yet this field is amazingly diverse. Here are just a few newsletter titles, to demonstrate that diversity:

Advertising World	*Association Sales and Marketing*
Fund Raiser's Exchange	*Mail Order News*
Amusement Business	*Motorcycle Business Newsletter*
Inside Footwear	*Outlook in Education*
The Flea Market Advisor	*Government Training News*
Personnel Management	*Investment Collectibles*
Travelgram	*"Insider's" Tax Loophole Report*

Of the thousands of newsletters, some are published daily, some weekly, some monthly, some quarterly, and some semiannually. Probably most are monthly publications. They are published by a wide variety of publishers, including all of these:

- Large publishing firms, many of whom publish a number of newsletters
- Firms in other businesses, publishing newsletters to help their marketing efforts
- Trade associations, professional societies, and similar organizations
- Government bureaus and community groups
- Small publishing firms, publishers of only a few—or even only one—newsletter
- Individuals, self-employed, and one-person enterprises, full- or part-time

For example, the American Bankers Association publishes 11 newsletters for its banker members. The American Health Consultants, Inc., publishes six health-and-medicine-oriented newsletters as a for-profit enterprise. The *Towers Club Newsletter* is the full-time enterprise of a person who conducts his enterprise in his home, and the *International Wealth Success* newsletter is one of the spare-time activities of a person who is employed regularly at a job.

THE TRUE BASIS FOR AN ADVICE ENTERPRISE

Although technological development has created a great deal of the demand for advice and furnished the basis for many enterprises, as you can see from the titles of the few newsletters listed here, the thirst for information and guidance is by no means limited to technological areas.

An expert in any field that affects a great many people probably already has a basis for such an enterprise. But it is not always necessary to be an expert, either; in many cases, simple access to or even the ability to gain access to useful information is ample underpinning for selling advice profitably. That would be the case, for example, in a subject field that did not require special training and education over some years to become proficient. So the publisher of *Biomedical Safety Standards* is a Doctor of Science, as he probably must be to handle the newsletter adequately, but the publisher of *Consumer New$weekly* does not need to be expert in any highly specialized field. And, of course, this is as true for other advice-selling media and enterprises, such as seminars and consulting, as it is for newsletter publishing: There are many possibilities for such enterprises where you do not have to have highly specialized skills or even knowledge to consult and advise clients on an individual basis. In many cases all that is necessary is a general awareness, a reasonable amount of related experience, an alert mind, and access to good information—the ability and means for research, that is. Here are a few examples of subject-matter areas in which people without special credentials in highly specialized fields have established and operated successful consulting practices, seminars and lectures, and/or newsletters and related products:

Marketing, general	Marketing, specialized
Sales techniques and methods	Dieting and weight loss
Antiques	Art appreciation
Household and personal security	Mail order
Industrial security	Small business start up
Newsletter publishing	Interior decorating
Office organization	Crafts, various
Business writing	Computer programming
Technical writing	Proposal writing
Editorial functions	Advertising
Indexing and abstracting	Music appreciation
Brochuremanship	Painting

FIVE GENERAL OPPORTUNITY AREAS

In the broad view, the targets of opportunity appear in five general areas, although each of these may be subdivided:

1 Consulting services (i.e., direct contact with and services to clients)
2 Publishing (newsletters, books, magazines, specialties, training programs)
3 Training services (seminars and other training presentations)
4 Free-lance writing (books, articles, other for-hire writing)
5 Free-lance lecturing (lecturing for fees)

In fact, the five areas designated are so broad that they verge on being oversimplified. Nothing is quite as simple as these terms make these specialties appear to be. On the other hand, the divisions are purely arbitrary because one can argue that lecturing is closely akin to training services, as are writing training programs. However, the basis for making these discriminations here is that the packaging and marketing requirements are distinctly different in each case, as are the skills called for. Lecturing on the "mashed potato circuit," for example, is not the same as lecturing in seminar and training sessions, and writing a training program is quite different from writing a magazine article or book. But let us have a brief look at each of these areas so that we can explore the different requirements of each specialty.

Consulting Services

To many, *consulting* and *advice giving* have identical meanings. Purists tend to believe that a consultant is one who confines his or her activities to rendering counsel, although that itself might entail doing some extensive research and study. However, the end product the consultant delivers, in this definition of the function, is advice, pure and simple, albeit perhaps in a thick report that has required much labor to write and assemble.

Not everyone shares that view. There are many practitioners who consider themselves to be consultants who do actual work for their clients, although the work, true enough, tends to be based on giving advice, directly or indirectly.

For example, a client might retain a publications consultant to design a newsletter or plan an annual report. The design developed by the consultant of itself is a recommendation—counsel or advice. Usually, in such a case, the design would evolve after several meetings between consultant and client, with recommendations by the consultant, until agreement is reached. So even if the consultant does that which purists believe he or she should not do—actual work—advice giving is almost inevitably a part of the function.

Of course, it may be argued that consultants also write, lecture, train, give seminars, publish newsletters, and do other things which have been listed here as different ways of packaging and selling advice. That is entirely beside the point, however; one may do these other things as a consultant or as another kind of specialist—writer, lecturer, author, publisher, or entrepreneur generally.

For our purposes here, to keep things in perspective, let us agree that a consultant is one who provides custom services directly to a client, under a contractual or fee arrangement, utilizing technical or professional skills. In general terms, that satisfies nearly everyone's definition of consulting.

Marketing is somewhat specialized, usually somewhat difficult, for the consultant because consulting is based on trust and confidence, and it is not easy to persuade total strangers to trust you and have confidence in you. For that reason alone, marketing your services as a consultant requires several special measures, at least in the beginning, that inspire trust and confidence. These measures include winning assignments through recommendations by others and as a result of marketing methods that build a prestigious image and visibility for you. (Later, we explore these marketing methods in greater detail.) The marketing hinges entirely on methods for generating a feeling of comfort and confidence in prospects. There are a number of ways of doing this, which it would be premature to go into now. Moreover, it overlaps some of the other four areas cited and can be discussed better after we have had a general look into those four areas.

Publishing

Publishing is a broad term, and it encompasses a broad range of activities, diverse in both products and functions. But let us first be sure that we understand the term: Publishing is entrepreneurial, not creative, consisting of finding, producing, and "distributing" (marketing) certain types of goods, including printed materials and recorded materials of various kinds, mass produced for resale. The publisher may buy material and/or creative services, but he or she is akin to the producer of a play or movie, in getting it all together—the creative effort, the production of the end item(s), the financing, and the distribution (the latter term being a euphemism for *marketing*).

We tend to think of publishing as the creation and distribution of printed materials—newspapers, books, reports, manuals, newsletters, and other such items. But there are also publishers who distribute tapes, records, sheet music, art lithos, computer programs, and many other items. It is the function, not the end item, that defines publishing.

At the same time, for our purposes, it is unlikely that anything other than printed matter—newsletters, reports, books, manuals, and possibly magazines—is truly relevant to our overall theme, that of packaging and selling advice. So let us confine the discussion to such items as these, and let us bear in mind that while as a publisher you may also be the creator—writer, for example—of the items, you may also do as many publishers do, and pay others to create the materials that you publish.

Like consulting, publishing can be done on a modest basis financially. You do not need to make a major investment to launch a publishing enterprise, particularly if you plan to publish a newsletter and/or various reports, which are generally among the least expensive items to produce. Of course, you may wish to produce training programs, with or without visual and audiovisual elements, magazines, or books, in which case a somewhat more substantial investment is involved. But even that is relatively modest compared with the investment required to capitalize many other small businesses.

Publishing does not require you to own the tools of production—printing and binding facilities—nor even your own distribution facilities if you choose to distribute through others who are organized especially for that purpose. In fact, it is possible to operate even a fairly substantial publishing enterprise from a modest set of offices, and that is one of its attractions for a great many people. (Many, in fact, operate small publishing ventures from their own homes.)

Even in the matter of preparation for printing—editing and typesetting—great economies (as compared with a few years ago) are possible. The reason is that for a great many types of publications, it is no longer necessary to use formal typesetting. Today, the modern electric typewriter and similar equipment—microcomputer/word processors, with their printers, for example—produce text of acceptable quality for many purposes, and few newsletters, for example, are typeset today:

typewriter composition has long been accepted for newsletters and reports.

On the other hand, by its very nature this type of publishing is most suitable for the small entrepreneur who will distribute the advice on a limited basis, for a relatively large price, usually via the mails (although the modern microcomputer and telecommunications in general have opened up other opportunities for distributing information). Where the large-city newspaper is sold today at an average price of 25 cents for 30 to 60 pages, the typical newsletter or report is likely to command $3 to $10 for a half a dozen pages, because the information is sold on a limited basis to a specialized audience. Those who buy such newsletters and reports are not paying their money to be entertained or diverted for a few hours; they are buying specific information or advice that has value for them commensurate with the price they pay—in about as pure an application as you can find of the advice business in practice.

Training Services

The market for training has been growing steadily for many years, and will almost surely continue to grow, as the world continues to become more complex and we need more and more to have specialists explain those complexities to us and show us how to cope with them.

This is distinct from the market for education, and if there is some confusion about the distinctions to be made between the two, let us define the terms now: Education is general, imparting to learners generalized knowledge of the world, its history, its societies, and other matters that most of us need as basic information stored in our memories for everyday living. Even when the education is designed to prepare the learner for a specific career, such as law or automobile repair, it is relatively general information, covering the field in a somewhat abstract sense.

Training, on the other hand, is specialized instruction, generally bearing on a specific application of certain skills and knowledge, so that one may learn to type as part of a general-education course in high school, but another may learn to type at a later time in a typing course designed to teach typing alone. In general, training is usually job oriented and specifically designed for immediate application.

Of course, there are many schools in the United States which are training institutions, rather than institutions of education, according to the definitions just offered here. Some of them are known as "trade" schools or "vocational" schools, as a clear indication of their special nature. But even the regular institutions of education—colleges, universities, and especially junior and community colleges—offer special training courses. These are often referred to as "adult education" and are often brief seminar-type courses of only a single session or at most, a few sessions. Many of these institutions publish an annual or semi-annual catalog of offerings, broken down into a variety of categories.

If you are on enough mailing lists, not a week will pass that you do not get at least two or three solicitations to attend seminars, of anywhere from a half-day to a week's duration, and held at a variety of locations, including on board cruise ships. There are also many correspondence courses available offering training in a wide variety of subjects, some of them given by accredited institutions, and many by institutions not accredited by anyone.

The seminars announced to you by elaborate brochures and broadsides are generally of the "open registration" variety. That is, anyone may attend by paying the stipulated registration fee, which is likely to average $200 per day and may run higher. (You may also see these seminars advertised in newspapers and magazines.) But many of the people who produce and present these seminars for the public also present these seminars on a custom, in-house basis for companies and other organizations, such as government agencies and associations, for substantial fees.

The chief reason that this need is growing steadily is that for many of us, if not most of us, our own basic education, no matter how complete, grows obsolescent almost as rapidly as do many other things today. A few years after we enter business or career life, we find ourselves in need of acquiring knowledge—information—that did not even exist when we were exposed to our original education. School children today are getting some education in computers as part of their basic education, but the rest of us must acquire that knowledge in some other manner. Some do so by intensive reading and self-study, but many others need the help and guidance of an instructor.

Change is continuous, even in those areas that appear unaffected by burgeoning technology although technological changes, such as the advent of the microcomputer, tend to touch all lives, all industries, and all careers. Every lawyer, for example, must somehow keep up with changes in the legal field as legislatures at all levels of government continue to enact new laws and modify old ones, while courts continue to make interpretations and establish precedents.

Business competition is directly or indirectly responsible for a great deal of the demand for special training, because a large percentage of the special seminars offer instruction in business-getting activities—sales and marketing functions, such as proposal writing, advertising copy-writing, setting up trade shows, and many similarly oriented sessions.

As a rule, the producer of seminars and other such sessions is also the author of the materials and often the presenter. However, the service is that of presenting the program, and it is on that basis, as well as for the materials themselves, that the producer of seminars and other training sessions charges.

One key to understanding the market for such ventures is the obvious shortage of and demand for certain skills. For example, help-wanted advertising reveals the shortage of word-processing operators. Since the skill is relatively new, and word processing is one of the most popular applications of microcomputers today, it is difficult to find skilled operators. Many people are therefore willing to pay fees to acquire this skill, and many employers are willing to send employees to courses to learn the skill.

Free-lance Writing

Perhaps some people still cling to the ancient vision of the free-lance writer as something of a romantic character, but the free-lance writer of today is much more likely to dress in a three-piece suit and interview executives and professionals in their offices than to journey off to faraway places or climb mountains. That is, probably the majority of free-lance writers today write about computers, business, political affairs, government activities, and other mundane subjects. More than one-half of the thousands of books published today, for example, are not only nonfiction, but tend to be in business, technical, professional, and reference classifications, designed for utilitarian use as conduits of information, not for the diversion of the reader. A great many of these books are written by people who have full-time jobs or careers not related to writing, who write these books for objectives and benefits other than direct financial return.

Much the same thing can be said for shorter pieces of writing, destined for much shorter life than that of books—for articles appearing in magazines and other periodicals, that is. Although many people have lamented the shrinking number of general-interest periodicals, such as the *Saturday Evening Post* and *Collier's,* the shrinkage is not in the number of periodicals overall. In fact, there are almost surely a great many more periodicals published today than ever before. But the vast majority, even those that appear on the newsstands, are of special interest rather than general interest.

It is possible, therefore, to be a free-lance writer in whatever your specialized field happens to be (or whatever field about which you have special information available to you), and be completely unknown to those whose interests lie outside that field.

In short, free-lance writing is writing *anything* you sell as a product, whether you sell it by the page, by the column inch, by the word, or by negotiation for each piece. There are those for whom free-lance writing is their entire career and sole occupation, and there are others— many more others—for whom it is a part-time or even only an occasional occupation and not necessarily for the fees paid.

What hinders many in this field is not their writing ability per se —one need not be Ernest Hemingway or Henry James to be a successful free-lance writer—or a lack of good ideas and useful information, but the market's lack of appreciation for their writing. One particular bit of naivete is the insistent effort to sell work only to those periodicals that are highly visible—found displayed in many places.

The computer field is a good example. There are perhaps a half-dozen to a dozen periodicals about computers to be found on well-stocked newsstands. But there are, reportedly, some 200 computer periodicals that qualify as magazines or tabloids, not counting the dozens of newsletters on the subject. Probably the latter periodicals do not pay quite as much to contributors as do the more visible ones, and of course the writers in them do not get the same "exposure" because the periodicals are not highly visible outside their own circle. (Many have circulation limited to a few thousand readers.) Still, they represent a vast market, relatively, and therefore offer correspondingly greater opportunity to the free-lance writer. Even so, it is not necessarily true that these less visible, less widely circulated periodicals do not pay as well for free-lance writing. Such periodicals have often paid me as well as have the more popular ones.

Also, free-lance writers need not think in terms of articles and books only; there are many other requirements for which clients will pay free-lance writers. Publishers of audiovisual materials—films, film-strips, slides, sound tapes, videotapes, and other such material—buy material from freelance writers. A great many such producers and publishers are in the training industry, in fact. Others in that industry buy training materials of other kinds—manuals, lecture guides, tests, exercises, and complete training systems.

Free-lance Lecturing

Lecturing on a free-lance basis is somewhat different from lecturing at your own seminars and other training presentations and is, in some ways, more akin to presenting a custom, in-house seminar to the staff or members of an organization. There are, in fact, a large number of people who are full-time lecturers or public speakers, who speak for fees.

The analogy to free-lance writing is an obvious one and a nearly perfect one: Like free-lance writers, some lecturers pursue public speaking as a full-time career, earning their entire living from it, whereas others speak as an adjunct to their main careers, and not necessarily for fees or because of the financial rewards.

Too, as in writing, there are "stars" who can command remarkably large sums for an hour or two of their time on the platform, but this is usually because they are celebrated or notorious rather than because they are especially gifted as speakers. Fortunately, however, it is not necessary to be a well-known public figure to be successful as a speaker.

As in writing, too, there are lecture bureaus—individuals and organizations who act as agents or brokers for speakers, arranging speaking engagements for a commission. Many speakers use such lecture bureaus or agents, but many claim that they can do better acting as their own agents.

The colleges and universities of the country represent a major market for speakers, but they are by no means the only market. There are many thousands of associations of various kinds, and they represent another large market for speakers to address audiences at their many functions—meetings, dinners, conventions, and other such occasions. Cruise ships often hire entertaining speakers to constitute part of their on-board programs. And there are a number of organizations who are conference or convention managers—they handle all the planning and other details of staging major convocations.

Fees vary quite widely, and like consulting fees, it is up to the person to decide what his or her fee must be. However, as in the case of consulting, seminars, and many other such services, clients tend to judge the quality by the price, and setting the price too low may have an adverse effect on the marketing of the service, rather than a beneficial one.

As in the case of writing, mentioned some paragraphs ago, some speakers are purely entertainers, diverting their audiences. But many are deliverers of useful and interesting information, and the quality of the presentation is geared to the quality of the information delivered as well as the quality of the presentation per se. That is, harking back to a point made earlier, clients and audiences do want the information itself, but are paying for an *interesting presentation* as well as for the specific information. The ideal is to be able to do both—present useful and interesting information and yet be entertaining.

YOU CAN SUIT THE PACKAGE
TO YOUR OWN PREFERENCES

The requirements placed on you, as an individual, vary somewhat in each of these applications. Some of them—consulting, lecturing, training services, for example—require direct contact with your clients (for they become "clients," instead of "customers," when you provide custom service at rates you designate as *fees*), whereas in others you never need to meet customers face to face. Some put you under the pressure of appearing before audiences, traveling, living in hotels, doing a great deal of personal, face-to-face marketing, whereas others permit you to lead a far more sheltered existence. Some require you to do what many find distasteful—write—while others permit you to hire others to do that job. Some are creative enterprises, with all the pressures and stresses that creativity imposes; others are purely entrepreneurial.

In short, it is possible to adapt your venture and the way in which you package your information/advice to suit your personal preferences. For example, one person who is highly regarded as a motivational speaker and whose audiocassettes sell widely is actually ill at ease on the public platform and speaks rather poorly before a live audience because he is nervous in that situation. Yet, alone in the quiet of a recording studio, he is perfectly at ease and speaks flawlessly into the microphone, to produce highly professional recordings. He avoids speaking before live audiences but goes on making and selling his cassettes.

Many individuals combine two or more of these activities—they lecture and write, perhaps even publish newsletters, produce seminars, and write books. In fact, many lecturers find that it doubles their incomes to sell books and newsletter subscriptions in "back of the room" sales at their seminars and lecture presentations, and many seminar producers record their seminars and sell sets of cassette tapes by mail.

In the final analysis, ignoring the fact of how you package the advice you sell, you can pursue the advice business in one of two ways: by providing the service itself, for specific fees; or by creating the product, as a producer/entrepreneur, and selling the product. That is the major distinction between lecturing for fees and producing seminars or lecture presentations for which you charge admission or registration; or between writing for others, as a free-lance writer, and publishing your own writing as newsletters, books, and reports. And, of course, you can do both, if you wish, as many do. But we are now verging on the broader subject of the markets and selling to them, and that is the subject of the next chapter.

Chapter 3

The Markets for Advice

"Markets" and market "segments" are not easy to define, but marketing success depends at least in part on how well the proper markets and segments are identified.

POSITIONING

Advertising people speak of "positioning," and those who lecture on the subject are quick to point out that positioning is something one does to the prospect's mind. More precisely, perhaps, positioning is something one does (or tries to do) to the prospect's perception—to how the prospect perceives the product or service offered and to how the prospect perceives the offeror, as well.

For example, suppose that you wish to offer advice on buying a personal computer. You can offer it to prospects in a variety of ways, each a different "position" or perception. Consider these, for example, as alternative ways to present your offer to impart information and advice on buying and using a computer:

1 *As necessary basic education:* "What everyone needs to know about computers today"

2 *As goal-oriented instruction:* "How to find the computer best suited to your own needs"

3 *As a secret of success:* "How to advance your career by learning about computers"

You can position an item as one with snob appeal or as one for the working person. You can appeal to prospects using a wide variety of positions. What you cannot do is use all the positions—not at the same time. You cannot be Cartier's and Macy's basement simultaneously. That is, you can sell the same product in Cartier's and in Macy's basement, but you will have to package it a bit differently for each. Many businesses do just that. For example, a certain well-known distiller of alcohol packaged his product expensively, named it after a city street, and sold it as the leader in its class. At the same time, he bottled the same product in cheaper packages under several different labels and sold them each at a lower price. This is not at all unusual. It simply takes advantage of human foibles: There are those buyers who insist on buying only the most expensive item in a line, firm in the belief that its price tag reflects its quality, whereas there are others who trend in the opposite direction, firm in their belief that the lower-priced item is a greater bargain. It is not a moral issue but an advertising and marketing problem: You must establish a position for your product or service, and you do so by guiding customers' perceptions of your offering. And at least part of that depends on packaging.

Companies also position themselves, helping customers perceive them according to whatever images they wish to present, such as innovative, modern, go-go companies or staid, conservative, old-line organizations. Some want customers to see them as the biggest in their industry or the oldest in their industry. Some want customers to think of them as being young and eager. One insurance company uses the Rock of Gibraltar to help customers perceive them as absolutely solid and reliable; another uses cupped hands to convey the idea of being safe and secure when covered by one of their policies.

Every product or service needs to be positioned, to provide prospects with the reasons—the motivation—for buying. But there is another, related idea that advertising people and other marketers consider. They call that idea *segmenting,* or they refer to market segments; and that can mean at least two different things, in application. First, it refers to the fact that a "market" consists of potential buyers who can be classified by segments and, in fact, must be so classified to plan an intelligent marketing campaign. Suppose, for example, that you offer advice/information on buying a personal computer. First of all, personal computers are sold both to individual consumers for at-home use and to businesspeople for personal use in their work. (Many large corporations have been supplying their executives with personal computers, for example.) Already, you have identified two major market segments for that information. But even that is only the beginning, for each of those can be further subdivided. Among those who buy computers to use at home are people using them primarily to play games, whereas others are using them to manage investments, and still others, to write books or plays.

So you might position a given microcomputer as the expensive, high-quality one, as the inexpensive one, as the one best suited to word processing, as the one best suited to portfolio management, as the one most versatile and suited to a wide variety of uses, or other such images. Obviously, there is a direct relationship between that positioning and the market segment you have identified and opted to pursue; and equally obviously, they must match.

PACKAGING

Positioning involves what you say about your product or service—about your offer. But what you say in words is only part of your message. The other part is what you say implicitly in your packaging. The way you package your product must contribute to the position you are trying to establish, to how customers perceive your product. Customers react to what they perceive, not to what you perceive. They do not perceive goods arriving in a "plain, brown wrapper" as high-quality.

Of course, that is packaging in its most literal sense. Advice is packaged in a more poetic sense, as seminar and lecture presentations, as books and periodicals, as audiovisual presentations, as slides and transparencies, as films, as videotapes and audiocassettes, as trade shows and conferences, and perhaps even as other kinds of packages.

Each of these represents an appeal to a different market, and even that is only a first step, because each of the markets is made up of segments, and the packaging and positioning must be directed to specific segments if they are to achieve maximum effectiveness.

THE BOOK-BUYING MARKETS

The book you are now reading appeals to one segment of the advice and information market; it is the segment that consists of people who buy books to make an independent, self-actuated study of a particular subject. Some do so out of curiosity or general interest in the subject, some out of a goal-oriented desire to gather information for career purposes, some to study business opportunities in the field, and others for perhaps other purposes and objectives.

There are other segments of the book market. One major segment is that represented by textbooks. The buyers of these books buy them to support formal studies of subjects related to advice and information. They—the buyers—may be institutions of learning, buying the books to resell or to issue—on loan—to students, or they may be the students themselves, buying through a distributor. (All campuses have bookstores that sell textbooks, among other volumes.)

There is a definite market segment for technical, professional, and reference books. Some of these are closely akin to textbooks, yet they are not quite the same, although it is possible that some books conceived and written as professional and reference books may be adopted as textbooks. However, those books designated technical/professional/reference books are intended for use by technical/professional specialists and by reference libraries.

Libraries are another segment, and this segment includes both public and private libraries. These institutions buy books because the books appear to be important, have been requested by users, or fall into special categories, all of which are bought because the library has a specialized purpose. That would generally be the case with libraries maintained by government agencies, large companies, and other organizations.

And there are yet other segments, miscellaneous ones, such as book clubs and organizations who buy books to use as premiums or gifts. (In my own case, the chief executive of one company bought 150 copies of one of my books to give to customers, provided that I would autograph each copy!)

Although I choose to consider each of these to be a segment of the book market generally, a case may easily be made of considering each of these as a market rather than as a segment of a market. In fact, there is some justification for this, especially in the case of the textbook, for textbooks tend to be quite different in many ways from other books, and most properly, a market segment ought to be some element of a market that will accept the same product, albeit in different packaging. That is not always true with textbooks, which are not usually quite the same product as a more "popular" book on the same subject.

Technical, professional, and reference books fall into the same category, in some respects, because they are so highly specialized. As a result of their high degree of specialization, many of these enjoy a rather limited market, and so must command a high cover price, if they are to be successful at all. Ergo, the publisher, knowing that the book will require a high cover price to recover its costs, tends to make the product one of high quality, with expensive paper, type, and binding—with expensive packaging, that is—since the book must be positioned for a certain price range by virtue of certain specific conditions and characteristics.

To some degree, this is true of book clubs also, although in reverse, since book club editions are often special, less expensively made editions of the book.

But even these segments have segments—are made up of subclassifications. Take that first book-market segment, for example. Those who buy books independently do so for a variety of reasons, which reflect both their objectives and their personal situations. Here are some reasons, for example, why a person might buy a how-to book of some kind:

- In preparation for a career in a given field—or perhaps a second career there
- To further personal knowledge and skills and to enhance one's opportunities for advancement in a career already directly related to the subject covered by the book
- To evaluate and perhaps guide one's efforts to launch an independent venture based on the information and advice given in the book
- To expand personal knowledge of the field because one teaches it or related subjects, and one must "keep up"
- To satisfy personal curiosity or general interest about the field
- To use as a teaching guide or textbook

How does all this affect one's packaging and positioning efforts? Just so: The person who chooses to "read up" on some field rarely chooses to buy a textbook, nor is he or she likely to find formal text-books in a general trade bookstore. Bookstore browsers do not buy textbooks, and bookstore owners are well aware of that. So the market for textbooks is definitely different from the market for general-interest books, or even for professional and reference books, which also tend to be stocked only in stores offering textbooks rather than in those catering to browsers and casual, impulse buyers.

Some marketers identify market segments by finding adjectives to describe the buyers in each segment. We might identify prospective buyers by such adjectives or titles as the following:

Small business proprietors	Browsers
Public libraries	Impulse buyers
Private libraries	Technicians
Company libraries	Engineers
Government libraries	Teachers
Opportunity seekers	Computer owners
Students	Hobbyists

The list could go on, depending on the book, and you might identify a large number of potential buyers in that manner. However, this would not represent an equal number of market segments because many of the names would belong to individuals of the same segment. The segment defines a position or a portion of a market to which you can at least theoretically sell the same product or service in the same package.

Most of these terms—market, segment, position, and several other terms used commonly in advertising and other marketing activity—are difficult to define and do not have agreed-upon meanings. To use them here, we must establish our own understandings of what the terms mean, for even that is entirely arbitrary: It proves difficult—perhaps impossible—to set up an organized and logical set of definitions that would not have many exceptions. So we must use the term *market* rather loosely, as most people do, to fit the situation or need of the moment. So there is a book market and a seminar market, on the one hand, but there is an opportunity-seeker market and a college-student market, on the other hand. In short, sometimes we identify markets as groups of potential buyers, but other times it is more useful to identify markets by what can be sold or what appears to be in substantial demand.

Segments within a market are identifiable subgroups which may require different packaging, different positioning, or different appeals from each other, even though the product is the same. Segmenting an appeal—identifying the segments within a market and addressing each segment separately—serves more than one purpose. One of the most important purposes that can be served by marketing to segments is testing to determine which segments respond best and/or to what kinds of appeals response is best. (We probe the details of marketing in Chapter 9 and we cover testing there, too.) But there is also the consideration of how to reach your market—to present your offer to the market —and segmenting is often the answer to that problem.

Packaging Advice for Book Buyers

You can see now that the book is not a single package, but several. That is, the book may be packaged as a trade book, one sold through bookstores to general browsers and impulse buyers. It may be packaged as a textbook, sold generally through special bookstores and distributors, after the publisher has won approval from relevant educational institutions. It may be packaged as a technical/professional/reference book, which is a not-too-distant cousin to the textbook. It may be a specialty book sold through the mails and by other direct-marketing means (although trade books can be sold this way, too).

Each of these necessitates a different way of packaging the book, and some mean a somewhat different product, as well, as we explored earlier, depending on whom you have selected as the best prospects for the marketing effort. But let's look at other products and services, in the advice business and others.

THE SEMINAR/WORKSHOP MARKET

Although the market for seminar attendance has had its ups and downs, with economic trends, over the long haul it has trended upward. This is true for several reasons, aside from the fact that all advice business has trended upward:

1 Many people cannot, or believe they cannot, learn a subject by reading alone, but must listen to an instructor in a classroom setting.

2 Some who come to seminars are motivated largely by the desire to ask specific questions and get direct answers, to probe certain areas in extended discussions, and even to get some practical experience, as a result of the practical workshops—exercises—which are part of many seminars.

3 Some are motivated by the handout materials, especially manuals which, they are often assured, are unobtainable by any means other than attendance at the seminar or workshop.

4 Seminars and workshops are often made attractive by presenting them as retreats, scheduling them in special settings such as on cruise ships and in resort areas.

5 Attendees often like the idea of "getting away" from their normal pressures and stresses for a day or a few days, and believe that the isolation will be conducive to learning.

6 Some seminars offer attendees a chance to meet and listen to distinguished presenters they might otherwise never have the opportunity to hear.

Size of the Market

No one actually knows how large the seminar market is, whether in dollars or by other standard of measurement. However, there is one firm in the Washington, D.C., area that does a business of well over $5 million annually in seminars, and there are several others of at least equal size and volume. In addition to that, there are hundreds of individuals and small organizations presenting seminars regularly, and thousands who present seminars and workshops occasionally. Overall, it seems safe—a conservative estimate, that is—to guesstimate the total at several hundred millions of dollars annually, at least. One person whose chief activity is lecturing on the subject of consulting, in half-day and full-day seminar sessions, has a volume of some $250,000 annually.

Market Segments

In broad terms, there are at least two major market segments: one made up of those individual customers who pay for their own attendance for whatever reasons induce them to attend such sessions, and the other which is made up of the many organizations who send their employees to seminars and workshops to enhance their skills as employees and make them more valuable to their employers.

It is necessary to distinguish between these two segments for at least one overpowering reason: Marketing aimed at one of these segments is totally different from marketing aimed at the other, in more than one way. For one thing, reaching each of these sets of prospects is a separate problem, requiring a different approach in each case. But for another, the fee structures—what one can charge these registrants—is also different.

It is commonplace today for seminar producers to set registration fees at $200 to $300 per day when the fees are to be paid by employers seeking to improve the quality of their employees' performance on the job. But it is rather difficult, in most cases, to induce individuals to pay such prices for seminars and workshops, and when these are directed at individuals, fees tend to be a great deal more modest.

On the other hand, when seminars are produced and presented by public institutions, such as community colleges, registration fees tend to be quite small—as low as $25 to $50 per day. However, the sessions tend also, under these circumstances, to be quite spartan, with few if any handouts, and presenters of no special merits or qualifications.

Custom, In-House Seminars and Workshops

The custom seminar, designed especially to meet the needs of a given organization and presented on a contract basis to the staff of that organization, is somewhat different from the seminars and workshops discussed to this point. Here, the client is an organization who is engaging the presenter/producer for a fee, under contract and under controlled conditions. There is a definite and growing market for this type of session, as there is for the open-registration type of seminar/workshop, because the custom seminar is generally an economy for the organization who has at least 10 people to be trained in such a session. (Fewer than 10 people for a custom, in-house session is difficult to justify economically.)

Although such sessions are normally custom-designed for the client organization, to make the project economically feasible for both parties—vendor and client—such programs are rarely developed entirely from scratch but are usually adapted from existing programs and materials. That is, the client engages the services of a seminar presenter, who has a standard seminar of the general nature desired and who can modify and customize it for an acceptable cost. There are exceptions to this, but it is relatively rare that private organizations are willing to sustain the cost of developing entire programs from scratch.

On the other hand, the federal government is an exception to this, and many seminars, workshops, and other training programs have been developed especially for government agencies. Federal agencies tend to perceive their own training and orientation needs as quite unique and therefore not properly satisfied by any training materials not designed and developed especially for their own needs. This is quite the opposite of the position taken by most private-sector organizations, which tend to believe that proprietary, off-the-shelf materials ought to be available somewhere to satisfy their needs, even if they require slight modification.

NEWSLETTERS AND SPECIALTY PUBLISHING

The market for information in the form of newsletters, reports, and other specialty publishing—publishing of items directed toward highly specialized audiences, as compared with general-interest materials directed toward the general public—is a great one. As in the case of seminars and workshops, the market is growing because the increasing complexity of our society continues to create more and more special interests, and many of those special interests tend to proliferate and diversify into others. The computer, for example, created a number of special interests, most of which are today subdivided. In the engineering aspect of computers alone, there are specialists in small computers and large, "super" computers, but there are also specialists in microminiaturization, in memory devices, and in sundry other aspects of the hardware end of computer design and development.

A great many of these interests are not well served by general publications. One engineer who was especially interested in dry cells and batteries in general discovered that there was little information published on the subject, even in the many journals on electronics and allied technological fields. He therefore launched his own newsletter on the subject. A woman in Illinois publishes a newsletter on needlepoint. A Pennsylvania newsletter publisher covers trends in trademarks. And a Washington, D.C., newsletter deals with taxes levied on nonprofit corporations.

Newsletter subscriptions are relatively expensive. While there are many monthly newsletters selling for as little as $12 to $24 per year, there are many others costing many times that amount. To a large degree, the cost of a newsletter subscription is proportionate to the degree to which the newsletter specializes in information not readily found elsewhere. That, in fact, is the sole reason for the existence of the newsletter: It offers information and ideas that are difficult to discover and are of interest to a relatively small population of readers. It is the fact of that relatively small population of interested readers that is responsible for the lack of coverage of the subject in other publications, and that also makes the newsletter a feasible venture. When information and advice on a subject are difficult to find but are of great interest to a small group of people, that group of people will pay any price within reason to get that information and advice. It is that which enables the publisher of a four- or eight-page monthly newsletter to get as much as several hundred dollars a year for a subscription.

Many newsletter publishers do not rely on the subscription fees alone for their income, but also publish periodic special reports, elaborating on a topic and charging readers a separate price for the report. The publisher of a newsletter on health care programs and related subjects, for example, publishes a hardcover book once a year, which he sells to his newsletter readership, and which reportedly produces more income than does the newsletter itself.

Newsletter publishers also often maintain mail-order "bookstores" for readers, which carry specialized books that are not commonly found in the general bookstore. Many newsletter publishers also produce and offer seminars and workshops periodically, as an adjunct to their publishing venture.

The newsletter market is therefore quite a diverse one and includes at least portions of other markets. That is one of the factors that makes it so difficult to define such terms as *market* and *market segment*. Figure 3-1 illustrates that overlap in something known as a Venn diagram. This shows that the three sets of activities, identified here as markets, overlap each other in a variety of ways. It illustrates, too, that among those who launch ventures in these markets there are some who confine themselves to that set of activities alone, whereas others diversify into other areas.

But this is only one way of illustrating markets and diversification. This, in fact, illustrates and exemplifies markets only in terms of types

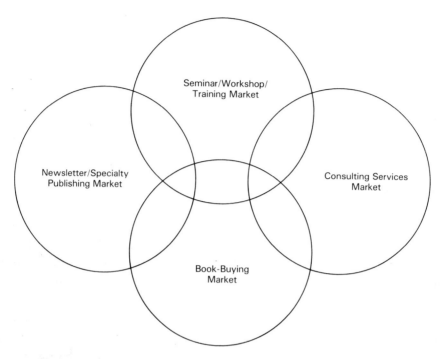

FIGURE 3-1   How markets overlap and intermingle

of products or services. But it is possible to identify markets and market segments in other terms, such as by types of user or customer.

IDENTIFYING MARKETS BY TYPES OF USERS

Earlier we discussed the two broad types of customers for seminars and workshops, identifying both the individual and the organization. This kind of discrimination can be employed for a great many ventures, including publishing, consulting, and writing, for example. But it does not work for all advice ventures. It is not economically feasible to try to sell free-lance lecturing services to individual customers, for example; such services can be sold only to organizations of some sort. (Of course, one can rent a hall and try to sell tickets to individuals, but that is not a promising venture today, although it once was.) In any case, markets can be identified in this manner, although the identification must be a bit more specific than merely discriminating between individuals and organizations as customer-prospects. To be useful for marketing purposes, it is necessary that the identification be carried at least one step further in perceiving types of individuals or organizations.

Sometimes these are indicated automatically by the nature of the information or advice. Advice on how to maximize personal exemptions and deductions—the most advantageous interpretations and applications of the current tax codes applicable to personal income and tax returns, that is—would obviously be of interest only to those who prepare such returns. That would include those people who prepare their own returns and those who prepare returns for others, whether the latter are individuals or organizations, such as accounting firms. But this is not always the case: Advice on how to make best use of a personal computer is applicable to a much wider and more diverse universe of prospects, and some research and thought is necessary to identify best potential markets for this.

At the same time, it is possible to point to a few markets, in broad terms, and to determine what those markets are likely to buy. That is, instead of discussing a product or service and to whom it may be sold most readily, we can turn that around and look at various identifiable markets or market segments and list some of the relevant products or services those markets are known to buy.

GOVERNMENT MARKETS

The federal government is a very large market in and of itself. Divided into its three main branches—legislative, judicial, and executive—each branch represents a market, but by far the dominant market is that of the executive branch—those departments, bureaus, commissions, and other agencies that report to the president. They represent well over 90 percent of all federal procurement of goods and services.

In total, federal procurement today is well in excess of $200 billion annually. The precise figure is not available, and, in fact, it is doubtful that anyone in or out of government knows the precise figure. For one thing, there are certain federal agencies, such as the Postal Service and the Pension Benefit Guaranty Corporation, which are not required to report their procurements to the Office of Procurement Policy and its Federal Procurement Data Systems branch, which publishes procurement figures. However, $200 billion is a figure that represents the bulk of today's federal procurement.

This figure represents purchasing by more than 60 departments and "independent" agencies, but because most of these agencies operate a number of offices, and many are subdivided into many "offices" and "administrations," there are some 15,000 federal procurement offices, employing about 130,000 procurement specialists of various kinds. It requires a great many people to spend $200 billion a year. From October 1, 1982, to March 31, 1983, for example, the federal government's executive agencies made 8,750,000 purchases, totaling $81,674,302,000. Not surprisingly, the largest spender was the Department of Defense. It always is.

There is no reliable way of determining precisely what the federal agencies spend for information and advice, since these are not specified among the broader categories reported. However, some idea of the volume and rate of growth in related fields may be inferred from this fact: In 1982, for the entire year, the federal government bought $1.1 billion worth of ADP (automatic data processing) services, and for the first half of 1983 the figure is $0.6 billion, an increase of nearly 2 percent. But that increase does not reflect the true degree of growth because there will almost certainly be a surge in spending during the last quarter, as there is almost invariably, making the actual increase considerably larger. Overall, the annual increase in government spending for goods and services is generally considerably more than inflation alone would account for.

On the other hand, figures for R&D (research and development) —which is inherently heavily oriented toward being an advice and information service—for the first half of the 1983 fiscal year reveal $10,926,919,000 spent in 14,276 separate procurements for a wide variety of fields: agriculture, defense, energy, environment, education, housing, and transportation, to name a few.

Nature of the Federal Market

The federal government market represents a fair cross section of all commerce and industry. There are federal customers for just about everything, and in some cases the federal government is the only customer—the only one who will buy the item or service today. However, a hastily drawn profile of government market segments suitable as buyers of advice and information products might appear somewhat as follows:

Libraries: Most agencies of any size have libraries of their own, and these libraries buy a variety of books, reports, newsletters, and other publications. Many also buy cassettes and other products that fall into the information/advice arena.

Training and Publications: Most agencies have both training and publication responsibilities, the latter of which includes public-information and/or PR (public relations) duties. In larger agencies, these duties may be assigned to separate departments for each of the functions; in smaller agencies, the duties may be assigned to a single department, or even fall under the aegis of the agency's personnel office. In any case, those responsible for the functions are prospective customers for all advice/information products, both proprietary and custom designed, and may very well buy the same things the library buys, to be sent to them directly. (On the other hand, some agencies buy such products by requesting the librarian to institute the purchase.)

Program Divisions: Each agency usually has one or more programs that reflect its main mission(s), in contrast to the support functions already mentioned. These program offices are also prospective buyers of many products and services of interest here, including consulting and other services to support and implement their programs. In this respect it ought to be made clear that in a great many cases federal agencies do not have enough personnel to carry out all the duties and functions necessary to their programs, but must contract out a great deal of the work. The result frequently is that the program staff of the agency spends most of their time overseeing the work of contractors. The Department of Defense is a good example of this, as are most of the more "visible" agencies. (For example, the National Cancer Institute finds it necessary to use contractor help to respond to telephone and mail inquiries from the public.)

State and Local Governments

The Bureau of the Census recognizes nearly 80,000 "governments" in the United States. This includes some 3000 county governments, about 18,000 cities and towns, and many other governmental entities, such as school districts, which operate more or less autonomously.

Overall, including the federal government, all these governments are estimated to spend in excess of $575 billion annually for goods and services. The state governments usually maintain a centralized purchasing facility in the state's capital city, and local governments generally maintain a purchasing official in their seat of government, and in many cases a fairly sizable purchasing staff.

Practices and policies vary. In some cases, virtually all purchasing is done via that centralized facility, although many of the bureaus are free to utilize the purchasing facility to satisfy their own special needs. In other cases, the various bureaus are empowered to buy independently, although this authority is usually limited by statute. However, certain types of agencies are almost invariably permitted at least some independent buying, even though they are public institutions. For example, publicly owned and operated colleges and universities usually do their own buying, as do penal institutions and systems, state and local legislatures, transportation departments, school systems, and a few other such governmental entities.

In general, then, government represents probably about 15 to 20 percent of the total domestic market overall, and by extension probably represents the same approximate percentage of the domestic market for the advice business—for consulting, for newsletters, for seminars, and for other such goods and services.

ASSOCIATIONS AS A MARKET

There are thousands of associations in the United States—Gale Research Company lists 16,800 of them. Associations are local and national—even international—in scope. Generally speaking, associations tend to fall into distinct groups:

- *Trade associations:* These are associations of people engaged in related businesses, such as food processing or computer software development.
- *Professional societies:* These are associations of professionals, such as physicians, lawyers, and architects.
- *Special-interest groups:* These are associations of people having some strong

mutual interest, such as a desire for more (or less) government control or more (or less) nuclear weaponry and international agreements.

- *Miscellaneous:* Some associations tend to fall outside these definitions or descriptions, such as those made up of people sharing a mutual hobby and not having a clearly defined special mission other than a general desire to meet with and become acquainted with others sharing their avocational passion.

All of these represent a general market, although each is a segment of that market, with somewhat different interests from those of the others. Associations usually have regular meetings, and someone is in charge of planning the meetings and arranging a program, which may include speakers, seminars, workshops, panels, or other activities. Moreover, most associations of any size have annual conventions or conferences, and these annual convocations invariably entail a major program of activities, for which the association usually hires specialists and/or makes special purchases.

Some associations also buy services on a regular basis. For example, some organizations retain specialists to prepare and manage a monthly publication of some sort—a rather costly and fully professional magazine, in some cases.

Typical convention activities of associations include an exhibit hall, where space is rented to exhibitors for booths, seminars on a variety of subjects, and other special sessions, as well as a banquet—often an awards banquet, where the association honors individuals in their sphere of interest.

Doing business with associations is a somewhat specialized marketing activity, and there are some professed experts who offer to train "outsiders" in this fine art. There is, in fact, at least one periodical devoted to association activities in general, and there is an association of association executives headquartered in Washington, D.C., which is host to some 2000 national associations' headquarters.

NONPROFIT CORPORATIONS

Associations are nonprofit corporations of one kind, although they are clearly distinguishable as a special kind of nonprofit organization. But there are other types of nonprofit organizations, including the following:

- *Colleges and universities:* These are of somewhat limited value as markets for the goods and services discussed here, except as noted for seminars and, to some degree, textbooks and newsletters.
- *Community groups:* Organizations of local citizens, banded together to do something on a community basis; also limited in usefulness as markets.
- *Business organizations:* There are a number of major business organizations which are nonprofit groups, such as the Rand Corporation, Battelle Institute, and Research Analysis Corporation. These and similar groups were organized to serve specific needs, as "think tanks"—organizations of scientists and other professionals who contract with the Department of Defense and other federal organizations (their chief sponsors and sources of revenues, although not their only ones) to support major programs.

Some of these groups were organized by the leading companies in an industry, just as a number of leading computer manufacturers are today cooperatively financing and organizing a research group to develop "supercomputer" technology, as a nonprofit laboratory. Some are foundations or other types of nonprofit corporations founded by single companies, as a nonprofit arm of the corporation. And some are organized independently by groups of people with a common interest in carrying out certain kinds of work.

Many of these institutions are excellent customer-prospects for the kinds of products and services considered here, although collectively they are not a large market. Still, they are a market to take account of.

FOR-PROFIT ORGANIZATIONS

According to whichever account you read and choose to believe, there are somewhere between 11 and 15 million organized business ventures —companies and corporations—in the United States today (13 million appears to be the number most favored, especially by the government agencies who publish such figures). Again depending on whose numbers you like best and on whose definitions of small business you agree with, somewhere between 90 and 97 percent of all these business organizations are small businesses. (If we use the Small Business Administration numbers, we have to agree on 97 percent as the right number.)

Of course, even among those 12,610,000 small businesses (using the 13 million and 97 percent figures) there is quite a large variation in sizes of those ventures. There are many self-employed independents—

one-person enterprises—many "Mom and Pop" retailers, and many ventures employing a handful of people. There are also ventures keeping as many as 500 employees busy, but lumped together with the tiny ventures as "small business." The latter term is fairly elastic, since it includes firms paying their proprietors a bare living, as well as firms counting annual revenues in the millions.

Those ventures at the smaller end of the spectrum do not represent a very substantial market, but those in midrange and higher are sufficient in number and in annual market share to represent a very substantial market for advice and information. This is not to say, however, that the remaining 390,000 corporations counted as big business are not also representative of a large market, for they are. Even the individual, self-employed entrepreneur can sell to major corporations. (I can certify this from my own success in selling advice/information services to a number of major corporations.)

It would, accordingly, be a mistake to assume that selling to major corporations is beyond your reach because yours is a tiny enterprise by comparison; the reverse is true, as you will see later when we discuss marketing per se: Smallness is often its own advantage.

Given the enormous diversity of American industry and business, it would be impractical to consider America's businesses as *a* market. They represent a large number of markets and must be so regarded for any intelligent effort to sell to them. Even if we were to try to subdivide them by types, we would identify only groups of industries. We could, for example, use any or all of the following types of identifiers and still not have furnished much of a lead as to how the market relates to what we have to offer:

Manufacturing industries	Small companies
Service industries	Large companies
Heavy industries	Food processors
Light industries	Electronics laboratories
Distributorships	R&D contractors
Retailers	Aerospace contractors
Chain stores	Trucking firms
Multinational companies	Airlines

In general, for-profit organizations offer the most attractive markets, despite the fact that there are some exceptions to this general rule. One reason for this is that for-profit organizations are more guided by the principles of expediency and efficiency than are organizations whose motives are other than profitable operation. Another is that there are so many for-profit organizations and that the array is so diversified, it is possible to find an adequate number of almost any type of industry or commercial pursuit desired.

But all of this has been directed toward organizations and/or business ventures, for whom the service you offer represents something of usefulness in their own ventures. We have not yet addressed the largest market of all: individual citizens and consumers.

THE INDIVIDUAL AS A MARKET

We are today a nation of some 240 million people. A large percentage of these represent prospective buyers—customers—as individuals, whether they are employed by an organization, are self-employed, are retired, or are still preparing for their careers and have not yet entered the work force. Some of these individuals represent two prospects, since some are buyers or potential buyers as agents of their organizations and again as individuals. (Remember that individuals usually make buying decisions for government agencies, associations, companies, and other organizations, as well as for their own families and for themselves personally.)

Classifying individuals as prospective markets poses the same problems as classifying companies and other organizations does. The classification makes sense—marketing sense, that is—only in relation to what you have to offer. If you are marketing a newsletter offering advice on investments, your marketing will only be of interest to people who have surplus income which they choose to invest. It will not be useful to address your offer to those whose economic status precludes their ability to make investments.

Obvious though this may appear to be, many people, even those with some experience, fail to study their markets and market segments and waste much of their marketing efforts soliciting people who are not likely to be interested, or they address prospects with the wrong appeal.

Deciding what appeal is most appropriate for each market segment is another consideration, one that will be covered in more depth in the chapter dealing with marketing and advertising per se. However, it bears heavily on identifying markets, for flexibility and imagination in designing the appeal can broaden the market considerably, adding segments. For example, you might be able to add to your market for an investment-advisory newsletter some people of lower-income status, by promising information about penny stocks, which enable almost everyone to invest at least on a modest scale. So it is not efficient to study markets purely on demographic considerations or on any basis that does not include consideration of ways in which an appeal—and, therefore, the market base—can be broadened.

MARKETS FOR CONSULTING SERVICES

There are some who think that the "advice business" and consulting are one and the same. Essentially, these are purists, people who tend to insist that consultants render counsel and guidance—advice, that is—and nothing else. And, these savants continue, anyone who goes beyond the giving of advice—who ventures to actually perform *work*—is no longer a consultant but has become a free-lance worker.

That is in itself one reason that *advice business* is a better and broader term than *consulting*. The latter term has been badly compromised by those purists who believe that their professional dignity is sacrificed when they assume postures other than that of the sage. A controversy rages to this day over just what consulting is and just what a consultant does that distinguishes him or her as a consultant.

Perhaps nowhere has the argument been more apparent than in the federal government, where, under the Carter administration, the OMB—the Office of Management and Budget—waged open war on consulting as a service performed under contract to federal agencies. The furor subsided considerably with the demise of that administration and its replacement, but the controversy has in truth never been resolved, and even today the various agencies have different views of what consulting is and is not.

Even in the narrowest view, the market for consulting services to federal agencies is probably well over $3 billion annually. And in the broader view, in which consulting includes actually performing some of the tasks that call for special knowledge and skills—such as developing standards for a research study or evaluating technical proposals in some complex field—the annual total is probably in excess of $12 billion.

So even at its minimum, consulting is a substantial share of the advice market among the federal agencies. There is also a major market for consulting services in other areas—state and local governments and private-sector organizations. There is also a market represented by individuals, at least for some kinds of consultants. (For example, those planning to enter into a free-lance or self-employment venture often solicit consulting services—advice, that is.)

Consulting is therefore very much a part of the advice business. At the minimum, even under the strictest of interpretations, it is the rendering of advice on an individual, custom basis, in response to individual, specific situations and needs. In more general terms, it is basically advisory, but may include problem solving and other hands-on working functions, applying the special skills and knowledge that are the basis of the consultant's practice.

Types of Consultancies

The consulting specialties—and consulting is by nature an activity that is based on specialized skills and/or knowledge—are growing steadily. This is not surprising because consulting is by its nature the consequence of complexities that require special training and experience for proficiency. For example, the medical profession, with its many specialties, uses consulting services regularly. The physician who encounters a complication or symptoms outside his or her special field almost reflexively calls in a specialist in that other field. In fact, medicine is perhaps the classic case of the use of consultation, but it is certainly not the only one—not today. Today, a field that may have been a consulting field a few years ago is fragmented into many such fields. Electronics, for example, has itself spawned many specialties. No one attempts to be a generalist in that field today. But even in less technological fields, there has been an increasing sophistication and complexity, which have been the natural causes or bases for consulting services. Here are just a few illustrations of that:

- *Political consulting:* There are specialists who advise candidates for public office and who perform a variety of duties concerning organizing and conducting campaigns.

- *Polling and surveying:* There are many specialists, some of them working primarily in the political arena, who are experts at public opinion polling and surveying.
- *Management:* Management consulting is itself a broad field which has fragmented into subordinate specialties, such as those in which clients are advised on office procedures, organization, work-flow systems, and sundry other matters concerning management.
- *Financial matters:* There are many financial consultants. Some advise clients on financing businesses—the best, most economical ways of funding enterprises; some aid clients in one-time funding requirements, such as floating a stock or bond issue; and some act as brokers or agents in finding funds for business.
- *Investment counselors:* There are many investment counselors, serving individuals largely, but also serving organizations, especially those charged with taking care of trust funds or otherwise managing other people's money.

These are less than a handful of examples; there are literally hundreds, perhaps even thousands of consulting specialties, depending on how you choose to define the term.

It is significant that general interest in consulting, as a profession, has grown steadily in recent years. It is not surprising, perhaps, in view of the fact that more and more people are trained as specialists, often in relatively narrow fields, and they are increasingly aware that many of today's activities depend entirely on the services of people trained in specialized fields. The entire computer industry is one outstanding example of that, but it is not the only one, nor is technology the only cause of increases in complexity and specialization. There are few general practitioners in many fields today—law and medicine are not the only fields in which practitioners must choose their specialties if they are to survive and prosper.

Coupled with the relative ease with which one may become self-employed in an independent consulting practice—little or no capital investment, working from one's home, starting part-time with contacts resulting from earlier employment, and with no license requirements, in most cases—the growing popularity of consulting is not difficult to understand.

So we may consider consulting to be a part of the advice business, for its basis is, indeed, advice, and we may consider it to be a market unto itself, with its own segments.

Consulting Market Segments

The first major subdivision of consulting is, as already noted, into the market segments represented by organizations and by individuals. Which is the major market segment—and perhaps the only attainable market segment, in some cases—depends largely on the nature of the field. It would be difficult to find individual clients seeking help in designing major inventory systems, or to find large companies interested in paying fees for marriage-counseling services, despite the fact that some consulting fields do lend themselves to both organizations and individuals as clients. But those two major subdivisions are too gross a set of definitions to serve usefully as guidance for marketing efforts, and it is necessary to subdivide these again.

In my own case, for example, most of my clients are companies seeking to do business with the federal government, and they want either help in training their staffs or help in developing specific proposals—or both. There is an occasional individual client, but by and large the clients are companies seeking government business.

On the other hand, size of the client company is not a factor in this case: Client companies include some very small enterprises, employing a relative handful of people, and some super-corporations, even Fortune 500 corporations. The chief factor, in this case, is the client's desire to do business that requires the preparation of proposals. It is that area of skill and knowledge in which the client feels the need for help, and even some of the largest corporations are not confident of their skills and knowledge in this field.

On the other hand, because it is possible for self-employed individuals—free-lance entrepreneurs of many kinds—to win government contracts, and many do, there is also a market for services to such individuals, if one wishes to pursue this market.

POSITIONING, PACKAGING, AND MARKETS

Consulting demonstrates, as clearly as any example could, the interdependency and interrelationships among positioning, packaging, and market identifications. To a large extent, market identifications depend on how you choose to position and package what you offer to sell. In some cases, you can diversify your offer to make it a candidate for many markets, whereas there are some cases where the item you offer simply is not adaptable to more than a few markets. At the same time, everything is a trade-off: To diversify and multiply the number of markets or market segments to which you can appeal, you must give up something else. And one thing you almost always must give up in this kind of exchange is the degree to which you are specialized. In becoming a bit less specialized, as you must in diversifying and broadening your markets, you lose some of your appeal, some of your exclusivity. That costs you something.

Later, when we discuss marketing per se, you will be able to see this a bit more clearly, probably, as it applies to your own situation. You will see that in most cases, markets and market segments are not inevitable consequences dictated by circumstances, but are to at least some extent the direct result of your own decisions and choices. The point is to make those decisions and choices with full knowledge of their consequences—to choose the trade-offs consciously and deliberately.

Chapter 4

How to Develop Packages:
Printing and Publication

It's been a long time since the invention of movable type, and the once-romantic arts of printing and publications are almost a mundane routine today, with modern refinements making them increasingly simple.

EVEN PRINTING HAS YIELDED
TO TECHNOLOGY

The technological revolution of this century has not been confined to electronics, to air travel and space exploration, or to other exotic and romantic fields, but has invaded even the most mundane human activities, such as printing. The storied "ink-stained wretches" of earlier times are no longer, nor do printers now employ "printer's devils," those errand-boy apprentices who once learned the printer's trade in that manner. For printing is today no longer the craft it was when a major portion of the printer's craft lay in those skills and that knowledge necessary to know all the various typefaces and type fonts, and in the ability to set copy rapidly by plucking the type from the various bins in the standard "California case" of the days of type set by hand in metal "chases." Today's printer is likely to know little or nothing of type and typesetting, and no longer uses metal type, in fact, but prints from inexpensive paper or plastic plates made in an automatic or semiautomatic platemaking machine, mounted on an automatic or semiautomatic offset printing press.

In fact, for much of the printing done today, the printing presses are not much more complex or sophisticated than the mimeograph machines of old, and the skills required to run them are of the same order. One no longer need apprentice for years to print efficiently and effectively, and typesetting is itself radically different and simpler than it once was and requires correspondingly less special training and experience.

The effect of this on the advice business—and on many other businesses, for that matter—has been revolutionary. It has, for one thing, had a profound effect on the ready availability of information in printed form. That is, it has vastly increased the amount of information available in inexpensive forms to anyone interested. That is because it is now less costly to produce printed matter, especially specialized material required in small quantities. (Per unit cost for printed matter in small quantities was formerly quite high because of the great amount of labor required to set type and make printing plates.) Too, it is now possible to produce printed matter far more rapidly than formerly. A printing job that once took days can now be done in hours, and there is an abundance of while-you-wait print shops today.

Strictly speaking, it is not absolutely necessary to understand the printing process to enjoy the advantages of today's systems and services. But it is an advantage to understand them in principle, at least, if you are going to prepare copy to be printed by today's offset systems, for you then have a far more useful understanding of what must be done and why it must be done when preparing copy. The following, then, is not intended to be an exhaustive examination of offset printing, but an orientation to the method and its basic principles, including an introduction to the special terms used in the industry.

LITHOGRAPHY

Perhaps you have heard the term *lithograph* or its more popular contraction, *litho,* referring to the print of a famous piece of art. Lithography is the method used to make such prints, and is based on using a specially prepared flat stone as the printing plate.

In conventional printing, as exemplified by Gutenberg, the typefaces were raised. Ink was applied to the typefaces and the paper pressed against the inked surfaces, transferring the image of that surface to the paper. Quite a simple method, basically.

Early type was carved from wood, but soon type was made from soft metals—lead, principally, alloyed with other metals to harden it—which melted easily and could be cast. Printers set the copy, character by character, by hand, in a *chase,* a metal form which was then mounted on the press and used as the printing plate.

Before long, the *linotype* machine came along. Here the operator used a typewriterlike keyboard to cast type in column-width lines, and these were set in chases, for small presses, or forms, for large presses. (Plates would be made from these forms.)

Lithography works on a completely different principle from that of inking raised-surface typefaces and transferring the ink to paper pressed against those raised and inked surfaces. Lithography makes use of the fact that oil and water will not mix. The material that is to be printed is created on the flat stone as a greasy image, and water is applied to the stone. The water is rejected by the greasy image but clings to the rest of the stone surface as a wet film. Then a greasy ink is applied to the surface of the stone. Now the wet areas reject the ink, but the greasy areas accept it. Paper is then pressed against the stone, and the ink, clinging to the greasy areas, is transferred to the paper.

PHOTO-OFFSET LITHOGRAPHY

The principle that is used almost universally in printing today is referred to as *offset, photo-offset, offset lithography* (despite the fact that the printing plate is not stone), and related terms. Instead of stone, plates are made of thin metal, paper, plastic, and foil-covered paper. Metal and foil-covered paper plates are "burned" in a platemaker using a photographic film negative; paper and plastic plates are made in other machines, using cameras, to make plates by a method known as *photo-direct.* There are two methods in use for that. The older one uses sensitized paper, similar to that used for printing photographs taken with a camera. The more recent and more popular one today, an electrostatic or xerographic process, is similar to the system used for making copies in most offices. (In fact, it is possible to make printing plates on office copiers.)

In all these methods, a camera copies whatever is placed before it—typed material, material drawn, materials pasted up, or anything else created by such methods—and the image appears on the printing plate as a copy of the original. However, the image on that printing plate will accept oily or greasy ink but will reject water. Hence, when it is treated as was the stone in the original example presented here, the image rejects the water and accepts the ink, but only the image is inked. However, the plate is a "positive" of the copy, and were that image transferred directly to paper, it would be reversed—a mirror image—on the paper. So it is first "offset" to a soft roller, called a *blanket* or *blanket roller,* as a reversed image, and the paper is then pressed against that blanket roller, producing a final, positive image—hence the name *photo-offset lithography.*

TYPESETTING AND COPY PREPARATION

The photo-offset method has not only revolutionized printing, but has made even more revolutionary changes in typesetting and other copy preparation. Today, type is set by typewriter almost as often as it is by any other method, especially since modern electric typewriters and one-time-use carbon ribbons have brought such order-of-magnitude improvements in the quality of typed copy. Offset printing methods will, in fact, reproduce anything that the camera can see. (In fact, it was this consideration, rather than simplification of the printing process per se, that impelled the rapid development and adoption of offset printing.)

Today you can prepare your copy—a newsletter, perhaps—in the morning, take it to a quick-service shop in the afternoon, have it printed while you wait, and have it in the mail that evening. Technology has made this possible.

Of course, an even later development, the xerographic or electrostatic office copier, has also entered the picture. Copies made by this method in the early machines were of relatively poor quality, but the technology has advanced rapidly, and most modern office copiers produce copies of a quality equal to—and sometimes even exceeding that of—the original copy. In many cases it is more practicable to use this method of reproduction. For example, if you need only 25 or 50 copies of a page or two, you can probably get them faster and at no greater cost by using an office copier, and the copies will usually be of quality equal to that of the offset press.

OFFICE COPIER TECHNOLOGY AND LASER PRINTING

The technology of the office copier—xerographic/electrostatic copying technology, that is—would be of little other than possible academic interest here were it not for the recent advent and the probable rapid evolution of what promises to become an important new technology: laser printing. But to understand laser printing, in principle, it is necessary to understand the basics of xerography.

This technology has nothing to do with offset printing technology, despite the fact that it produces the same result—printing whatever the camera sees. For office copiers do use a camera to photograph the copy you place on the viewing glass plate. However, instead of the image seen by the camera being presented to a photo-sensitized (silver-salt–coated) film, it is presented to a selenium-coated metal drum (although a few copiers use a slightly different system of "masters"). The drum surface is electrically charged, but where the light strikes it, the charge is dissipated. The remaining charges represent the image on the original copy and are, in fact, an invisible, electrostatic image or "photograph" of it. And now, when a dry powder is brushed across the surface of the drum, it clings to those charged areas. A sheet of paper, with the opposite electrical charge, is then pressed against the drum (or master), and the powder clings to the paper. Using heat, the powder is then fused to the paper, to create a permanent copy.

The emerging technology known as "laser printing" is a marriage of computer technology—word processing, in fact—the laser, and the electrostatic copier. However, instead of the word processor driving a printer to produce "hard-copy" output, which would then possibly be copied by an office copier, the word processor drives a laser output, which "paints" the copy on the charged drum as an electrostatic photograph or image, and the copier produces the required number of paper copies (see Figure 4-1).

The immediate advantage is speed. The process eliminates that preliminary step of producing a paper master or original to be copied,

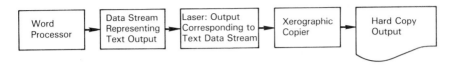

FIGURE 4-1 Basic steps/functions in laser printing

by translating the computer output directly to electrostatic images, saving both time and labor. There is some slight sacrifice in quality, inasmuch as the characters are painted on as a series of dots, in a dot-matrix pattern, but this is compensated and (it is claimed) overcome by using extreme dot densities, ranging to 300 by 300 dot matrices (per square inch), for a total of 90,000 dots per square inch.

The method offers an advantage in many situations. For example, J. Dick & Company, of Highland Park, Illinois, publishes a directory, *Leading Consultants in Computer Software,* using the laser printing method. This enables the publisher to keep the directory up to date because the method permits printing the directory in a small quantity, with frequent updates ("binding" is in a three-ring binder). The company reports, in the front matter of the directory, that it is printed on a Xerox 9700 Electronic Printing System in approximately 1 minute. (For those interested, the company is at 500 Hyacinth Place, Highland Park, IL 60035, and publishes other directories.)

TYPESETTING/COMPOSITION METHODS

Composition—probably a more appropriate term, in many instances, than the word *typesetting*—is most often done for small-scale publications, such as reports and newsletters, by electric typewriters. Even the military manuals ordered by the various armed services to guide service personnel in installing, operating, and maintaining equipment are usually composed by that method or its equivalent.

At an earlier time there were other "cold type" machines (so called to distinguish typewriterlike composition from the cast-metal type fonts of earlier days, often referred to today as "hot type," "hot metal," or just "metal"). They were, in fact, all patterned on the typewriter in their basic characteristics, in that all were "impact" or "strike on" machines, which struck a metal typeface against paper through an inked or carbon ribbon of some sort. With the advent of the IBM Executive typewriter, with its carbon ribbon, followed by the versatile Selectric, with its changeable font or "element," and followed later by the IBM Composer, a true setter of cold type, emphasis began to shift away from these manually operated cold-type typesetters.

Meanwhile, competitors began to produce "electronic" type-writers, still very much in vogue today. These have fewer moving parts than the earlier electric typewriters because they use electronic controls to replace many of the mechanical controls of earlier machines. They also have memories, which can store a few pages of copy and remember a number of characters for correction by means of the "lift-off" feature, automatic centering and underlining, and a few other special refinements.

Meanwhile, typesetting began to become a photographic technology, which produced cold type on sensitized paper, which could then be pasted up to produce final master copy for platemaking. In fact, one machine was called a "linofilm" machine, to dramatize the fact that it does at least as much as the older linotype machine did for type-setting and composition. True typesetting was soon primarily the product of systems based on this principle.

With the steady progress of computer technology, something called "word processing" came into existence. In this method, computers are used to compose copy electronically, presenting it on a TV-like screen for review, editing, and correction, and finally printing it out on a typewriterlike device.

The latter system really came of age with the development of microcircuits and the resulting microchips and microcomputers. Suddenly, almost overnight, word processing was a practical reality for even the smallest office and, for that matter, even for the self-employed free-lance writer working at home. (In fact, word processing is today the most popular application of microcomputers.) Typically, the modern word processor is a computer with a CRT (cathode-ray tube) display screen, a typewriterlike keyboard for inputting the words, external storage (usually disk drives), and a printer of some sort (see Figure 4-2).

Word processing is often regarded with skepticism by those long accustomed to producing copy via typewriter and satisfied with the method. They tend to regard word processing as little more than automatic typing, and hence treat it with some disdain. However, few of

FIGURE 4-2 The popular Tandy Corp/Radio Shack TRS-80 word processor (Courtesy of Tandy Corp/Radio Shack)

those who finally succumb to the lure and actually buy and begin to use word processors fail to become champions of the method. Isaac Asimov, for example, insisted that word processing would neither speed up nor in any way enhance his already prodigious output. However, he confessed that he thoroughly enjoyed other attributes of the system, such as being able to make corrections before printing the copy out, and thus offering his publishers cleaner manuscripts. And he enjoyed the never-ending "magic" of the system, as well. Most people do. It is so easy to insert a paragraph, drop a sentence, rework a page, change words in the middle of a description, add or delete punctuation, and make hundreds of other changes by pressing a few keys before printing the copy. It is marvelous, too, as another writer pointed out, to have the system do "global searches" to see if you have used a certain term before or to count how many times you used it before; or to have the machine go through all the dozens of pages already input and change all those "principles" to "principals."

Word processing is, of course, far more than automatic typing. It enables you to do a great many things you cannot do with an ordinary —or even extraordinary—typewriter. And it enables you also to do most things you can do with an ordinary typewriter much more efficiently, rapidly, and effectively than you could do them with a typewriter. It is the modern way to compose and prepare manuscript and even final copy.

Word-Processing Output

Two general types of printers are used with word processors: the dot-matrix printer and the "letter-quality" printer. Typically, dot-matrix printers use a matrix of blunt needles, which strike the paper through a ribbon to form characters (see Figures 4-3 and 4-4). This offers a number of advantages, despite some sacrifice in overall quality (although there are ways to improve the quality until it approaches letter-quality quite closely). In general, dot-matrix printers are faster than are the other types, can vary sizes readily, can mix fonts without changing elements, and tend to be less expensive. They are also usually more flexible in printing out graphics.

Letter-quality printers generally use a "daisy wheel" element, which may be replaced easily to change type fonts. Daisy-wheel printers produce the same quality as that produced by ordinary electric and electronic typewriters. They are, in general, considerably slower in operation than are dot-matrix printers and are not quite as well suited

FIGURE 4-3   Outline of a typical dot matrix printer: Quantex Model 7030 (Courtesy of North Atlantic Industries)

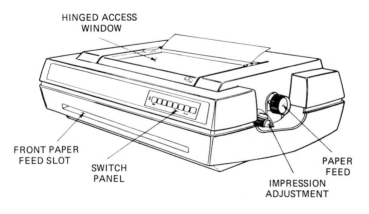

HINGED ACCESS
WINDOW

FRONT PAPER
FEED SLOT
SWITCH
PANEL
IMPRESSION
ADJUSTMENT
PAPER
FEED

```
Performance Characteristics are:
    120 Characters Per Second Print Speed
    Bidirectional Print Technique
    Short Line Logic Seeking
Standard Features are:
    96 ASCII Character Set
    True Descenders in Lower Case -i.e. great, printing, output
    64 Block Graphic Characters
    9X9 Dot Matrix
    4 Programmable Character Sizes
    Parallel AND Serial Interfaces
    6&8 Lines Per Inch Vertical Line Spacing
    Friction AND Pin Feed Paper Handling
    Electronic Vertical Format Unit (VFU) - 12 Channels
    Top of Form - 10 Switch or Program Selectable Lengths
    Platen Knob for Easy Paper Loading
    Paper Out Switch for Detecting End of Paper
    Column Indicator to Line Up Text
    Accommodates 1 to 4 Part Paper

Optional Items are:
    OKIGRAPH I Dot Addressable Graphics Kit
    OKIGRAPH II Graphics Software Package
    9600 Baud Serial Interface with 2K Buffer & Current Loop
    IEEE-488 Interface with Address Capability
    Tractor Feed for Paper Handling
    Printer Stand
```

FIGURE 4-4   Dot matrix printing (Courtesy of Okidata Corporation)

to printing out graphic devices. They tend also to be more costly than dot-matrix printers, although there are many exceptions to this (see Figure 4-5).

FIGURE 4-5   MorrowWriter system, complete with letter-quality daisy-wheel printer (Courtesy of Morrow Designs)

Note in these figures that the printers do not have keyboards. That is because inputs to the printers are from the computer, which has its own keyboard for inputting. However, there are printers available which do have their own keyboards. In fact, they are generally electric or electronic typewriters which have been adapted especially to serve as word-processing printers. This means that the machine can be used as both the output printer for the word processor and as an independent typewriter. There are many small tasks which are accomplished much more easily and efficiently by typewriter than by word processor, and word processing does not eliminate the typewriter by any means; but some word-processor owners prefer to have a single machine that can serve as both printer and typewriter.

Modern Typesetters

Today, the phototypesetter resembles the word processor quite closely, and in fact they are not readily distinguishable from each other in external appearance. Nor are they greatly different from each other in their major functions. The principal difference is the output: The typesetter produces high-quality output that is at least the equal of metal type in all respects, and, of course, it can do the font changes that are normally accomplished with metal type, switching from whatever is the body type to small capitals, boldface, italics, foreign characters, or whatever else is required.

Like most modern word processors, phototypesetters today use disks, both the plastic "floppies" and the higher-capacity hard (metal) disks for mass storage. In this and in other ways, phototypesetters are compatible with many word processors and thus can accept data directly from word processors.

The significance of this is in the ability of phototypesetters to take data directly from word-processor sources and turn out type spontaneously. In fact, there are a number of ways that word-processor output—manuscript copy—can be input to phototypesetters to produce typseset copy for pasteup, preparatory to making plates and printing the output product. In fact, there are a number of levels of such interface relationships. Figure 4-6 and Table 1 illustrate this, starting with the lowest level of intersystem compatibility (and resultant efficiency) and progressing to the highest level of compatibility and efficiency.

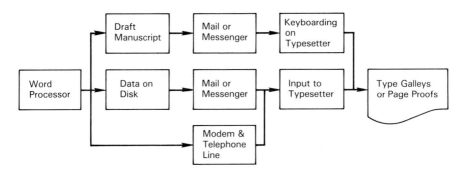

FIGURE 4-6 Several alternative ways of getting copy to typesetting

Unfortunately, by far the majority of situations today are those of the first of the five stages of compatibility/efficiency presented, primarily because there are still a limited number of word-processor systems that can input to a phototypesetter with even a partial degree of compatibility. However, in time, the compatibility will grow to the point represented by the fourth and fifth stages shown in the table. (For those not yet familiar with these systems, a *modem* is a *modu-lator–dem*odulator device which enables two computer systems to "talk" to each other via a telephone connection.) This will certainly change, in time, and our current systems of progressing from the writer at the typewriter to the printed copies in the mail will also change, with all the consequent improvements in efficiency.

TABLE 1   Possible Stages of Word Processor/Phototypesetter Compatibility

SOURCE DATA	TRANSMITTAL METHOD	INPUT METHOD/ REMARKS
Typed manuscript	Mail, messenger, shipment	Keyboarded by typesetter operator
Floppy disk	Mail, messenger	Converted/translated for phototypesetter input
Floppy disk	Modem and telephone	Converted/translated for phototypesetter input
Floppy disk	Modem and telephone	Copied directly by photo-typesetter computer, stored on disk for outputting
Floppy disk	Modem and telephone	Output in real time (while being transmitted)

The reason there are so many separate levels of compatibility and resulting levels of efficiency is that the computer industry has only limited degrees of standardization. Therefore, the floppy disk on which you record your manuscript may not be compatible with the phototypesetter. Sometimes compatibility can be established by another bit of software, which translates the input floppy to terms the phototypesetter computer can "read" and utilize. In this case, the phototypesetter computer can either copy the data on its own floppy disk and in its own language and according to its own operating system, or it may even be able to respond spontaneously to the input and do the typesetting immediately, in "real time," as the data are received.

The latter is most efficient, normally, although it is not always possible, either for technical (compatibility) reasons or because of schedule conflicts. However, we are approaching this level, and one day the bulk of our typesetting will be done by sending data in over the telephone to drive the typesetter directly or to be recorded for later typesetting.

DOT-ADDRESSED GRAPHICS

One of the advantages of dot-matrix printers over daisy-wheel printers is that the former are more flexible than the latter in printing out graphics. Figure 4-7 illustrates some of the simpler graphics capabilities. However, it is possible to do far more sophisticated graphics than these, including a variety of charts—bar charts, pie charts, and others—as well as the graphs and plots suggested in the figure.

This ability is an enormous advantage when preparing reports and other documents and publications. A complaint raised by some is that word processors are severely slowed down by commands to print out graphics. However, in the worst case, the slowest printer will almost surely outspeed the fastest illustrator in producing such graphics. But the benefit does not end there; even if an illustrator turned out a chart or diagram as rapidly as a word processor, there is still the delay of fitting the copy together, compared with the efficiency of having the text and illustrations produced together, in a single, coherent output. (If that is not yet crystal clear, it will be clearer when we discuss the assembly of all final camera-ready materials to produce the "mechanicals," or masters from which printing plates will be made.)

FIGURE 4-7   Examples of dot-addressed graphics printouts (Courtesy of Oki-data Corporation)

Figure 4-8 shows the full dot matrix of which a 5 by 7 dot matrix printhead is capable, enlarged, of course, because the overall dimensions of the full matrix are no larger than the largest character in the font. For a 12-pitch printer—12 characters to the inch, the most popular typewriter size—that means that the print matrix must not be more than ½ inch.

In the case illustrated, the matrix is a 5 by 7, for a total of only 35 dots maximum, to outline a character. However, many printers have larger matrices—a 9 by 7 matrix, for example, would print up to 65 dots, and even larger matrices are possible. However, even with a 5 by 7 matrix, many printers can do other things which increase the number of dots. In a "double pass" mode, for example, the printer can utilize twice the number of dots by printing each character twice, the second time slightly offset from the first, so that a 5 by 7 matrix can produce 70 dots, a 9 by 12 matrix can produce 130 dots, and so on.

The adjective "dot addressable" means that the program can specify each dot to be printed, and it is because of this ability that a printer can draw plots, charts, and other graphics—even simulate half-

FIGURE 4-8   Expanded view of 5x7 dot matrix

● ● ● ● ●   Printhead:
● ● ● ● ●   Set of seven "needles"
● ● ● ● ●   Total number
● ● ● ● ●   of dots possible
● ● ● ● ●   in matrix
● ● ● ● ●
● ● ● ● ●

tone photos, as witness the sketch of the late Winston Churchill in Figure 4-7. And when referring to graphic printing, as when referring to dot-addressable graphics presented on the CRT monitor screen, it is customary to talk about resolution in terms of dots per square inch rather than per character or per printhead matrix. You may recall that the laser printing description specified a matrix of 300 by 300 dots per square inch, for a total possibility of 90,000 dots per square inch. This offers a relatively high resolution, claimed in advertising to be equal to typewriter quality.

LAYOUTS AND MECHANICALS

The very word *publication* has a wide number of implemented definitions, from the one-page, all-text newsletter set totally by typewriter, to the complex, multivolume set of case-bound books with process-color illustrations, tables, and other manifestations of the bookmaker's art in its highest form. It should be obvious that in our discussions here, we are not suggesting anything approaching the latter extreme. Yet, with the help of developments of recent years, neither must we confine ourselves to the near-primitive methods of the opposite extreme. It is now possible to produce highly professional publications at costs which are within reason for even the smallest of enterprises. To produce something much more sophisticated and polished than that example of a simple one-page newsletter, however, it is necessary to become aware of and utilize a few of the basic methods used in producing publications. And since we have already discussed several methods for producing text—body copy—and even touched on graphics, the logical next step is to discuss layouts and mechanicals. This covers the steps required to plan the actual publication and prepare the copy physically for the platemaking and printing operation—or even for duplicating on an office copier, if that is to be the method of production.

Definitions

A *layout* is a plan for assembling all the elements of the publication, and is particularly appropriate—and necessary—when the publication combines a number of elements on a page, such as text, headlines, tables, and/or artwork—drawings and/or photos. In fact, a layout is also a sketch or diagram of that plan, and the term therefore refers to both the plan or design itself and to the sketch.

Of course, one cannot plan a multipage brochure or book with a single layout; there must be a layout for each page (sometimes referred to as a *page layout*). So it is possible for a publication to require several layouts—at least one for each page that will contain some mix of elements which must be fitted together.

For many publications, such as a manual or proposal that is to have only a limited number of copies, a simplified plan is used to avoid the expense and consumption of time that is required to prepare layouts. In this simplified plan, there are no layouts per se because elements are not mixed on a page, or if they are, the simplest possible arrangement is used. But customarily, for this type of publication, each page of text has only text on it, and any special elements, such as a table or illustration of some sort, appears on a separate page, without text.

That makes the publications planning quite simple. Whenever a table or illustration is to appear, the text introduces it, and it appears on the next page. (In some cases, the introduction is made at the appropriate place in the text, but the table or illustration appears at the back of the publication or even in a special appendix. This is the exception, however.)

There are three kinds or levels of layout: rough, comprehensive, and mechanical. In general, the rough layout is, as its title suggests, a preliminary plan and sketch, prepared primarily to be reviewed and evaluated. Once it has been reviewed and final decisions made, a comprehensive layout is prepared. The *comprehensive,* as it is commonly called, is the final plan and shows precisely where each element of the page fits. Headlines and titles are sketched in also. Figure 4-9 illustrates a comprehensive.

Finally, a *mechanical* is prepared. The mechanical is the camera-ready master copy that the comprehensive was the plan for, the actual page that will be photographed and printed. Figure 4-10 shows the mechanical of the page planned in the comprehensive of Figure 4-9.

Note that the comprehensive is still a sketch, largely freehand, but showing just how the copy will be fitted to the page. Headlines and other indicators identify the copy for each space. Indicators are placed,

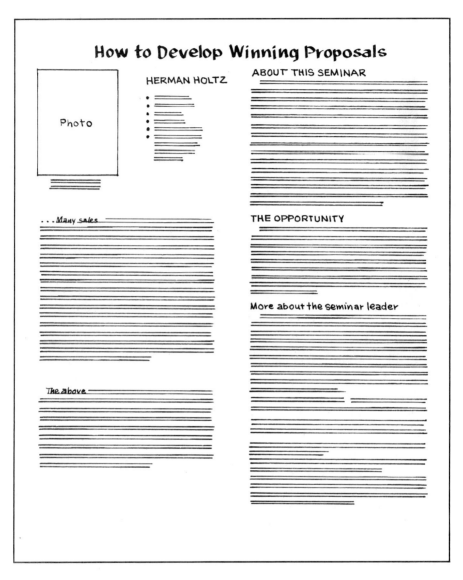

FIGURE 4-9 Comprehensive layout of copy for mechanical

also, for any artwork. If the artwork is a line drawing of any kind, it will be "sized"—enlarged or reduced (reduced, usually, since drawing the artwork on a large scale and reducing it by photography greatly increases the apparent detail and sharpness) to the actual size it is to be on the mechanical—and then pasted in place together with the text, which is also "line copy." But if a photograph or other continuous-tone

How to Develop Winning Proposals

HERMAN HOLTZ
SEMINAR LEADER

HERMAN HOLTZ

- Consultant
- Lecturer
- Author
- Engineer
- Seminar Leader
- Winner of over $125 million in government contracts

ABOUT THIS SEMINAR

In this seminar you will spend a full intensive day with one of the nation's foremost experts in the field of government contracts. You will learn about the entire marketing process for government business and will be shown how to write proposals that win. The main emphasis of this seminar will be on factors for success. Have you heard that all bids you see in the *Commerce Business Daily (CBD)* are wired? That it is futile to bid them? That you have to be a huge corporation to do business with the government? . . . myths, all of them (and other tales like them). Herman Holtz has been proving that for years, over and over. That's what led to this seminar. He decided it was time to tell other government marketers the truth. You will learn: how to develop streamlined marketing techniques; how to take advantage of hidden rules and regulations; how to obtain inside information; and, most of all, how to write superior proposals, the kind that WIN.

THE OPPORTUNITY

The government spends over $160 billion annually in goods and services. This money flows to literally thousands of companies—many very small, some very large. All of them have to learn the very special way the government does business. Either they learn it by listening to those who know, or they learn the hard way. This seminar offers you the opportunity to gain a competitive edge for your company; whether you are a small business or an executive with a large firm.

More about the seminar leader:

HERMAN R. HOLTZ, consultant, lecturer, freelance writer, and small independent government contractor since 1974, holds a B.S. degree in Electronics Engineering. He has been Director of Marketing at Volt Information Sciences, Inc. and Applied Science Associates, and has worked in various capacities as Editorial Director of the Educational Science Division, U.S. Industries. A participant in many major programs, including Apollo, Atlas and BMEWS Titan Missile programs, Mr. Holtz is also author of such recent books as:

GOVERNMENT CONTRACTS: Proposalmanship and Winning Strategies, Plenum Publishing Corporation, NYC, 1979.

THE $100 BILLION MARKET, AMACOM (publishing division of American Management Association), NYC, 1980.

THE WINNING PROPOSAL: How to Write it, McGraw-Hill, NYC, 1980 (scheduled).

ANYONE CAN DO BUSINESS WITH THE GOVERNMENT, Government Marketing News, Washington, DC, 1976.

PROFIT FROM YOUR MONEY-MAKING IDEAS: How to build a new business or expand an existing one, AMACOM, NYC, 1980.

DIRECTORY OF FEDERAL PURCHASING OFFICES: Where, What, How to Sell to the U.S. Government John Wiley & Sons, NYC, 1981.

". . . Many sales presentations are good up to the point of credibility. They get attention, they offer benefits (reasons to buy), they are easy to understand—and then they fall on their faces because they fail to convince. They fail to compel belief that they will deliver as promised.

"The chief problem is that so many writers mistakenly believe that CLAIMS ARE EVIDENCE. Typically, such a writer will say some such thing as, 'J. Black and Company is the largest tool manufacturer in our industry,' which is obviously a claim, the writer's opinion. The adjective, 'largest,' is the giveaway. Lay off the adjectives and adverbs, and stick to the nouns and verbs. As Walter Brennan used to say in one of his TV characterizations, 'No brag; just fact.'"

"Let's take that claim of being largest. Suppose we said it this way: "J. Black and Company employs 7,000 employees in 43 plants throughout the United States. That's EVIDENCE. No claims; just reporting the facts . . ." says HERMAN HOLTZ.

The above is just a sample of the kind of hard-hitting pointers on proposal development that you can expect to receive from Herman Holtz at this seminar. Holtz knows his business, and his business is the governments. His own proposals have won more than $125 million in contracts from such diverse government agencies as NASA, the FAA, Departments of Labor and Commerce, the Army, the Navy and HUD. An electronics engineer by formal training, Holtz has worked in various capacities for RCA, IBM, GE, and other large, successful outfits.

FIGURE 4-10   Mechanical: master copy ready for camera

material is to be printed, it must be screened as a halftone, and thus is not pasted down on the mechanical. Instead, a "mask" is pasted down of the exact size the photograph is to be. This is a rectangle of black paper (or, in some cases, ruby-colored paper, which the camera sees as "blacker than black"). When the page is photographed, to make a plate, the negative will have a "window," a clear space corresponding to the mask. Another negative, screened and with the screened photograph in the exact position that the window occupies on the first negative, is placed directly behind the first negative, for platemaking.

This procedure eliminates the labor of "stripping" the two negatives together, of actually splicing the screened photograph negative into the first negative, an alernative and classic way of making up "composite" negatives—negatives containing both line copy and screened or halftone copy. Of course, the printer does this, not you, but you simplify the printer's job if you prepare your mechanicals—use masks where photographs are to appear—for this easier way to making up the composite or combination negatives.

Note that we are talking about using negatives here, for platemaking, whereas we previously discussed methods of making "photodirect" plates, which do not require negatives and metal plates and are thus much less costly. However, there is no satisfactory way of reproducing photographs other than the screening and halftone process, and this can only be accomplished by first making a screened negative. It is possible to make a "line shot"—direct photograph—of a print of a photograph already screened and printed, and if the screen is a fairly coarse one, a fair quality of reproduction may be realized. But this is an expedient because there is usually a significant loss of quality in doing this, and it is generally considered much more satisfactory to make a screened negative of an original photograph.

Incidentally, "coarse" and "fine" refer to the screens used, since they are of various degrees of coarseness, depending on the number of "lines" in the screen. Photographs destined to be printed on newsprint or other coarse and highly absorbent paper are usually made on 75-line screens. If you look closely at a photograph (halftone) in a newspaper, you can generally make out the dots with the naked eye. On the other hand, if you examine a photograph printed in a magazine on smooth paper, you will probably need a magnifying glass to see the dots because a screen of perhaps as many as 225 lines was used to create the photo, resulting in a large number of very small dots rather than a lesser number of very large dots.

The screen size you can use, then, depends on the kind of paper you will print on. If it is important that your photographs be of high quality and reveal fine detail, you will have to plan to print on high-quality paper so that a fine screen may be used.

DUMMIES AND RUNNING SHEETS

Because publications vary so widely in styles, formats, and requirements, it is rare that you can simply turn over your copy, even if they
are mechanicals ready for platemaking, without specific instructions.
True, it is customary to begin a book or manual with a right-hand page
bearing the page number—folio—one, with its reverse side being page
two. But there are many customers who have special requirements.
Suppose, for example, that the copy is to be printed on one side only.
In that case, every page will be a right-hand page, and right-hand pages
will bear both odd and even page numbers.

That is not too difficult to specify. Simply advise the printer that
the copy is to be printed "one side only" or "front side only." Otherwise, he will take it for granted that you want to print "front and
back" or "two sides."

But suppose you want the manual printed front and back, but
there are some pages to be left blank on their reverse side. For example,
suppose that you want each chapter to begin on a right-hand page, with
an odd number, but some of your chapters end on right-hand pages.
That means that the reverse side ("verso") of those end-of-chapter
pages must be blank on their reverse side.

And there is front matter—title page, table of contents, frontis-
piece (if you use one), preface, foreword, or other: How is that to be
handled? (Front matter almost always requires a page or two to be
blank on its other side.)

There are two ways to instruct the printer as to how you want the
publication printed. You can supply a "dummy" or "printer's dummy,"
as it is also called, or you can supply a "running sheet." The chief difference between the two is that you generally use a printer's dummy
for a small publication, such as a small brochure or broadside that must
be explained, and a running sheet for a longer publication, such as a
book or manual of many pages.

The dummy is especially useful when the publication is one that
has no page numbers. In fact, it may be a broadside that opens up into
a large sheet, but is folded into a half-dozen or more "sides" or "pages."
Your copy, if it is a set of mechanicals (two, for a broadside, one for
the front and one for the back), is probably adequate for printing, but
you need a dummy to show the printer how to fold the printed sheet.

A dummy is simplicity itself: It is merely one or more sheets of paper, folded or otherwise arranged to represent the final publication, as you want it to appear, with each sheet and each side marked to make clear what copy appears there. In that sense, it is to the printer what the comprehensive is to whoever is fitting the copy together to make up the mechanicals.

A running sheet is a kind of schedule (see Figure 4-11), which serves the same purpose, guiding the printer in printing the copy and assembling the publication. As you can see, this form would be able to list all the pages of a sizable manual or brochure, even up to 168 pages. (For a larger book, additional pages of the running sheet would be used.)

This sheet is useful for a publication made up of single pages (front and back) assembled into a book or manual of some kind. However, not all books, manuals, and multipage brochures are printed and assembled by single sheets of two pages each; many are printed and assembled by *signatures,* a unit of two or more pages (although we are not concerned with any signature of fewer than four pages, for obvious reasons). In fact, many books are printed in signatures of 32 pages (signatures are usually multiples of 4). That is a sheet with 16 pages on each side, so two plates are required to print a signature, and it takes only eight signatures to make up a 256-page book.

For our purposes here we will not get into the complications of folding and binding books of 32-page signatures; we will use the saddle-stitched book, made up of a number of four-page signatures. The significance of bringing this entire matter up is that you will almost surely have to make up a dummy for your own use in numbering the pages and assembling the mechanicals for such a book. For the minute you depart from those single sheets of one or two pages each, you run into a somewhat more complicated problem of figuring out how to number your pages.

First of all, each mechanical for such a book is a *flat* containing the camera-ready copy for not one but two pages. Two such flats are required, one for each side of the sheet that will be the four-page signature. If the manual or book is to be an 8½-by-11-inch book, the flat must be 11 by 17 inches, so that the two pages are side by side on the flat. However, since the book is to be saddle-stitched, the pages must be numbered to reflect their relative positions in the bound book.

FRONT	BACK	FRONT	BACK	FRONT	BACK	FRONT	BACK
Title p	Blank	39	40				
iii	Blank	41	42				
iv	Blank	43	44				
v	vi						
vii	viii						
1	2						
3	4						
5	6						
7	8						
9	10						
11	12						
13	Blank						
14	Blank						
Blank	16						
17	18						
19	20						
21	22						
23	24						
25	26						
27	28						
29	Blank						
31	Blank						
33	Blank						
35	36						
37	38						

FIGURE 4-11 Partially filled out running sheet

Let us suppose, for the sake of argument, that the book is to be 64 pages, printed on both sides, except for the title page. A saddle-stitched book is one that consists of pages and cover folded in the middle and bound with a set of staples ("stitches") in the middle of the fold. Many magazines are bound this way, if they are not too thick, so you have almost surely seen and handled saddle-stitched publications, even if you did not know that term to describe their binding.

What this means is that the first page that appears inside the cover is the right-hand page of the flat that contains it, and the left-hand side of that flat holds the last page in the book. So that last page is the sixty-fourth page (see Figure 4-12) and the flat that contains that page also contains the first page. The flat that will present the camera-ready copy for the other side of that signature is composed of the next-to-first and next-to-last pages.

On the other hand, the signature that appears in the center of the book will contain consecutive pages on one side of the signature, with the lower number (the thirty-second page of the 64-page book) appearing as the left-hand page on the flat, and the thirty-third page appearing as the right-hand page of that flat.

Perhaps when you are thoroughly experienced, you can figure all that out in your head or with pencil and paper. But even experienced publications people tend to construct a dummy before laying out the flats for the signatures. It is quite difficult to do it any other way and

FIGURE 4-12   Flats making up one signature for saddle-stitched book

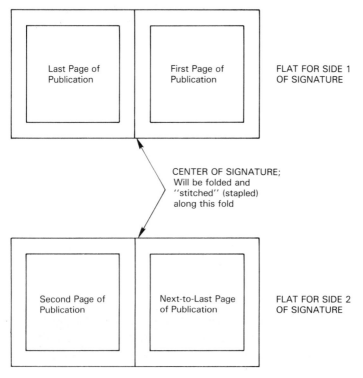

Last Page of Publication

First Page of Publication

FLAT FOR SIDE 1 OF SIGNATURE

CENTER OF SIGNATURE; Will be folded and "stitched" (stapled) along this fold

Second Page of Publication

Next-to-Last Page of Publication

FLAT FOR SIDE 2 OF SIGNATURE

get it right the first time—to match up the proper pages on the flats, that is. For even when you know the exact number of pages—arabic-numbered pages that make up the body text—you must take into account the pages that make up the front matter (title page, table of contents, preface, foreword, etc.), and the blank backs that appear. It is quite easy to slip up in your calculations and paste up the flats incorrectly, which turns into disaster rather rapidly. The few minutes required to make up a dummy before pasting up the flats is time well invested.

One of the problems is that the pages you have made up—for typically, you will make up the pages and then paste up the two-page flats from them, as the most practical way to do the job—account for all the pages on which there will be copy—all the pages that will print. But you tend to forget the blank pages, the backs of pages that print on one side only. So you may decide that all you have to do is to count the total number of pages you have and divide by two to determine which pages are the middle ones in the book. If the total number of pages is an odd one, you simply add 1, for then the last page in the book will necessarily be a blank page. So you count 63 camera-ready page mechanicals, and you add one, for a total of 64. That means that the thirty-second and thirty-third pages are your middle pages, and will face each other, left and right, on the flat. The other side of that signature will be the thirty-first and thirty-fourth pages, backing up the thirty-second and thirty-third pages, respectively; and so on, until you have all 64 pages pasted up. Then you discover that there are at least two other blank pages, and your flats are pasted up incorrectly. Actually, you must now plan for 66 pages, although only 63 print. If you make up a running sheet for this 66-page opus, you perceive this. But you also realize, soon enough, that you cannot make a saddle-stitched book of 66 pages because with a book made up of four-page signatures, the total number of pages must be a multiple of 4 (see Figure 4-13). So you add two more blank pages, to make a total of 68 pages, with 63 printing. Dividing that 68 by 4, you find that you will have 17 of those four-page signatures. Counting down the columns of the running sheet, you discover that the midpoint—the thirty-fourth page—will be page 26.

However, if you make up a paper dummy of the projected book, you will discover that the running sheet is of no help in making up the flats for the 17 signatures. In fact, the flats will work as shown in Fig-

FRONT	BACK	FRONT	BACK	FRONT	BACK	FRONT	BACK
Title p	Blank	41	42				
iii	Blank	43	44				
v	vi	45	46				
vii	Blank	47	48				
1	2	49	50				
3	4	51	52				
5	6	53	54				
7	8	55	56				
9	10	57	58				
11	12	Blank	Blank				
13	14						
15	16						
17	18						
19	20						
21	22						
23	24						
25	26						
27	28						
29	30						
31	32						
33	34						
35	36						
37	38						
39	40						

FIGURE 4-13 Running sheet for a 66 page saddle-stitched book

ure 4-14: The first page will be the right-hand side of the first flat, the left-hand side will be blank, and both sides of the flat for the opposite side of the signature will be blanks. The second signature will have pages iii and 58 (the last page that is printed) on one side, and pages 57 and a blank page on the other side. Make up a dummy for this book, and you will see why it works out this way.

Once you gain some familiarity with this, you may be able to use a form such as that shown in Figure 4-14, instead of making up a dummy.

SIGNATURE NO.	FLAT SIDE 1		FLAT SIDE 2	
	RH SIDE	LH SIDE	RH SIDE	LH SIDE
1	Title p	Blank	Blank	Blank
2	iii	58	57	Blank
3	v	56	55	vi
4	vii	54	53	Blank
5	1	52	51	2
6	3	50	49	4
7	5	48	47	6
8	7	46	45	8
9	9	44	43	10
10	11	42	41	12
11	13	40	39	14
12	15	38	37	16
13	17	36	35	18
14	19	34	33	20
15	21	32	31	22
16	23	30	29	24
17	25	28	27	26

FIGURE 4-14 Planning sheet for pasting up flats for 4 page signatures

But it does take some practice and careful checking to be sure that you have it all correct, before you make up the flats; it is remarkably easy to make a mistake in doing this.

Note that on all flats the right-hand side will be for the odd-numbered pages, the left-hand side for even-numbered pages. That is one thing to check almost automatically to verify that you have not made a mistake.

The cover has not been accounted for here, but it corresponds to the signatures because it prints the same way—two flats of two pages each, one for each side of the cover. Of course, the cover does not have page numbers of any kind, and many publications people refer to the four "pages" or sides of the cover as cover 1, cover 2, cover 3, and cover 4. Cover 1 refers to the outside front of the book—what might be referred to in general conversation as "the front cover." Cover 2 is the inside of the front cover, cover 3 the inside of the back cover, and cover 4 is the outside of the back cover. Flats are required for the cover, too, of course, corresponding to as many of the cover sides as are to be printed.

There are many other details involved in developing information packages for printing and publication, and this is not intended or expected to make you an expert in the field, but only to give you some basic orientation and familiarization with the basic techniques of getting your copy ready for printing and binding. Now let us get on to what are perhaps even more basic aspects of developing information and advice for publishing: developing basic ideas, doing the research, and developing the information for the packages.

CHAPTER 5

GIVING BIRTH TO
AND REARING IDEAS

*Marketing is one major key to success in any enterprise,
but first there must be something to market, and that
begins with an idea.*

A FEW FOR-INSTANCES

Plying the advice business as a lecturer and/or consultant has one immediate drawback if it is your goal to make a great deal of money: Those are primarily personal services, and no matter how handsome the fees you eventually are able to command, you are still limited to the number of hours you can bill clients for. You are therefore unlikely to make a great deal of money (although you may do quite well) unless you do either or both of two things usually necessary to earning a great deal of money: produce and sell a product and/or employ others and earn profits on their labor. For the average person trying to make rapid progress, it is generally more practicable to build a product line. The alternative of building a large consulting firm or a large lecture bureau is difficult and usually takes far more time.

This is especially true in this general field of the advice and information business, where the products—information presented in and by a variety of media—are generally relatively inexpensive to develop, produce, and distribute, and therefore offer a large markup. It is small wonder, in that respect, that there are such a large number of newsletters and other advice and information products offered to the public.

Almost anyone can launch such ventures, with extremely little capital, as a full-time venture, as a part-time or moonlight business, or as an adjunct and supplement to another business, perhaps not even directly related to the publications venture. Among those who publish newsletters, reports, manuals, books, booklets, and other such materials, we find entrepreneurs who fit all those categories.

Birmingham's Chet Lambert, now retired after a military career, publishes a monthly hybrid of a periodical that falls somewhere between being a magazine and being a rather large newsletter. He calls it *The Computer Trader,* and it is directed to ham (amateur) radio operators, computer enthusiasts, and others with related interests. Every issue carries some advertising and a number of articles relating to the two subjects and a few other electronics topics. There is also a classified section where readers can run advertisements to buy, sell, and trade equipment, parts, and components. Lambert gives free advertising space to those who write articles for him and has managed to build his publication to the point where it carries substantial advertising and is placed on newsstands in a number of cities.

J. F. Straw publishes the monthly *Business Opportunities Digest,* the chief feature and attraction of which are the myriad FOR SALE, WANTED, AGENTS, FRANCHISES, and other business offerings subscribers may place free of charge. The publication also offers a number of special reports and manuals that Straw publishes, and has been the springboard and key marketing medium for various other enterprises in which he is engaged, including a banking type of venture and something he calls the American Business Club, also related to furnishing financing for small businesses.

Richard Brisky, of Ischua, New York (near Buffalo), publishes *Moneyfax,* a monthly newsletter for financial brokers and consultants, and offers various related publications. Those who subscribe to *Moneyfax* become members of his NAFCO, National Association of Financial Consultants. Member/subscribers are entitled to place their own notices or classified advertisements without cost, and a large part of each issue's coverage is devoted to those notices. However, in expanding his inhouse capabilities to turn out his publications, Brisky has built a facility that includes integral printing and mailing capabilities that exceed his own needs, and is thus able to accommodate outside work for others, increasing his base of income-producing activity.

Ted Nicholas [Petersen] wrote the manual *How to Form Your*

Own Corporation without a Lawyer for under $50.00 several years ago, when most people found themselves compelled to pay at least several hundred dollars to have a law firm incorporate them. He published the manual himself, in paperback, and advertised it in magazines most likely to reach people who might wish to incorporate. Over the years, he sold hundreds of thousands of copies. For the most part, he advocated forming a Delaware corporation, which was famous for being hospitable to corporations, and therefore the chosen state of incorporation for many of the country's leading firms. (Most other states have since liberalized their requirements and tax bases for corporations.) He also established himself as a registered representative for out-of-state entrepreneurs who incorporated themselves in Delaware. Later, after writing and self-publishing other books, he formed a general publishing corporation, Enterprise Publishing.

Note that each of these enterprises has a core idea around which it is built, although some of these entrepreneurs have diversified considerably. Straw originally bought the *Business Opportunities Digest* from its originator, but he developed it and made many changes over the years, as he spun off other ideas from it. Still, it clings to the original core idea of being a "meeting place" and medium of exchange among small businesspeople who want to buy, sell, swap, and make other business exchanges. Lambert found that there were enough ham-radio and microcomputer aficionados to support a periodical devoted to them, with a focus on selling/buying/trading components and equipment. (Such swapping has been almost a tradition among ham-radio enthusiasts for many years.) Many of Straw's readers are financial consultants and brokers, but Brisky found that there were enough of them to make up a profitable market for a periodical specializing in servicing their needs. Petersen ("Ted Nicholas") had a great idea when he decided that a great many people would incorporate without delay if they knew that they could do so for as little as $50 by filing the really rather simple documents themselves.

IDEAS BEGIN AS NOTIONS

One commonality among the examples just cited is that each began with and was based on that rather simple core idea. But there is one other factor that each of these success stories has in common with all the others: In each case the entrepreneur did more than develop an idea: He took positive and aggressive action to put the idea to work, to implement it.

Without such action, an idea is not really an idea at all; it is simply a notion. Perhaps thousands of people said to themselves, "It's a shame that people don't know how simple it is to incorporate themselves, especially in Delaware. If they only knew. . . ." But it took Ted Nicholas Petersen to do something about that notion. Petersen decided that it was worth the risk of spending the time and money to develop the idea into a book, complete with all instructions and forms, and to publish the book himself. Of course, he has had a number of imitators since, but he was the originator of the idea.

Ideas do not suddenly spring full-blown from the brow, but often begin as little more than vagrant notions or observations. For most people, the notion does not progress beyond that stage, beyond the thought, "Why don't they [whoever 'they' are] . . . ?" But for the Petersens, Straws, Lamberts, and Briskys of the world, the process goes on, and the notion evolves into an idea and, ultimately, if the idea proves worthy, into a business venture. In fact, the process typically is somewhat as follows:

1   The first "somebody ought to" notion, noting a problem
2   Deciding that the problem could be solved by a certain action or product
3   Wondering how many people share the problem and would welcome a solution
4   Ruminating on the business potential of offering the solution
5   Scratching up a rough, preliminary business plan—thinking it out on paper
6   Growing conviction of feasibility
7   Working at refining the plan; making "serious" calculations and investigations
8   Researching market possibilities, financing, and other needs
9   Making the final decision to go ahead
10   Launching the effort

Perhaps not all of this is conscious—not discrete steps, that is. Perhaps the person has been dimly, semiconsciously aware of the problem for some time but never thought about it much. But one day something raises the problem to a higher level of consciousness, provoking more intense thought. Or perhaps one day something happens that the person suddenly perceives as an answer to the problem. Petersen, with his general business background, probably had known for years how to form his corporation without a lawyer for under $50. But one day something provoked him into wondering how many people would be willing to pay $10 or $15 for a set of instructions and forms that would enable them to form their own corporations for under $50.

In any case, an idea is the result of an evolutionary process, whether the phases and steps are wholly conscious or not, and is not a suitable basis for an enterprise until it is fully formed. To serve as the basis of a business venture, the idea must clearly offer prospective customers some benefit, such as the solution to a problem or a better way to accomplish something or other, or perhaps even to deliver a benefit heretofore not realized by the prospective customer. (Examine and consider the basic ideas of the enterprises described here as examples, and see what benefits each of those ideas offers customers.) There were a number of different office copiers before the Xerox Corporation introduced theirs, but theirs was so much better—faster, cheaper, and more convenient, as well as productive of a better copy—that it wiped out all the earlier competition almost overnight. And it is no secret that IBM owes much of its success to the truly peerless quality of its service. Xerographic copiers solved the problem of making copies, initially, but today they have gone beyond that and are now often regarded and used as a practicable way of solving the problem of getting ultraquick short-run printing. TV has made it easier, more convenient, and more comfortable to get the news (presenting news faster, even while it is happening), and that "better way" has put a great many large newspapers out of business over the past two decades.

In a sense, then, there is no such thing as a new problem to be solved, only better ways to solve traditional problems. Many problems are with us on a larger scale than ever before, but they are not truly new problems. One modern problem is disposing of trash, which has grown out of proportion to the population increase, at least partially as a result of the vast increase in throwaway packaging. But there was always a trash-disposal problem; it is not new, but is, instead, more difficult to solve. In fact, most new products and services are better solutions to old problems, and do not survive unless the buying public recognizes and accepts them as better solutions. So whether your idea offers to solve a "new" problem or a "better way" to solve an old problem depends largely on how you view and define the problem to be solved. Reduced to its most fundamental definition, every problem will be recognized as an ancient one. But in conceiving, generating, defining, and/or recognizing ideas, it is helpful to recognize this basic truth and sometimes to view the idea from both viewpoints—that is, to ask yourself the question in its several forms:

- What new problem does this solve?
- What old problem does this solve?
- How is this a better solution?
- What is/are the benefit(s) to the buyer?
- What does this do for the buyer?

BENEFITS: WHAT ARE THEY?

Benefits to the buyer are the key to the feasibility of an idea as a basis for an enterprise. Whether you define those benefits, in general, as a better way to accomplish something, to solve a problem, to do something desirable for a buyer, or in any other frame of reference does not matter as long as you can define the benefit(s) clearly, accurately, and unequivocally. That is of critical importance. If you believe that superior marketing or brilliant salesmanship will make a service or product a success, regardless of how good or bad the service or product is, you are already on the wrong trail. You might meet temporary success that way—many have—but in the long term, only that which provides worthwhile benefits will be truly successful.

Benefits are not easy to define, especially not from the seller's viewpoint. Definitions of benefits are meaningful only from the buyer's viewpoint. Buyers buy what they perceive, not what the seller perceives. For example, a "better" way to make copies may or may not have anything to do with the actual quality of the copy itself. "Better," to the customer, often means more convenient, faster, cheaper, or some other measure that has nothing to do with quality (except, perhaps, the quality of the service). Those three factors are probably in their proper order of importance, too: Convenience is an enormously influential benefit, followed closely by *faster,* as an inducement, with cost as much less of a motivational factor than the first two items.

Of course, this is not an unvarying truth. There are some people for whom cost is the paramount factor in their motivation, but they tend to be very much in the minority, when speed and other factors of convenience are offered as alternatives to low cost. On the other hand, there are certain fields in which cost is the main factor because most other factors are roughly equal among competitors—all offer about the same convenience and speed.

Consider tax law information, for example. Suppose that you were to offer two ways to get the latest information on IRS regulations under current tax codes, one as part of a larger program on taxes generally, the other as a crash course in latest IRS codes. There would be some who would sign up for the first course, some who would choose the second course. But a surprisingly large number of people would choose the crash course, even at a higher price, because of the convenience of spending far less time in the study. The cost would be a lesser consideration.

Or suppose you offered the latter program as a seminar, as a printed self-instruction course, and as a videotape. A great many would choose the videotape, if they had machines on which to play the tape, as the most convenient way to get the information. Others would attend the seminar. The smallest number, given the choice, would opt for the printed course, even if it were the lowest in cost. In general, this is true: A great many people, probably a majority, will opt for a passive way of doing something rather than an active way, given the choice. In terms of initiative, action, and aggressiveness, the requirement ascends from videotape, to seminar, to printed program. One can watch a videotape at one's leisure, and be almost a passive observer, not participating at all. The seminar requires being there at a given time and place, and being some part of the process, at least slightly more than a mere observer. Studying a printed program definitely requires active effort and some aggressiveness.

All of this is summed up in a standard bit of marketing/sales wisdom: Make things as easy for the customer as possible, to maximize the motivation to buy. The more effort the customer must make, the less probability that you will make the sale. Some people who run seminars and record them, offering the audiotapes to attendees and to others who have not attended the seminar, report that they do as well with the tapes as they do with the seminar—even at prices as high as $100 to $150 for the set of tapes.

Psychologists will explain benefits in terms of emotional needs and gratifications. All human beings need to love and be loved, to merit respect and enjoy prestige, to feel secure, to be free of guilt, to like themselves, to be recognized, to have their accomplishments acknowledged, and have numerous other kinds of ego gratification. Probably all these can be justified and explained as forms or aspects of the need for security, or the combating of the strong tendency most of us have to feel insecure. If it is helpful to think of benefits in these terms, do so. Men and women use cosmetics, clothes, automobiles, and numerous other products to achieve some of these emotional satisfactions. The product or service that does a better job in this respect—that affords the buyer greater satisfactions—is bound to succeed. (But remember that the customer must *perceive* these as greater satisfactions.)

SEARCHING FOR IDEAS

Few ideas are truly new or totally new. Most are rooted in existing products, services, methods, or systems. They are refinements, adaptations, new combinations, new applications, inspired by existing things. TV burst on the scene after World War II (it had been scheduled to appear earlier, but was delayed by the war emergency), an apparently radically new invention. But in fact TV was the result of combining the technology of the oscilloscope (a laboratory instrument) and well-known radio circuit technology. The microwave oven is an adaptation of a well-known effect of radio-frequency (RF) energy to agitate molecules and generate rapid and intense heat in organic matter that is placed in its field. (Many old-time radio experimenters learned about "RF burns" through unpleasant personal experience, such as inadvertently getting their hands in the energy field of radio frequency energy radiation, and the term *RF burn* became part of radio jargon.) Videotape development was inspired by audiotape success, which replaced the earlier wire-recording method because it was so much better. And the ultramodern microchip electronics that have made microcomputers and pocket calculators miraculous realities have their roots in early "solid-state" devices which were working in laboratories as early as 1870, over 100 years ago.

All or virtually all of our new ideas, including the most miraculous achievements, are the result of evolution, a relentless progression of improvements, adaptations, and new combinations. To quest for a new and valuable idea, begin with the mind-set that everything—*everything*—can be improved on. (Compare today's xerographic—office—copy with those resulting from the copiers of approximately 20 years ago: The difference in quality is nothing less than startlingly clear evidence of continuous improvement. Had the Xerox Corporation rested on their laurels and failed to continually improve their product, they would have lost their position of leadership long ago.)

One platitude endlessly recommended as the basis for a successful enterprise is to "find a need and fill it." Unfortunately, that is no more helpful than believing in God, motherhood, and apple pie. The platitude is true enough philosophically, but not really of any help because finding needs is easy enough—the world has an abundance of problems—but "filling them" is another matter. It means finding better solutions than those currently in use, or perhaps finding solutions to problems that have never been solved before.

One way to do this is to be alert at all times to the everyday problems that relate to selling advice and information in whatever areas you specialize. Suppose, for example, that you are an investment analyst/advisor. You can, of course, function as a consultant, rendering direct, personal services to clients. You can publish a newsletter and ancillary publications. You can lecture on the subject, and even conduct seminars or formal classroom sessions. You can do any, all, or some combination of these things, and you will not be breaking new ground, in all probability; it has been done many times by others, and is being done today.

But suppose you are seeking a new idea, something a little different from that offered by all those other investment analyst/advisors. You can blaze a new trail in any (or all) of four different ways:

1 A new and different way to package the advice
2 A new and different way to specialize
3 A new and different area of specialization
4 A new and different way to market your advice

Let's consider each of these, one by one, to illustrate how you might think them out and evolve a new and different idea.

Packaging Advice

Three basic packages have been named already: consulting, publishing, and lecturing (including seminars and/or formal classes). You might add to that tape-cassette packaging, either especially recorded or recorded from seminars and lectures. But that, too, is a well-established packaging method. Nothing new here, so far.

"New and different," however, does not mean that it must be radically new or truly new. (Remember that nothing is totally new.) Simply finding an improvement that delivers a distinct benefit to the buyer may be all you need to get a great advantage over competitors, develop an overnight reputation for yourself, gain favorable publicity, reach rapid success. Suppose, for example, that you ponder the problem of costs: A great many people cannot afford the cost of direct consulting, paying for many hours of your time. And many cannot afford the cost of the typical seminar, with its $100 to $300 registration fees. How might you arrange to offer direct, personal advice to clients at low cost without making personal sacrifices?

Perhaps you can run "miniseminars" of an hour or two, in your own home, for small groups at modest fees. Ten or fifteen clients can be accommodated in most private homes, and a fee of perhaps $25 each for an hour or two of your time is usually profitable enough. The small group gives you the opportunity to counsel each person, and the use of your home keeps your overhead costs to a minimum.

The rapidly growing incidence of microcomputers in people's homes, many of them purchased and used for portfolio management, suggests another way of packaging advice. There are a number of software programs already offered for use in portfolio management and related investment coverage. But suppose that you published an investment newsletter in floppy disk form, to be played on microcomputers? Or, instead of mailing the disk to buyers, you offered a communications service whereby a subscriber could dial up your system and get the information via telephone line?

Ways to Specialize

Many people specialize in the kind of work they do or in the kind of product they handle. But one way to specialize that rarely occurs to entrepreneurs is to specialize in the types of clients you serve. For an investment analyst/advisor, for example, it might be worthwhile to study the types of investors and decide whether there is one class or type in which specialization would be new, different, and worthwhile. For example, you might classify investors as high rollers, those who invest in risky stocks with high payoffs possible; cautious investors, who tend to buy only blue chips and watch them like a hawk; small investors, who apparently can afford to invest only small sums periodically; and perhaps several other types.

You might then consider which of these groups gets little service from such specialists as yourself—as, probably, is the case with the small investor. Consider how you might specialize in serving that group and yet doing well by yourself. Or perhaps you will discover that none of these groups are being offered all the services possible, or the quality of service possible. Study the problems of each of the types of investors you identify, and consider how you might improve the services offered.

Areas of Specialization

With the complexity and number of stocks offered today, specializing in an area is almost inevitable. High-tech stocks alone are a specialized field, but so are other kinds of issues. The investment advisor cannot really keep up with all and be equally expert and conversant with what is happening in all fields—electronics, mining, consumer goods, information industries, heavy industries, and so on. Find an area where specialization will be different from what is now traditional or usual, but will offer you some advantage over the norm of today.

Marketing Methods

More than one entrepreneurial success has been built on the basis of a better way to market the service or product. In fact, even if you offer a superior service or product, it will not sell all by itself. The "build a better mousetrap" platitude is false: The world will not "beat a path to your door." Everything must be marketed.

The traditional marketing methods are via direct methods—from manufacturer or original source directly to consumer—and through distribution—from original source down through one or more levels of jobbers, wholesalers, dealers, to the consumer. To support and implement these methods, marketers use print advertising, radio and TV "commercials," direct mail, trade shows, in-house demonstrations, and several other methods of presenting their offers and appeals to the prospective buyers, such as the salesperson.

Among the many new ideas that have been tried and used successfully and are among today's more or less standard methods of marketing are contests of many kinds, from pure lotteries to talent competitions. Many of these contests themselves show a great deal of originality and present new ideas. In fact, there are today specialists in designing contests, and they design contests to order for clients.

Find a new and better way to market—offer buyers more convenience or other motivation/inducement to buy, and you may find it every bit as effective in achieving success as a new idea for your service, your product, your package, or for any other area in which a new idea might be developed and applied. New and different ideas—if they are also better ideas—are effective no matter where they fall. Note, however, that there is a direct relationship among the four areas, so that they should not really be considered separately, but in connection with each other. Almost anything you do in any of the areas affects the others.

THE CREATIVITY PROCESS

A great deal of research has been done on the subject of creativity. One method has been to interview a large number of those with obvious creative talents—prominent inventors and designers, for example. Another has been to study the writings of such people, particularly their own accounts of how they developed their inventions, designs, philosophies, and other creations. From all of this certain principles have been induced, and there is general agreement that while many new designs have been developed by conscious, continuous, methodical procedures (often trial and error or empirical methods), a great many new breakthroughs and original ideas result from a three-stage process:

1 Concentration
2 Incubation
3 Inspiration

The brief explanation of this process is this: First you concentrate on a problem as intensely as possible, trying consciously to find an answer—or, at least, to consider all the possible answers and/or approaches to developing answers. When you have exhausted all possibilities you can summon up consciously, you drop the effort and go on to other things, allowing the problem to incubate in your subconscious mind. Simply forget it. At some future time, generally when you least expect it, unpredictably, and often when you are relaxing and have little or nothing on your mind, the solution appears magically—inspiration. (Some call this "illumination.")

The rationale is this: Unlike the conscious mind, the subconscious mind never forgets anything. (That is why people can "remember" long-forgotten things, such as childhood events, under hypnosis, which is a link with the subconscious mind.) That means that the subconscious has a great deal more data—a much larger "data base," to use the term now popular among computer specialists—to work with in seeking a solution. But it is not easy to reach one's subconscious; the hypnotist does so by relaxing the subject because it is evidently only when the conscious mind is thoroughly relaxed that it is possible to communicate immediately and directly with the subconscious. However, the intense concentration of the first stage of creativity also breaches the barrier and somehow imparts a request to the subconscious to work on the problem. This also explains why the illumination or inspiration comes about when the conscious mind is thoroughly relaxed and therefore out of the way of direct contact and communication with the subconscious.

It explains why, after you have tried to remember a name or something else and finally given it up in despair, the name later flashes in your mind suddenly. It explains why you occasionally wake up in the morning with some troubling matter suddenly crystal clear in your mind. It perhaps tends to explain all inspiration.

In any case, if you have tried to develop a new idea or solve a problem in a new and better manner and have not succeeded, do not despair. Keep at it as long as you can, but be ready to give it up—let it incubate, that is—when you have given it your all consciously. Expect the answer to appear magically at a later time, because it very likely will.

This is not to say that you may not get inspirations spontaneously and without a struggle and the three-step process outlined here. You may very well get such hot flashes. But you do not have to get new ideas that way, and should permit yourself to get them as described here. You should take the advice of some highly creative people, such as the late Charles "Boss" Kettering, a very creative individual, who invented, among other things, the self-starter for automobiles, the electric cash register, and improvements to the diesel engine. Kettering believed in education, but he warned all who would listen that education was not wisdom. He said that education was "all right" if you did not allow it to interfere or get in the way of your thinking.

What he meant by that was that too many people confuse education with thinking and tend to be intimidated by and confined to whatever they have been taught in formal education, without considering whether what they have been taught is, indeed, true. When he was commissioned by Ransome Olds, original manufacturer of the Oldsmobile, to develop a self-starter for automobiles, the conventional wisdom in the engineering community was that it was an impossible task because the starter motor (a self-starter is an electric motor) would have to be as large as the engine itself, making the whole idea impractical immediately. (Nor was that the only problem, although it was the principal one.) Of course, Kettering was well aware of the scientific truth that a self-starter smaller than the engine would overheat when used. The difference between Kettering's reasoning and that of the engineering community was that Kettering was sure that he could find a solution despite that problem, and he did find a solution, as we all know.

Thomas Edison faced the same kind of negative thinking and criticism in seeking a way to create a practical incandescent electric light, and Robert Fulton was called a fool for trying to invent a practical steam-powered boat. These are old stories, and throughout history achievers have been castigated by those who have allowed intellectual *rigor mortis* to set in immediately upon their exit from formal education. Pasteur, the Wright brothers, Einstein, and others were forced to run the gauntlet of such criticisms. (Admiral William Leahy confidently staked his professional reputation as an explosives expert that the atom bomb would never work.)

Yesterday's truth is not today's truth. When I attended school it was an immutable truth that matter could be neither created nor destroyed. This truth was expressed as a law concerning the "conservation of matter." But that was before man confirmed a theory held then by only a handful of scientists that energy was another form of matter, and that matter could be changed to energy. The atom bomb proved that theory true to even the most hardened skeptics, and the physical "law" was changed to reflect the new fact that it was possible to "destroy" matter by transforming it to energy.

Kettering did not prove that self-starters would not overheat: They did, and they still do. But he proved that overheating was not an insurmountable barrier to creating a practical, workable self-starter. And this illustrates another aspect of creative thinking that bears importantly on the subject: Even when the facts you employ are indeed facts, be careful about your analysis and reasoning process. Kettering's detractors reasoned fallaciously and drew an illogical conclusion, because they had been taught in academic engineering courses that overheating had to be prevented at all costs. But Kettering reasoned differently. Here are the two chains of logic, to illustrate:

ENGINEERING COMMUNITY'S LOGIC

Self-starters smaller than the engine will overheat.

Overheating cannot be tolerated.

Therefore, the self-starter is not a practicable idea.

KETTERING'S LOGIC

Self-starters smaller than the engine will overheat.

The self-starter must be invented.

Therefore, a way to tolerate overheating must be found.

Be careful of the conclusions you draw. It is quite easy to fall into the trap of reasoning from the conclusion, a classic logical fault, also known as rationalization. It is the result of accepting things without question, because that is what the professor taught you, or because that is what "they" or "everybody" says, thinks, or does. (Have a look at the copyright date on those textbooks and see how new or how old that information is.)

In this fast-changing world of ours, by the time anything has become so widely accepted as to qualify as "conventional wisdom," it is almost surely obsolescent already. That makes all those "they say" and "everybody knows" clichés almost automatically suspect. But even worse than this principle is the clear admission that bias, prejudice, or platitudes will be preferred to actual thinking. Whenever you permit one of those clichés to dictate your decision, you have rejected that most notable achievement of man: the power to think, to cogitate, to ruminate, to ponder, to intellectualize, and to create.

THE COURAGE TO BE CREATIVE

If creativity is being different—and it is, in its most literal definition—it means being the ugly duckling, cursed, sneered at, laughed at perhaps, for no other reason than the fact of being different. Whether you are trying to invent a telephone or merely a better way to keep records, you need courage to be creative. Even if no one knows what you are trying to do and, therefore, you are not suffering from detractors of any kind, you need the courage to fight your own doubts, for self-doubt is one of the classic burdens of creative effort. There is an apparent security in conformance, in doing what others do, in thinking as others think, and that is the chief reason creativity is a relatively rare characteristic. It is a latent talent. Most of us have the talent and the ability to be highly creative, but we must overcome fear. We must have confidence in what we are doing, where we are headed. But there is something else we learn from successful inventors: We must not fear to fail. For the record of all inventions is the record of a great many trials, most of which were less than successful. Even huge teams of engineers, armed with mountains of money, equipment, people, and other resources, as NASA was, undergo many trials, many errors, many disappointments before they even begin to achieve success. And in the case of such monumental development projects as NASA undertakes, initial successes, when they do come, are only partial successes.

THE IDEA BREEDER REACTOR

Nuclear breeder reactors are devices that produce more nuclear fuel than they consume—they breed nuclear fuel, that is. Creativity—getting ideas—is a process that emulates that. It is possible to start the idea-breeding process and have it feed on itself, turning out more new ideas than you can use, so that you have an abundance of new ideas from which to choose those most attractive or most suitable to your needs.

To do this you must do two things:

1   Expose yourself to a maximum number of stimuli—to a maximum amount of thought-provoking information.
2   Condition yourself to be always alert, always seeking new ideas.

The two conditions are mutually dependent, of course. The first is of no help without the second, and the second is of no help without the first. But the process soon becomes an unconscious one, almost instinctive, after you have conditioned yourself by the conscious quest for new ideas. You must read widely, for many great ideas are ideas borrowed from fields totally different from your own, but adapted to your field. Watch public TV, at least once in a while. Read serious journals, as well as popular magazines and books. Study advertisements and TV commercials. Compare bits of information from different sources. Seek out anomalies, identify common problems, think about solutions, study what others offer, and think about improvements. Soon enough, you will do this without conscious effort. Simply reading a magazine publisher's own advertisement gave one man a profitable idea for a mail-order offering. The advertisement listed offerings of sales literature from a number of advertisers and offered to order them for the reader for a nominal 50-cent charge to cover costs. This prompted one reader to research and compile a list of free publications of value, and to devise a mail-order offer. Explaining that the publications listed were free (although he did not specify the source of each, of course), he offered to have any of them sent directly to the buyer at a charge of 50 cents per item. It was a successful and profitable promotion, bringing orders ranging as high as $25.

As part of the input process—and your output of ideas will naturally be in some direct proportion to the volume of input information—talk to people. Exchange information, ask questions, probe, speculate, discuss, argue.

Write to people. Maintain correspondence. Keep your conversations and dialogues going via the mails as well as by telephone and in person.

Belong to groups, and attend meetings. Know as many people as possible. Be a gadabout. Attend as many functions as you can. Go to conventions, trade shows, conferences. Meet new people. Exchange cards. Get interested in all sorts of events. Keep your mind and your consciousness buzzing with as many new experiences as possible.

Write to advertisers offering literature. Get on mailing lists. Open that junk mail before you discard it, and have a look at what is inside. You may be about to discard a valuable idea, or the seed of one.

Before long you will be doing all of this without conscious effort or planning, and it will avalanche, breeding and growing, as will the base of new ideas that will occur to you.

But that is not all there is to it, either. There are some specific methods that will help you develop your own creativity and stimulate your imagination. One of these is a discipline called *value analysis*. The entire discipline and methodology are not, of course, presented here, but some of the relevant methodology is because it is entirely relevant and applicable to getting new ideas, especially to finding better ways to do and make things. (That, in fact, is precisely what value analysis is all about.)

FUNCTION ANALYSIS

The basic approach in value analysis is to examine the subject of the analysis, whatever that subject is (product, system, service, or other), and perform a *function analysis* first. The objective of this is to determine precisely what the basic or primary function of the entity is. The entire effort depends on making an accurate determination of that fundamental function, and it is necessary to state that function clearly and unequivocally.

Take, for example, a dictionary. What is its fundamental purpose or objective? If you were to ask a number of people that question, you would get a variety of answers, including some such as these:

- To look up words
- To look up big or uncommon words
- To find synonyms
- To explain words
- To look up spelling

Among the things "wrong" (for our purposes in value analysis) with these terms are at least these:

1. "Look up" is what the person does; it is not the objective of the dictionary.
2. Finding synonyms and "looking up" spellings are uses some people make of dictionaries, but that is not what dictionaries are designed for as their primary use.

The fundamental objective of a dictionary—what its compilers intend it to do as its primary function—is to *provide definitions.* A dictionary provides definitions of all words—big words, small words, uncommon words, and common words—within its constraints. (Obviously, small dictionaries cannot list as many words as larger dictionaries do.) Yes, dictionaries do offer synonyms for many words, as part of the function of defining them, a side effect. Inevitably, dictionaries also provide spellings and even alternative spellings, as they provide preferred and alternative definitions. But these are not their primary functions because it was not for these reasons primarily that the dictionary was compiled.

The function must be clearly and unequivocally stated, and to achieve that, the rule is that the function must be stated in two words only: a verb and a noun. (In cases where it is unavoidable, to achieve clarity, a noun or verb may be a two-word phrase, but this is the exception.) The idea is to avoid the use of adjectives and adverbs because these tend to introduce subjective opinions and to shade meanings. So, in the case of the dictionary, our statement of its primary function might be *define words.* ("Explain words" might serve the purpose, but "explain" is not as precise as "define.")

Those other things that the dictionary does, such as *provide synonyms* and *define spellings,* are *secondary functions,* which we will bypass for the moment.

QUESTIONS AND ANSWERS

Having finally decided what the primary function is—the reason the item exists at all—is the result of answering the second of several questions we ask ourselves in making the analysis. The first question was: *What is it?* The answer, in this case, was: *A dictionary.* The second question was: *What does it do?* And the answer was: *Define words.* We are now ready for the third question: *What else would do that?*

If we are a group of people performing the analysis, we would be working together and reaching agreement on answers. However, it is possible to do this analysis alone, even adapting the brainstorming method to individual, solo analysis, despite the fact that brainstorming was originally designed for group analysis and synthesis. In this case, simply begin to list, on paper, all the other possible ways of defining words. You might, for example, list microfilm or microfiche systems, computer systems, audiotape, videotape, and perhaps even others.

Once you have exhausted the list of possibilities, you can begin to sort out the ideas, making judgments and deciding which ones are worth further consideration. Finally, you will have narrowed the list down to a number of possibilities, from which to make final selections. You would then make comparative analyses among them, deciding on the pros and cons of each, judging, comparatively, such factors as cost, convenience, and other factors. (In considering costs, for example, you would consider at least two kinds of costs, development costs and per unit costs.)

In some cases, such as in the case of an item or service that has a great many secondary functions, you might decide that some of those secondary functions are of little use and add little value to the item. Perhaps you can eliminate some of them and have a product or service you can market at a much lower cost, thereby greatly improving marketability or sales appeal of the item.

Or perhaps by adding a function or making some relatively minor change, you can vastly improve value or even produce something entirely new. For example, whoever first used transparent yellow ink in a marker pen changed the item from a pen to a "highlighter." A minor change produced an entirely new—and successful—product. So during value analysis you might also ask yourself the question: *What else can this do?* (With or without changes, that is.)

One of the simplest inventions of all time is the ordinary paper clip, so simple and effective that it seems impossible to improve on it. Yet someone did improve on it by making scratches in the metal, so that friction is increased and the paper clip grips the paper just a little more firmly.

SUMMARY: THE IDEA IS THE THING

The basic media for packaging and selling advice are printed matter of one sort or another, personal (one-on-one) consultation, oral presentations to groups, and recorded presentations. Each of these offers a variety of possibilities for services and products, and the ideas revolve around any or all of: the service/product per se, the subject matter of the service/product, and the marketing of the service/product.

Ideas are important, and in this age, new and innovative ideas—progressive ideas—are especially important. They are important for everyone, but they are especially important in the advice business, for who should be more up to date and sparkling with the latest ideas than the specialist in advice and information? But you cannot afford to wait and hope that some vagrant inspiration will happen along fortuitously and land uninvited on your desk. Instead, you must do everything you can to invite ideas, to seek them out actively, to go in pursuit of them. And it is possible to do so. But you must make a distinct effort to stoke up the creative fires, using some of the methods proposed here and others which are available.

Chapter 6

How to Develop Packages: Research and Writing

Research is not only a key to writing success, but also produces some unexpected and surprising benefits.

IDEAS ARE FREE

A well-worn writer's saying has it that stealing from one or two sources is plagiarism, but stealing from fifty sources is research. Another saying is that there is more truth than humor in that idea. At least a large part of research into a subject consists of reading what others have written on the subject before you. Therefore, the public library is one prime resource for gathering information. So is your own library at home, of course, if you maintain a suitable library.

In my own case, I do turn to my own bookshelves as well as to those in the public library. But I also search the shelves of several local bookstores, and much of my personal library is the result of books I bought to support my own research in subjects about which I was preparing to write.

Don't stop at books. There is a far greater assortment of periodicals on the newsstands than you might have imagined, for most newsstands and magazine racks in retail stores carry only a handful of the periodicals published today. If you search energetically enough, you will discover one of those rare stores that carries a truly large assortment of periodicals—such stores/newsstands do exist—and you will have the pleasant surprise of gaining access to a great deal of information you did not even suspect was readily available.

You can also ask your librarian for help in unearthing some of those periodicals, many of which are circulated via the mails to only a few thousand subscribers (in the case of newsletters, sometimes to only a few hundred subscribers). There are publications that list all or nearly all periodicals, and your librarian can direct you to them and will gladly do so.

What you are reviewing in your literature research is information—ideas. Ideas and information are not copyrighted. Copyright protects only specific combinations of words. This does not mean that you can do some minor rewording of another's work and publish it as your original work; that is plagiarism. But you are certainly free to use the information and ideas you encounter and gather up through your research, and that is the objective of research.

UNEXPECTED REWARDS AND BENEFITS

Obviously, your research has as its objective gathering information to flesh out an idea you started with as the seed of some kind of advice package. You are going to be reading and reviewing a great deal of material, several times more than you can ever use. Perhaps the package you emerge with later will consist of two or three hundred pages, but you will probably have scanned many hundreds of pages—probably several thousand pages, in fact—to glean the information you finally organize into those two or three hundred pages. Along the way, you should have come up with at least another idea or two for other projects. For example, perhaps you read a chapter in some book or an article in some periodical on a subject you think would make a good book in itself—a subject that should be expanded and is suitable for expansion into a complete book. Or perhaps you were stimulated by some idea that you think might make a good seminar or the nucleus of a complete training program. Or perhaps you got an idea for a service to add to your own offerings or an idea to give your marketing a boost. The fact is that research is a stimulating exercise that often produces, for the alert person, many new ideas.

OTHER SOURCES

All the foregoing sources are only the beginning of research. In fact, research is almost a continuous process when you are in the advice business, for your principal commodity is information. Therefore, you should be gathering information continuously, as a retailer of merchandise must constantly evaluate sources of supply and new products to stock.

After you have been in your venture for a time, you will find that you have gotten onto many mailing lists, and every day will bring press releases, memoranda, advertising literature, and other items many people dismiss as "junk mail." But it is not junk mail to you; it is a mine of useful information. And as in the case of mining anything else, you must study the ore and select from it that which is worth keeping. To discard it all, without review, is often to throw away useful material.

You do not have to wait for this to happen spontaneously. You can help it happen by asking that your name be placed on certain mailing lists. You can do this directly, by specific letter requesting such action (for example, asking to be placed on distribution for press releases of an organization), or by sending for information, such as by sending in the request forms printed along with many advertisements. Once a marketing or public relations department has your name as an interested prospect, you will hear often from that organization.

You will find, to your surprise, that not all the mail you get will be press releases and other advertising literature. Inexplicably, perhaps, you will find yourself on more than one "complimentary" list for newsletters, manuals, sample copies of various things, free passes to conventions and trade shows, and numerous other such things. And if you publish a little newsletter, this will be all the more certain a result. Just award free—"complimentary"—subscriptions to certain people (even if you normally charge for subscriptions), and you will find yourself on others' "comp" lists.

If you want to accelerate this process, write to the publishers of other newsletters and offer to swap complimentary subscriptions. And you can go a step or two beyond this, also, and offer to swap freedom to reprint items from each other's publications (with attribution, of course). You might even offer to swap mailing lists of subscribers, if you are not in direct competition with each other but think that the other's mailing list will be useful.

USING CONTRIBUTORS

Writers who sell articles and other material to publishers are often referred to as "contributors," and most of the material you see published in magazines has been written by such contributors. The word "contributor," however, should not mislead you into believing that the "contribution" is a free one. Ordinarily, contributors are paid for their writing, and the free-lance writer sends his or her work in to an editor as an offer to sell it. So you may be able to get some good material written free of charge by people who want the publicity that such "exposure" may bring them, but in general you are likely to get better material and get good material more consistently by soliciting it from free-lance writers who sell their work.

There are several ways to solicit such work—to *announce* that you accept and pay for material that meets your needs, in fact. One way is to list your needs in the magazines, *Writer's Digest* and *The Writer.* Another is to list your newsletter and the fact that you pay for contributions with Howard Penn Hudson, publisher of *The Newsletter Yearbook Directory.* Still another is to list this information with John Hall for publication in his newsletter for writers, *The Inkling,* and with publishers of a few other newsletters directed at writers. It will not be long before you start getting queries and manuscripts.

As a newsletter publisher, you do not have to pay large rates for free-lance contributions. Many newsletters cannot afford to pay more than 3 to 5 cents per word, and that is at least a good starting place. But be sure to caution readers that all manuscripts (at least, those you have not solicited specifically or made agreements to accept) must be accompanied by return postage—preferably by a self-addressed and stamped envelope for return of any manuscripts you do not find suitable for your needs.

All of this applies to other publications, of course. Consultant Hubert Bermont wrote a small book on how to become a consultant and met with such success in selling it—some 45,000 copies over several years—that he wrote a second such book, founded a small book-publishing venture called Bermont Books, and finally decided to publish only books for consultants, thereupon founding The Consultant's Library. Although he has authored some of the books and co-authored others, he has also published a number of them written by others, for which he pays standard royalties to the authors.

DOING IT YOURSELF

Some people find writing of any sort a difficult and possibly even unpleasant task and recoil from it as others do from speaking publicly. On the other hand, a great many publishers of small newsletters—probably even a majority of them—do their own writing and editing, typing, and attend personally to other details of getting the publication out.

It is a popular misconception that one can learn to write by mastering the rules of grammar, punctuation, spelling, and something the schools call "composition." Or to view that from the opposite perspective—that to write effectively one must have mastered those subjects. From whichever perspective one views this, it is a mistaken idea, at least on balance.

WHAT IS "GOOD WRITING"?

For some, "writing well" means writing with professional polish, elegant phrasing, perfect grammatical constructions, and other such literary achievements, achievements that are, in sum, "style." There is no doubt that a graceful style is a worthy goal for anyone who writes, and that style is not reserved to professional writers; anyone may exhibit such a style as a natural talent.

On the other hand, in the world of business and technical writing, where the main purpose is communication—explanation, argument, instruction, or other such advice—style is or should be a secondary consideration. The first consideration is effective communication. And even before that—for "communication" is far less simple an idea than it appears to be—there is a consideration known as *having something to say*. And that idea begins to strike at the heart of writing for the reader who wants information or instruction, and it is properly the first and probably most important topic.

Having Something to Say

If you were to examine and analyze a few samples of the kind of writing that was labeled "gobbledygook" by the late Maury Maverick, you would discover that the problem with such writing is almost invariably that the writer had nothing to say. However, that phrase, "nothing to say," may or may not be a literal truth. True enough, some of that kind of writing reveals, upon analysis, that the writer really did have nothing to say, and took hundreds—sometimes thousands—of words to conceal that fact. But it is also often the case that the writer had something to say but had not really thought out the matter, sorted out the facts, or organized the ideas. The writing then clearly reflects this uncertainty. After all, what can you write except what you have mentally formulated? Is not what you write inevitably and inescapably the reflection of what you think?

It is clear enough, then, that the first law for writing well is to know exactly what you want to establish—what precise point(s) you are trying to make and the organization of your information and/or arguments for making those points.

In short, you must have a goal or objective for everything you write. It is when you do not have clear goals or have not thought things out and organized your thoughts that the writing comes out badly, even if your grammar, spelling, punctuation, and other usages are letter-perfect. Your writing will be bad writing even if you have a magnificent style; style is no substitute for substance.

Most of us who have had at least a high school education have no valid excuse for not being able to write reasonably well, unless we do have a language problem—are not fluent in English, although we may be fluent in some other language. And as far as the mechanics of usage—grammar, punctuation, spelling, and the like—are concerned, you need master only the basics, and even then you do not have to be able to cite the rules formally.

A Few Facts about Grammar and Related Topics

Grammar texts and dictionaries are not, contrary to popular and uninformed opinion, sets of rules for how to use the language. On the contrary, they are explanations and guidelines for how those considered to be authoritative do use the language. That is, those texts and dictionaries reflect *opinions* about spelling, punctuation, sentence construction, and other such matters. That is why you will so often find that a word has more than one definition and more than one spelling, with the "preferred" spelling or meaning a reflection of majority opinion, usually. The same thing applies to grammar and punctuation.

For example, there is the older "school" of "close" punctuation, which many of us were taught years ago. In that philosophy, one uses commas and other punctuation marks quite freely. But since that time a school of "open" punctuation has arisen, in which those punctuation marks are used much more sparingly and reflect how we actually speak: If we do not pause between two phrases when we utter them, we should not use a comma between them in writing the phrases, for example.

Even "sentence fragments"—phrases lacking all the requirements that qualify a string of words as a sentence—are acceptable today as a stylistic freedom. In newsletter writing, "telegraphic" style—omitting articles and verbs to achieve economy in the limited space a newsletter affords—is used quite widely, and sentence fragments are popular.

Guidelines

In general, you do not need to remember the formal rules at all if you have sentence sense and avoid controversial areas such as the use of sentence fragments. (Breaking the rules is risky when you are not an expert, and you will almost surely be well advised to stick to the basic rules of usage, at least until you feel quite at home in writing for publication.) Here are a few simple guidelines that will keep you out of trouble:

1 Know what your specific objective or point is in every item (sentence, paragraph, chapter, etc.) you write.

2 If you find yourself having trouble explaining what you mean, consider that difficulty as a possible indication that you have not really thought the matter out, do not know exactly what your point or goal is, have not done enough research and really do not know enough about the subject, or otherwise *are not yet ready to write.*

3 Writing well is almost always the result of rewriting, although there are occasional geniuses who write most things well the first time. But a good way to work is to write it all out, in detail, in a rough draft, and then self-edit it down to essentials—especially for newsletters, where you are limited in space.

4 In that rewriting, you can reduce the material to a telegraphic style by deleting all the articles (*the, an,* and *a*) and dropping any other words that are not truly necessary for meaning.

5 "Listen" mentally (or say the words out loud, if you prefer) to your sentences to determine how to punctuate them: a comma for a brief pause, a semicolon for a longer pause, and a period for a dead stop after a complete thought.

If you still feel somewhat shaky about your mastery of the mechanics of using the English language, you may feel a great deal better about it by having someone act as your editor and review your copy.

THE KINDS OF PACKAGES

Much of this discussion has centered on newsletters because they are popular, relatively easy to develop, and highly versatile, useful both for marketing promotion and as independent profit centers. At the same time, there was no intent to suggest here that newsletters were the only or even the most desirable advice package to develop and offer. There are other packages you can develop, perhaps even in addition to a newsletter, each offering certain advantages of its own. And, as many have learned, there are often distinct advantages in publishing both a newsletter and other advice packages because the combination often turns out to be synergistic—far greater than the sum of the parts.

One kind of package that offers many advantages to the small publisher is the report, called by some a *folio*. This may, in fact, be essentially a book or manual, but need not be bound as such, which is itself a major advantage for the small publisher. In fact, for a small report of a few pages, a corner staple and a "self-cover" (a title page or the first text page, acting as the cover) is generally sufficient. But even for the larger report, such as one of 100 or more pages, a cover and "side stitches" (staples) or any of the patent binders sold in office-supply stores is satisfactory.

The concept here is that it is not a book the customer is buying but information (advice), and therefore should not be asked to pay for paper and binding. The report is an excellent medium for marketing that advice, for such reports do not require formal typesetting, but are entirely satisfactory composed by typewriter or equivalent, as are most newsletters. Nor must they be printed in great quantity, but may be printed quite economically in small quantity, for binding as described.

ILLUSTRATIONS

The subject of illustrations is much misunderstood. Those not thoroughly indoctrinated in or knowledgeable about publications tend to consider illustrations as devices to elaborate on text descriptions, in a sense illustrating what has been written. In fact, the reverse is true: Words and illustrations are both methods for presenting information. The writer should consider, for each case—for each idea or concept to be offered—which is the better way. In general, words (text) are usually the more economical way to present information. But there are many cases where either the concept is such that it is difficult to present it effectively with words alone or it is uneconomical to do so. In short, there are situations where it is necessary or at least far more efficient to use an illustration to get the information across.

The degree of abstraction is one indicator. Abstract ideas are often difficult to present effectively with words alone. The idea of a right triangle and the naming of its parts—the hypotenuse, for example—would be extremely difficult to present effectively without a drawing.

Try, even, to explain in words alone exactly how to make out a personal check to someone who has never seen one and does not have one available to view. But with a simple drawing of such a check, the explanation is not at all difficult, especially when the drawing shows a check made out properly as an example.

This principle also serves as a standard by which to evaluate an illustration: An effective illustration requires little in the way of explanation: the less it requires, the more effective it is. (Truly great illustrations, like great art, require no explanation at all, but explain themselves without comment.)

Types of Illustrations

Several types of illustrations have appeared in earlier chapters—photographs, line drawings, flowcharts, and examples of various items referred to in the text. But there are still other types of illustrations, including many which are especially useful in typical advice publications—various types of charts and graphs, for example, used both to present information and to assist the reader in visualizing the concept or understanding the information. Newspapers and magazines often use little figures (called "icons" in computer usage) to represent items, such as armies, airplanes, and missiles, making the size of the figures proportional to the quantities they represent, so that the reader can grasp the relative sizes of Soviet forces and U.S. forces, for example.

The bar chart (see Figure 6-1) is used quite often to show quanti-

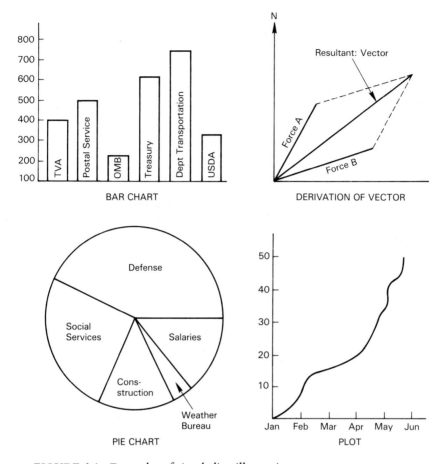

FIGURE 6-1 Examples of simple line illustrations

tative relationships among several items. But other kinds of charts also serve the purpose—the pie chart is another way of comparing quantities. The government may use this to show how a budget is divided, for example. The plot is still another useful graphic form, used to show the progress of a factor and/or trend. A simple drawing helps a reader understand the somewhat abstract idea of a vector, which is something more than mere direction and rather difficult to explain without at least one illustration.

It is not necessary to be a commercial artist or even to hire one, necessarily, to handle the development of illustrations. For one thing, there is the possibility of being able to generate at least some of your graphic illustration needs via a word processor. Modern software programs for graphics are capable of producing such illustrations as these and even more sophisticated ones if you are properly equipped. But that is not your only recourse; there are still other ways that you can manage to produce such illustrations yourself and achieve good results— if not quite as good as a professional artist can achieve, at least good enough to qualify as suitable for publication.

Artist's supply stores today offer a wide variety of do-it-yourself aids. For example, you can get "rub down" or "transfer" (decalco-mania) type and make up headlines and other text yourself. Such type

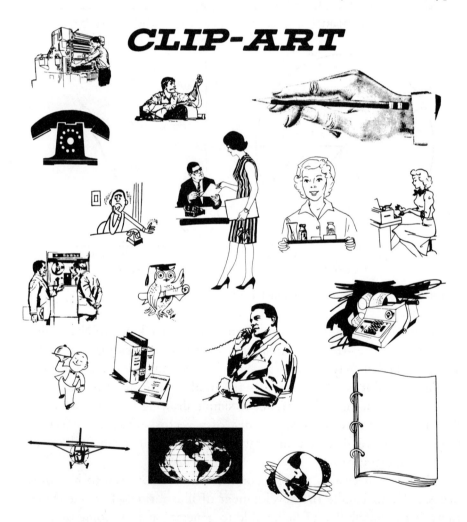

FIGURE 6-2   Examples of typical clip art

fonts are also available as vinyl characters, with a "stickyback" (self-adhesive) feature to enable you to paste the characters up.

There are also many kinds of symbols available in decalcomania and other forms that are easy to use to make up illustrations—symbols used for engineering drawings in various fields, symbols used in the construction industry, mathematical symbols, and others, including some of those little figures mentioned earlier. In addition to this, there are many kinds of templates and stencils available if you prefer to use these for developing charts and graphs.

There is also something called "clip art." This is artwork—cartoons, forms, and other drawings—sold for the express purpose of helping illustrate publications. Some of these are shown in Figure 6-2. Such material is, of course, not copyrighted because the entire intent is to provide ready-made artwork. So once having purchased this, you are free to use it as you see fit.

WHAT MAKES A GOOD REPORT?

Whether a report is "good" or "bad" is a pragmatic consideration, and there are two factors that are most influential in steering a report to one or the other of those two extremes: how *useful* the information is to the reader—and perhaps that might be even better expressed as how directly *usable* the information is—and how exclusive the information is.

Reports tend to be quite expensive compared with other publications if you consider the small size and informal, inexpensive bindings used on most reports. An ordinary typewriter-composed and corner-stapled report of 15 pages might easily cost the buyer $10, for example. That cost is justified only if the buyer finds that the information in the report can be put to work directly, to earn its keep, and the information is not readily available—perhaps (and preferably) not available elsewhere at all.

There is perhaps one more qualification that should be stipulated here with reference to the exclusivity of information. Quite often a successful report deals with a subject on which a great deal of information has already been published, but little or none of it in everyday English, language that the average person is likely to be able to understand readily. A successful report may therefore be one that interprets or translates technical information into everyday language or otherwise explains something. Following are a few examples of successful reports such as those described:

- *The OPM Plan:* "OPM" is a fairly common abbreviation for "other people's money," and it refers to financing a venture. This little report discussed some ways to finance small business ventures, but focused on ways to do it without borrowing or giving up equity, through pursuing certain methods for getting advance payments from customers.

- *The Truth about Copyright:* This was a small report for small publishers, discussing the then-new copyright law (as revised) and explaining what it meant in practical terms to the small publisher.

- *Cash in on Closeouts:* This was a fairly extensive explanation of the closeouts business, together with a directory of closeout buyers and sellers.

Some reports have a short shelf life, and what makes them successful is that they can be produced quickly, while the information is fresh and useful. For example, when the federal government awarded $6 billion in grants to local governments for public works, it was of great value to contractors and suppliers to get the information quickly. (It was of little use several months later.) The government did not issue a complete listing and directory of those grants until more than a year after the last grant was awarded, by which time the information was of little practical value to anyone. In the meantime, an enterprising small publisher turned out reports of the awards every few weeks, as more awards were made, and sold these quite readily. So timeliness is also a major factor, especially in a situation where the ease and speed with which a report can be generated gives you a distinct advantage over those who are confined to publishing by more conventional, far slower methods. But this matter of shelf life brings up another consideration.

SHELF LIFE AND LIST POSITIONS

In the book-publishing world every book has a list position, at least as long as the publisher continues to offer it for sale at its regular price. New books that sell well, especially those that manage to reach bestseller lists, are on the front list, and they remain there until their sales begin to fall off and/or stabilize.

Books that sell modestly but steadily, month after month and year after year, are backlist books (although they may have begun life as frontlist books and even as best sellers). They generally remain in print and are offered for sale for a number of years, some for many years, although probably with occasional updating and revision. There are some books that fall between these two positions, and these become the midlist books.

Very much this same situation is applicable to your reports. Some will sell extremely well, but will expire soon—those, for example, mentioned earlier as owing their success largely to being timely and getting on the market before the larger publishers can get a book or other publication on the shelves. Some will never sell well, for what reason you are not likely ever to know with any certainty. And some will sell well for a long time.

In some cases, then, you will know or at least be reasonably sure that the item will have a short shelf life. You will have to judge whether the investment in time and money is worth the risk, for the risk is that you will have only a short time—a *relatively* short time, that is—to recover your investment and earn a profit. However, whatever the reason that sales of an item begin to decline suddenly and rapidly—or even gradually, for that matter—it is necessary to abandon the item and go on to other things. Nothing is forever, and nowhere is that more true than in the advice business, especially in the publishing end of it. Publishing is, by its very nature, a high-risk enterprise, and most publishers know that only a certain percentage of their products will be entirely successful. In fact, what makes this aspect of the advice business so attractive to small, independent publishers is that for them the risk factor is relatively small because it is quite expensive to turn out books and magazines, but much less expensive (if handled wisely) to turn out newsletters and reports.

CONSISTENCY OF COVERAGE

Of course, if you publish a newsletter, your newsletter subscribers are probably your best prospects as buyers of your reports. Certainly, they are the most accessible prospects and the least costly to reach. This consideration should be a controlling factor and should influence you in conceiving ideas for your reports. That is, try to make your reports such that they will be likely to appeal to your newsletter subscribers. (More than one small newsletter publisher owes his or her success more to the publishing of compatible small reports than to the newsletter per se.)

SELECTING TITLES

The title you select for a publication is a factor in its success or failure, sometimes a decisive factor. Later, when we discuss marketing, we will talk some more about titling in terms of marketing considerations. But let us consider titles and titling in general here.

The purpose of a title is, ostensibly, to help a prospective reader (buyer) understand what the publication is about. *The OPM Plan,* for example, meant something to most of those who were interested in the subject of financing a venture, because "OPM" is a widely used term. *The Truth about Copyright* and *Cash in on Closeouts* are fairly obvious definitions of what the reports are about.

There is an understandable tendency on the part of some writers to get "arty" and select somewhat cryptic titles, on the supposition that these are poetic and therefore appealing. A book titled *Five Acres* was doing poorly until it was retitled *Five Acres and Independence,* an obvious improvement in definition which helped its sale considerably. Try to bear in mind, when choosing a title, that you are selling advice—information—and a cryptic title that the reader does not find enlightening as to the probable content of the publication is hardly a recommendation for your services or products.

One myth that lures some writers into selecting cryptic titles is that the title must be short so that the prospect will remember it. Whether brevity makes the title more memorable or not is itself moot, but is not even germane, nor is it relevant; many publications with long titles have sold quite well. Ted Nicholas's *How to Form Your Own Corporation without a Lawyer for under $50.00* has been highly successful and has remained in print for many years. Nor is it an isolated case or an exception: Howard Ruff's *How to Prosper during the Coming Bad Years* was a best seller for many weeks, as other books with long titles have been.

Blurbs and/or Subtitles

There is one way to make use of a short title and still get the message across—define the coverage, that is—by using subtitles and/or blurbs. *The $100 Billion Market,* for example, is not entirely definitive until you read the subtitle, *How to Do Business with the U.S. Government.* Many publications thus bear both a title and a subtitle.

Another alternative is the blurb. A blurb is a short paragraph—it may even be a sentence fragment or a phrase, usually in telegraphic style—that describes the content, illustrates the coverage, or otherwise offers the reader some inkling of what a publication is about and furnishes some inducement for reading it. Blurbs are often used in magazines and even newspapers, following the title or headline of an article, story, or column.

The book title *2001 Sources of Financing for Small Business* was certainly definitive enough. However, the jacket of the book carries a blurb: "Bank loans * Venture capital * Grants * Federal and state programs * Foundations," which certainly elaborates on the title and helps the reader determine more precisely what is covered in the book. A recent magazine article titled "Where the Tongue-Tied Can Get Help" used the following blurb immediately after the title: "There are lots of public speaking courses, but talk isn't always cheap."

In terms of helping the reader grasp what the subject and coverage are, the descriptive title (whether short or lengthy) is probably the most effective, since many readers will not read the subtitle or blurb unless the title or headline has captured their interest. The title and subtitle are next in order of effectiveness, and the title and blurb are clearly last, since the reader must be induced to read that far—far enough to reach the blurb—before the latter can help in any way.

Obviously, there is some advantage in using all three: a highly descriptive or definitive title, a subtitle that elaborates on the description/ definition, and a blurb that carries it still further. If each of these elements induces the reader to go on and read the next element, there is a large possibility that the reader will beome a buyer of the publication.

Chapter 7

How to Develop Packages: Canned Presentations

There is a steadily growing appetite for the convenient alternative.

THE CLASSICAL METHOD: TAPE RECORDING

There is a substantial market for cassettes—"canned" presentations. Many who cannot or prefer not to attend such presentations as seminars, lectures, lecture series, and other forms of training delivery will often buy audio- and/or videocassettes of such presentations. In fact, many seminar presenters simply tape their seminars, as presented to an audience, and duplicate the "live" recording with little or no editing. It is not at all unusual for them to charge buyers $150 or more for a recording of a one-day session, even for a rough, unedited cassette. The market is that good for such material if the material itself is good enough.

Naturally, such a cassette is not exactly a polished or highly professional recording. A truly professional recording would be made under studio conditions, with careful control of audio levels (lighting and video, too, of course, if it is a videocassette) and professional editing of the product. For even under studio conditions, a tape cassette must be edited to bring it to final perfection.

As a compromise, you might make a tape of your live presentation and have it edited by a professional studio before making duplicates for sale. The result will be something a bit better than the raw, unedited tape but still a far cry from a truly professional tape cassette. To produce that, you must stage your presentation(s) under studio conditions and have the product professionally produced for you.

Actually, such cassettes are generally sold in sets rather than as single tapes. For example, Dottie Walters, who is active in the public-speaking field, publishes a set of four tape cassettes, titled *How to Enter the World of Paid Speaking,* representing eight lessons, one on each side of each tape.

Generally, such a set is made up in a booklike package—a box that resembles a book superficially—within which are shaped receptacles for the cassettes, and often a space for a booklet of some sort, to explain the system to the user or to provide supplemental information, such as suggestions for studying, illustrations, and anything else deemed necessary or helpful.

Such packages may be developed very much as you would develop any other kind of advice or information package: You may start from scratch and develop lectures or other presentations, but it is the exception, rather than the rule, for cassette packages to come into existence that way. (We are referring here primarily to audiocassettes, for while almost everyone has an audio tape player-recorder—since they are so inexpensive now—relatively few people have videocassette recorders. Still, what is said here for audiocassettes is or can be equally true for videocassettes.)

By far the majority of cassettes come into existence as adaptations from other media. That is, they are taped versions of seminars, lectures, and training programs, or they are adapted from published books. In fact, more than one company is mass-producing audiocassettes from successful self-help books, and distributing the cassettes widely as rack merchandise in a wide variety of outlets.

ADAPTING TO THE PERSONAL/ HOME COMPUTER

We are, of course, now well into what may be someday called the "Computer Age." Sales of home computers have climbed into the millions and threaten to go higher and higher, until they become as common in the typical home as TV sets are today. A new market for the advice business is rapidly opening here, and already some inroads have been made into that market by those who have produced training and education programs for home/personal computers.

Those who have home computers can, of course, buy programs—on floppy disks and/or on cassette tapes—to fit their computers and can thus get both audio and video (depending on the systems they own). Or, as an alternative, they can "dial up" information using modems—devices that permit them to link their computers to information sources and/or other computers through telephone connections—for even greater convenience. There is a young but growing market for such materials, as there is for videocassette recordings.

In sum, the tape market is definitely here and well established, especially the market for audiocassettes, but the other markets for canned presentations are growing and will unquestionably be important markets eventually, given the demonstrated appetite of the buying public for convenience. There can hardly be a convenience greater than dialing a telephone number and having the information or training materials you want presented to you on your own computer screen, where you can manipulate it, interact with it, and otherwise apply to it whatever purposes you wish.

Except for audiotape cassettes, then, this is a market largely for the future, but the not-too-distant future.

CHAPTER 8

How to Develop Packages: Seminars and Workshops

Seminars and workshops are almost an industry by themselves.

SPECIALIZATION IS ONE KEY

Over the years, seminars have become more and more a part of the industrial scene. One reason is that society in general has become so technological that many of us—perhaps even most of us—are compelled to become specialists of one kind or another. As specialists, we are in a constant effort to "keep up" with the dizzying pace of changes taking place in many fields. In my own case, I present seminars on government marketing and proposal writing.

I generalize within this specialized field—I offer instruction on writing proposals for almost any government agency and for almost any kind of government contract. But there are others in my field who specialize further than I do, presenting seminars on proposals strictly in the military—Department of Defense—areas of interest. And if that is not specialized enough, there are those who specialize even further than that: One man I know works only on certain aspects connected with security of military equipment, and is kept quite busy because there are few as expert as he in his own narrow field.

So there are probably few limits to how narrowly one may specialize if the specialty is well chosen as one for which there is a demand. But those are the very conditions that constitute a sound basis for a seminar or workshop. By and large, seminars are offered for the purpose of assisting people—often professionals—in catching up with new developments in their field or in learning some specialized aspects of their field that only a specialist is likely to know. That may be something related, directly or indirectly, to the attendee's field, as in the case of proposal writing.

SOME TYPICAL SEMINAR SUBJECTS

Proposal writing is not a subject normally taught in formal courses of education, yet a great many professionals find themselves required to participate in or contribute to the writing of proposals because the requirement is not inherent in the profession, but in the employment—in the kind of job or company that employs the individual.

Of course, the art of proposal writing is only one of the many types of special subjects in which seminars are offered. Frequently, a seminar program results from an event or some new trend. When the government decided to create special organizations to combat the pollution of our environment, it led to needs that were new—in fact, to the creation of new technical and professional disciplines, under the broad umbrella of "environmentalists." Again, this is not a subject that is itself taught in formal courses, but is an application—an entire range of applications, in actuality—of many professional and technical disciplines.

This situation is a common one, and more often than not, seminars are geared to the applications rather than to the basics of a subject. Here is a tiny sampling of subjects in which seminars are frequently offered:

Contract law and administration	Office organization
Speed reading	Word processing
Labor relations	Personnel management
Construction management	Purchasing
Computer familiarization	Computer programming

Inventory management	Public relations
Direct marketing	Copywriting
Public speaking	Personnel recruitment

TWO TYPES OF SEMINAR ATTENDEES

There are, of course, as many types of people who attend seminars as there are types of people. But from a broad marketing viewpoint, there are just two types of seminar attendees: those who attend at their personal expense, and those who are sent to attend at their employer's expense. It is important to recognize this distinction if you are to market seminars successfully. This is only the beginning of market analysis, of course; there are many other considerations, as each of these two broad classes of attendees is subdivided into classes.

The person who attends a seminar at his or her personal expense does so, of course, with the expectation of achieving some benefit worthy of the cost and the time invested. But the employer also sends employees to seminars with the expectation that the time and cost—which includes the employee's salary, of course—are merited by the benefits to be achieved. Whereas in the first case you address your marketing appeal to the prospective attendee, who is to be the customer, in the second place it is the employer, rather than the attendee, who is to be the customer. (Still, even then it is necessary to "sell" the proposition to the employees, for the employer will not send employees who do not themselves think their attendance will be worthwhile.)

Of course, not all seminars address subjects pertaining to business or professional pursuits. Often the appeal is to a personal interest that has nothing to do with business or careers. Some people attend speed-reading courses, for example, simply because they want to improve their reading ability in general, often because they are abnormally slow readers. And seminars have been offered to train people in real estate basics so that they will be equipped to make an intelligent search for a house to buy and will have a full understanding of all the legal processes of closing a real estate sale.

Later we will discuss marketing of seminars, with specific examples, and you will find that there are many differences merely in the process of reaching each of these two broad classes of seminar prospects.

HOW LONG SHOULD A SEMINAR BE?

Seminars range widely in length, from as little as two hours to as much as an entire week. The factors that affect and control this are partially the nature of the subject, but costs and other considerations affect this also. It is not at all easy to persuade anyone to spend a full week in a seminar class, and it requires rather powerful motivation to do so. The individual paying out of his or her own pocket is likely to be reluctant to spend that much money, and the executive who cares little about the cost—or who is not unduly concerned about it, at least—is rarely enthusiastic about being absent from his or her office for an entire week.

In considering this, bear in mind that for many kinds of seminars the attendees have traveled far from home or from their offices, and are paying for hotels and meals. Even the executive for whom the cost is not a major item of concern must be convinced that the time and money are merited—probably the time even more than the money.

There is another side to this, however: If the seminar is too short —a half-day, perhaps—you may also lose appeal for this reason. The executive is not likely to agree to the expense of travel and hotel expenses to attend a half-day seminar. You must consider this also when planning the event. You must consider what attendance will cost a typical attendee—and you should, of course, have a clear idea of the prospects to whom you address your appeal—and make sure that you have a match of program, appeal, attendee, and cost in both time and money. That compatibility is an important factor, for all the salesmanship in the world will not sell a bad product in sufficient quantity to produce a success.

PROGRAMMING A SEMINAR

Bear in mind that a seminar is intended to be a learning experience for the attendees, not formal training. This means that there must be a clear training objective for the session—something specific that the attendee will know, understand, and/or be able to do as a direct result of the seminar. The seminar is not likely to be a success—and that means success in the eyes of the attendees, of course—unless the attendees are informed in advance of what the beneficial results—objectives—

TABLE 2 General versus Specific Seminar Objectives

GENERAL OBJECTIVE	SPECIFIC OBJECTIVE
Explain new labor laws	Present and explain 1984 changes in labor laws
Teach government procurement	Explain two general types of government procurement methods (advertised and negotiated)
Instruct in headline writing	Teach AIDA concept in headline writing, with exercises
Present basics of news releases	Instruct in news-release formats and need for release to be "newsworthy," with exercises
Explain critical path method (CPM)	Present concepts and exercises in use of critical path method (CPM), with exercises

of the seminar are, and they agree after the session is over that the objectives were achieved.

It is seductively easy to generalize objectives, and there is a great temptation to do so because it is the easy way out. We tend to take the easy way out unconsciously, but that does not change the fact that we seriously compromise the seminar's chances for success by so doing. Formulating and articulating specific objectives is hard work, admittedly, but it is necessary hard work. Table 2 presents several examples of overly generalized objectives and suggestions of how they might have been made suitably specific. There should be some specific overall objective or goal for the seminar, and a follow-up set of more detailed objectives in outline form showing how the main objective will be met.

Figure 8-1 illustrates this concept. Note that the general objective is stated first: "How to Develop Winning Proposals," which is followed by a detailed outline, in which each item listed therein is a specific objective—a statement, in fact, of what will be presented. Note that the reader of this brochure—for this is an excerpt from a brochure which was used quite successfully to market an actual seminar—is told what to expect, and told in highly specific terms. Note, too, the relationship of the detailed outline to the overall goal or objective. The detailed outline actually explains how the overall objective will be achieved, in an orderly and logical progression of steps.

SEMINAR OUTLINE

Proposals for Government Contracts
How to Develop Winning Proposals

8:30 a.m. - REGISTRATION, coffee and pastries
9:00 a.m. - Session Begins

I. The $160 Billion Market
   a. Understanding the market
   b. What the government buys
   c. How to sell to the government.

II. Locating Sales Opportunities
   a. How to uncover selling opportunities.
   b. Getting on the appropriate bidder's list.
   c. How to use the *Commerce Business Daily* as an effective marketing tool.
   d. How to use the Freedom of Information Act to market.

III. Proposed Strategy Development
   a. Why proposals?
   b. What is a proposal?
   c. What does the customer want?
   d. What must the proposal do?
   e. What makes a winner?
   f. Why strategy makes the difference.

IV. The Stages of Proposal Development
   a. Bid/no-bid analysis and decision.
   b. Requirement analysis—understanding the requirements.
   c. Indentification of the critical factor(s).
   d. Formulation of the approach and technical/program/pricing strategies.
   e. Formulation of the capture strategy.
   f. Establishing the theme.
   g. Design and presentation strategy.
   h. Writing the proposal.

V. Persuasive Proposal Writing
   a. What is persuasion?
   b. The art of persuasive writing.
   c. What makes others agree?
   d. What turns them on? And off?

VI. How to Write a Winning Proposal
   a. Writing to communicate.
   b. Writing to sell.
   c. Writing to arouse and sustain interest.
   d. Your proposal should promise desirable end-results.
   e. Your proposal should, preferably, be a unique claim, one your competitors can't match.
   f. Your proposal must be able to prove it's validity.

VII. Formats and Proposal Content
   a. Recommended format.
   b. Front matter and other elements.
   c. How to use format for best results.

VIII. Cost Justification in Proposals
   a. Understanding costs.
   b. What the government expects in cost proposals.
   c. Technical vs. cost proposal.
   d. Construction of the quote.
   e. How to make bids.

WHO SHOULD ATTEND: If you are a small business executive and would like your company to increase its sales or profits in the enormous government market, or if you're a marketing executive in a major corporation, this seminar will be of tremendous benefit to you. New employees will shorten their learning curve. This seminar is designed to benefit marketing executives, contract administrators, engineers, systems analysts, computer specialists, trainers, editors, proposal writers, accountants, lawyers, contract specialists, manufacturers, service companies, consultants, and individuals seeking government contracts. Our faculty's expert advice has helped companies win contracts worth $1 million to $25 million and that expertise can be yours by attending this fact-filled seminar. Just one tip or one idea can be worth thousands of dollars to you.

MATERIALS: Each participant will receive an exclusive Handbook on Proposalmanship, authored by Herman Holtz, along with a host of other valuable materials.

FIGURE 8-1 Seminar outline that specifies objectives

Elsewhere in the brochure is other information, and we will return to this when we talk about marketing. For the outline serves two purposes: On the one hand, it is necessary to present this outline here for marketing purposes—to present to prospects a suitable explanation of what is being offered—but it is also necessary to reason out for yourself what you will offer, and the outline shown here is the plan of presentation.

WHO SHOULD ATTEND

Note the admonition "Who Should Attend," which is included in this brochure. This is an item found quite commonly in seminar advertising, intended to help readers "identify" with the copy as being addressed to and suitable for their own needs and interests. In this case, as you may have noted, this is addressed to business executives, suggesting that they attend or send employees, in the interests of their own companies. To reinforce this idea and ensure that the reader fully understands this message and knows to whom it is addressed, specific functional titles of people who ought to attend are listed—marketing executives, contract administrators, engineers, and many others.

Again, this is a step taken in the interest of good marketing and sales principles, but it is also significant in that it demonstrates that the seminar is intended to be of interest and value to a number of specific individuals, who were identified by the seminar producers in designing and planning the seminar. Identifying those to whom the seminar is addressed—"who should attend"—is not an afterthought but part of basic seminar planning, and no seminar ought to be undertaken until and unless the whole class of "who should attend" has been identified.

HANDOUT MATERIALS

Handout materials are an important item in a seminar. Most attendees do not feel that they have received full value if they do not get some kind of manual or other handout materials to carry away with them when the seminar is over. Despite their note taking, they tend to feel that the substance is ephemeral if they do not have it documented, at least in summary, in some type of permanent medium.

My own preference is for a seminar manual, with space provided for taking notes. The manual sums up all the important points of the session, including reproductions of several of the transparencies used to illustrate key points, and as such is a permanent reference and refresher the attendee may use later in applying what has been presented at the seminar. However, there are others who prefer to give out a series of individual handouts as the day progresses or even bind them together in a single package, and some even provide a three-ring binder for the handouts.

Each procedure has its merits and disadvantages. One reason some prefer the individual handouts is that is is often possible to get many handouts free of charge. For the seminar described in Figure 8-1, for example, it would be quite easy to get supplies of free government literature to give out, and some who present seminars in government contracting do, in fact, follow this procedure. However, anyone can get that literature by simply asking for it, so it loses the exclusivity of a manual or other material developed especially for the seminar and available only to attendees of that seminar.

Still another alternative for handout material is the practice of using a published book as a handout. Frequently, when the author of a highly successful book, such as one on making money in real estate, decides to present the information in a seminar format, the logical thing to do is to use the book as a handout. But there are also other situations in which a commercially published book makes an excellent handout.

Still another alternative is that of using free materials supplied by companies seeking free advertising. For example, if the presenter of a seminar on writing proposals approached companies whose products and services would be useful to writers of proposals—printers, stationers, and art-supply retailers, for example—it is likely that those companies could and would offer some handout materials and even more active participation and help, such as other materials and even speakers to help make presentations. There is, in fact, almost a superabundance of free help to be had in virtually all areas of programming and presentation of seminars and workshops, and we will consider each of these in turn as we proceed to discuss all those other areas of programming and presenting seminars. There are a great many missed opportunities resulting from the failure to thoroughly think out the problem, as well as all the possibilities.

PRESENTATIONS

Seminars are essentially lecture presentations, but are not necessarily solo performances. There are some who prefer to make the entire delivery alone, even if it is a day-long seminar or one of more than a single day. But there are also those who prefer to offer an array of speakers, presumably each especially qualified in a different area. This can become an expensive proposition if you are compelled to pay regular speaking or consulting fees to each of several speakers. But there are at least two alternatives:

1 It was mentioned earlier that many companies and other organizations—government bureaus, associations of various kinds, and for-profit companies who see a PR or advertising advantage in helping you—will often furnish speakers free of charge. In fact, many such organizations maintain rosters of staff people who are willing and able to speak publicly on subjects of interest, and are eager to offer the services of these people.

2 Many consultants and other small, independent entrepreneurs are willing also to speak for nominal fees—small "honorariums"—in exchange for the sales promotion they thus achieve.

There are some advantages in using several speakers. One is that the change of pace and various viewpoints are welcomed by the attendees, and the mix of speakers tends to liven up the session. And, of course, there is the fatigue factor, which you obviously avoid by having other speakers than yourself.

On the other hand, there is the drawback that perhaps some of the speakers you get free of charge are not worth any more than you paid for their services: They may be poor speakers and put your attendees to sleep, something you certainly want to avoid. There is a risk in using speakers you know nothing about and have never heard.

There is also the problem of building your seminar around a specific group of speakers who may or may not be available the next time you want to present your seminar. It is difficult enough to be sure of the availability of anyone not in your direct employ, let alone that of someone who is being paid only a nominal fee or none at all for making a presentation.

This second consideration becomes even more serious if and when you find your seminar so successful that you want to "take it on the road." Most successful seminars are presented in an itinerary of many cities, since that is the fundamental way of making a successful seminar produce satisfactory income and profit. The problems are twofold: (1) those who speak free or nearly so are not going to travel to other cities, even if you pay their travel expenses, because they will usually not be willing to donate that much of their time to an activity that is not directly profitable, and perhaps not profitable at all, especially when presented out of town; and (2) the expenses of travel and lodging may very well place an intolerable burden of expense on your seminar venture and make what promised to be a successful venture an unsuccessful one.

Hence there are distinct advantages in doing your seminar as a solo performance. It gives you total or, at least, nearly total control. You can plan more effectively when you depend little or not at all on others, your expenses are minimized, and you are free to take your seminar on the road or do what you will with it. All you require is the stamina to handle the entire lecture requirement by yourself. But even that does not mean that you must lecture without ceasing all day; there are ways to ease the burden of lecturing all day, too.

HINTS FOR THE LECTURER

It has been noted that there are people who would sooner face a charging rhino or climb a sheer cliff than speak before a group in a formal or even semiformal setting. Somehow, the very idea of standing up and speaking publicly terrorizes a great many people. Without a doubt, a degree of insecurity lies at the heart of such fear. Many people are sure that they will make fools of themselves, that they cannot "speak well," that everyone will focus their stares on some physical flaw of the speaker—perhaps the most insignificant mole on the speaker's neck— that a slight lisp will bring great embarrassment, that they will forget their speech, or that any of a hundred other disasters, real or imagined, will happen.

So intense are these fears, quite often, that many speakers never manage to overcome their fears, even though they compel themselves to speak publicly despite their fears, and even after they have spoken publicly hundreds of times. (Many noted stars in the entertainment field, for example, confess that they never have managed to overcome their "stage fright," despite years of experience and performance.)

There is no point, therefore, in promising you that "you'll get over it" or "you'll get used to it." Probably you will "get used to it" after a while, and probably you will overcome stage fright if you have it, but that is not, of itself, important—as long as you do not let such fears prevent you from speaking publicly. (Although there is one very well known person whom many think of as a public speaker but who never speaks publicly because of his fear of appearing before a live audience: What he does is record all his speeches in the solitude of a studio, and these recordings are played for all his radio broadcasts and other such events.)

Whether you are nervous and fearful about speaking publicly or not, and whether you ever become free of these fears or not, there are some things you can do to offset and ease the anxiety of making public appearances. Bear in mind that a large part of the anxiety is based on the feeling that you are totally exposed, standing on a dais—virtually naked, psychologically, before an assembled crowd who are staring at you, waiting for you to make even the smallest slip. That is a completely false image, but it is, nevertheless, one that a great many people have when they stand before an audience or even contemplate standing before an audience. If we reduce that to essentials, it reduces to the two stress factors of being defenseless and being the object of intense scrutiny or attention. If you can do things to combat those two stresses, you will make a beginning at easing the tension and the anxiety, and there are things you can do to combat and reduce those two stressful illusions.

You can erect several shields. The best one is to be seated, preferably behind a table or desk of some kind. If that is not feasible, the next alternative is to stand behind some kind of lectern, which acts as a shield. Any of these measures is better than standing on a platform, feeling totally conspicuous, unsure of what to do with your hands, fumbling with your clothes, and otherwise fidgeting like a child reciting before a class. It is almost always possible to use a lectern if you cannot employ any of the other measures; you have a place to rest your hands (on the lectern) while "shielding" yourself with the lectern.

Combating the other stress factor, that of being the sole object of attention, is even easier, for there are several ways you can draw attention away from yourself:

1 When possible, especially when you are getting your earliest experiences at public speaking, try to make your first few appearances on the platform as a member of a panel, and share the spotlight with others.

2 Use as many visual aids as you can—transparencies, slides, posters, film clips,

models, demonstrations—so that you share the spotlight and get frequent relief from being the center of attention.

3 Get the audience to participate, with exercises, discussions, questions (invite questions and comments), and any other way you can think of to involve the audience.

GOOD AND BAD ADVICE

There is probably as much bad advice accepted as conventional wisdom as there is good advice available. One piece of advice often offered novice speakers is to select someone in the audience and address the presentation to that person. That is bad advice. It can only make that person entirely uncomfortable and offend all the rest of the audience, who are thus signaled that they do not count. The right thing to do, in this respect, is to keep moving your eyes about the audience, and talk to all of them. However, it is important to make eye contact, so make eye contact with many people in your audience. Do talk to all of them as individuals, but do not single anyone out for more such attention than anyone else. You will be surprised at the friendly looks and smiles you get when you do this. Most audiences want you to succeed, and they are not being critical in their gazes. It helps to learn that.

When you are advised to be prepared, that is good advice. The problem with it is misunderstanding by many as to what being "prepared" means. It does not mean to have your speech memorized. Memorized speeches are generally bad ones. Unless you are a good actor, your speech will sound like what it is—memorized and hence thoroughly mechanical. Instead of memorizing it, prepare a set of notes to guide yourself—many speakers use 3 by 5 index cards—but speak more or less extemporaneously, although with complete awareness of the points you wish to make.

You do not need to have "pear-shaped tones" and perfect diction to be a successful speaker. Quite the contrary, many successful speakers have lisps, gravelly voices, and other such minor flaws—yes, minor flaws because those defects have not prevented these people from becoming successful speakers.

What you should have is great enthusiasm, for enthusiasm is contagious; your audience will catch it from you. But "enthusiasm" does not mean false heartiness, for audiences are quite sensitive to any phoniness and will detect any effort to present a false enthusiasm. The enthusiasm must be real, and it will overcome any small defect that you may have as a speaker.

Of course, you should also know what you are talking about. That is part of being prepared. The late Paderewski was reported to have said that when he missed practice for a day, he knew it; when he missed two days, his audience knew it.

PRESENTATION MATERIALS

The type of material you use in your presentation depends on several factors, some of which are under your control, some of which are not. In some cases, a seminar presenter can get appropriate and useful audio-visual materials—films, filmstrips, slides, or other aids, just as in the case of handout materials—either inexpensively or at no cost. Obviously, it makes good sense to take advantage of such opportunities when they exist. On the other hand, you might wish to make up slides or film-strips of your own. It is possible to do so, quite often, at an acceptable cost, although it would be impractical to make a movie solely for your seminar.

But even in the case of slides, audiotapes, and filmstrips, cost is not insignificant, and the practicality of absorbing that cost into your seminar is determined primarily by just how costly they are and by how often you will present the seminar. As a rule, it is not a practical idea to go to the expense of making up such materials for only one or two pre-sentations of the seminar. Such costs are investment costs, costs that (your accountant will probably advise you) should be "capitalized." That means, simply, treated as an investment that has to be amortized. We will discuss that and related terms later, when we discuss the eco-nomics of the business, but in simple terms, it means that it is usually too large a cost to try to recover in a single use. Even a relatively simple audio-visual program can cost you several thousand dollars (although it is possible to make simple slides up cheaply if you are equipped with a camera and know how to use it well).

A practical and popular presentation aid is the *transparency,* also referred to often as a "vu-graph" or "view graph." Transparencies can be made up inexpensively and are essentially the same as slides in what they do for you and your listeners. They offer certain advantages, in addition.

Slides are generally 35mm slides, made by using a 35mm camera to photograph whatever the scenes, objects, drawings, or text materials are that are to be presented. However, you need a slide projector to present them, of course, and the only flexibility you have with them is the order in which you present them. (However, if you borrow or rent slides, you may be offered lantern slides, which are larger, mounted on glass flats, and require an entirely different kind of projector.)

Transparencies are made of a thin, flexible plastic—acetate, generally—and may be clear or tinted in any of several colors. They are most popularly about 8 by 10 inches and may be mounted on cardboard "holders" or frames, although they can be used without these. They can be made on an ordinary office copier, by placing the acetate in the paper tray and copying whatever you want on the transparency by the usual method for making copies on these machines.

Transparencies are used with a machine called an *overhead projector*. Because they are projected onto a screen, as are slides or films, the room is normally darkened. However, one advantage of transparencies over slides and filmstrips is this: The transparency is exposed on the projector table, and readily accessible. Moreover, it is large enough to work with and make notations on (with a grease pencil, for example) or to point out items on. And there are other ways you can use this flexibility. For example, many lecturers use a transparency on which there are a number of items to be discussed, but which the lecturer wants presented only one at a time. With slides, the only practical way is to have a new slide for each item, so 10 items requires 10 slides. Not so with transparencies: With a transparency, you can use a sheet of paper or a card of some kind to cover items 2 through 10 while you discuss item 1, then move the cover sheet down to expose item 2 and discuss it, and so on (see Figure 8-2).

For small groups—25 to 50 people, that is—even posters work well if they are on the order of 3 by 4 feet in size and are lettered boldly. Of course, you can have posters done up by a professional illustrator, but you can also do them yourself if you want only lettering on them.

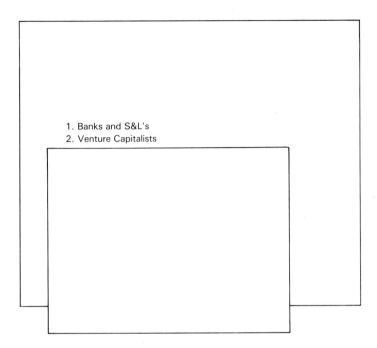

FIGURE 8-2 Presenting items one at a time using a transparency

There is a wide assortment of marking pens to select from, with a wide spectrum of colors. With respect to colors, you will do well to stick with dark colors on white or light-colored paper. (Black and yellow have been shown to offer greater contrast than black and white.)

If you do not care about having posters made up in advance, you may prefer to use the easel—a pad of large sheets of paper, mounted on a stand, on which you can write, and which you can then flip to expose a fresh, clean sheet for further writing. Or you may prefer a blackboard, which does the same thing but needs to be wiped off before you can enter fresh material on it.

Each method has its pros and cons, but in the end you must select that which best suits your own purposes and preferences. Do not lose sight of the basic criterion: what suits you best.

There are some miscellaneous items in this regard: In some instances, models are appropriate exhibits, and perhaps demonstrations are helpful and relevant, in which case you may need some special materials.

EXERCISE MATERIALS

Many seminars ought to combine a workshop element—give the participants some work to do, so as to enable them to get some firsthand experience in actually *applying* what they are learning. To accomplish this, you generally need to have a few exercises made up in advance, although part of the workshop may consist of spontaneous discussion and Q&A (question and answer) sessions, too. Ordinarily, it is a good practice to hand out exercise instructions (if you use written instructions for your exercises) when the time arrives to conduct the exercise, rather than in advance. And most seminar or workshop leaders critique the exercise results and discuss them, with a follow-up Q&A, frequently.

Again, whether you include exercises and whether these are supported by formal, written instructions is entirely up to you and to your situation and aims. There is no universal rule, of course. In my own case, formal written exercises would not be especially helpful, but informal, spontaneous ones are—open discussions, based largely on asking my audiences questions and inviting spontaneous answers. That works well in my situation, but might be all wrong for your need.

THE LITERATURE TABLE

For many kinds of seminars, a literature table is appropriate and helpful in several ways. This is simply a table somewhere in the room (usually at the back of the room) on which is deposited appropriate literature—brochures, business cards, pamphlets, and whatever else appears to be relevant to the session and may be offered to the participants without charge. The sources for this literature are several:

- Some of it may be your own advertising literature, offering your services or products for sale.
- Some may be that free literature mentioned earlier, which you choose to deposit on a literature table rather than include in the handout package.
- Guest speakers who are speaking without charge or for a nominal honorarium are generally invited to deposit their own literature on such a table. (In fact, this is one of the inducements.)
- When appropriate—when participants are likely to be able to do business with each other—they may be invited to leave their own cards and other literature on the table.

The result of all this is usually a well-stocked assortment of literature and, for some at least, an added inducement to participate in the seminar.

SALES AT THE SEMINAR

Many seminar presenters use the occasion to sell their books and other products (and many of my own seminars produced consulting contracts for me) at the time, and they set up a back-of-the-room sales booth at which they sell their own books, tapes, newsletter subscriptions, or whatever they have to offer. For some, the income from this activity at least equals the seminar income.

Nor is that the only way to gain income. Mailing your sales literature for whatever other products or services you offer together with the brochure or sales letter soliciting seminar attendance often produces orders for those items as well as seminar registrations.

THE ADMINISTRATIVE DETAILS

There are three functional aspects to consider in producing and presenting seminars: the program aspect, which we have just reviewed; the marketing aspect, which we shall discuss in the next chapter; and the general administrative aspect. These are not small matters, either: There are many details to attend to when planning a seminar, and most of them must be planned and executed well in advance, for a seminar presentation requires advance planning. (This refers to the "open registration" seminar, which anyone may attend by paying the registration fee, as compared with the custom or in-house seminar presented to an organization via contract agreement.) Some of the matters that require attention have a direct linkage to each other and are therefore interdependent.

One example of this interdependency is the need for an early arrangement of a place to hold the seminar. No announcements, brochures, or advertising of any sort can be ordered until the date and place are fixed reliably. Nor can any announcements or advertising materials tell the readers very much—or even make a very strong appeal—

PHASE I — PLANNING	PHASE II — COORDINATION	PHASE III — MARKETING
Program Approximate Date Approximate Location Fees Handouts	Select and Reserve Room Draft Advertising & Literature Order Printing Draft News Releases	Order Advertising Mail out Literature Mail out Releases Sign up Registrants

FIGURE 8-3   Administrative phases and functions of seminar ventures

until other planning is completed. For example, the program cannot be described or the highlights of the program featured in the brochures and other advertising unless the program has been designed and planned in detail well in advance of the event. In fact, the administration itself breaks down into three general phases of activity which are mandated by these cause-and-effect interdependencies. Figure 8-3 illustrates these separate phases. Note that it is not possible to carry out Phase II before Phase I, or Phase III before Phase II.

Estimating Date and Location

It is rarely possible to fix exact seminar dates and locations until you have checked to see what facilities are available in the general locations and on the approximate dates you have tentatively selected. For example, you may decide that your seminar will appeal primarily to individuals (rather than organizations). Because of that you decide that Saturday, a non-workday for most people, is the best day of the week for your seminar. You decide, too, that the only practicable way to reach prospects and solicit their attendance is via print advertising. You also decide that March 31 is a good date for your purposes. But before you settle on that date, even as an approximate date, you must check on your advertising and see how much lead time you need. If you are planning advertising in any daily publication, such as a newspaper, you will not need much lead time; you can usually place your advertising a few days in advance. But if you are planning to place your copy in something published on other than a daily basis, you had better check on lead time first because you may be required to place your copy weeks in advance.

The same consideration applies to other methods of advertising your seminar and soliciting attendance. Even if you are going to use direct mail, which is a practicable enough approach in cases where you can rent or otherwise gain access to suitable mailing lists, you need to allow time to have your materials written, composed, and printed. It is wise to allow some margin for error here, too; slipped schedules are common in printing as they are to most human activities.

So obviously you cannot set even a tentative date until you have settled these other matters of lead time. Having done that, you can go on to investigate availability of suitable facilities.

Meeting Rooms

For most seminar producers, hotel and motel meeting rooms prove to be most convenient and most readily accessible, with the added advantage of offering attendees from out of town lodging at the same site. In fact, if you can guarantee the hotel a minimum number of room rentals, or if you are serving a luncheon for attendees, many hotels will let you have the use of a meeting room without charge.

In general, meeting rooms vary in cost according to several factors:

- Day of week
- Time of year
- Size of room
- Location of hotel
- Individual hotel policy

Some hotels charge more for weekends than they do for weekdays, whereas other hotels have an opposite policy. It depends on which days are in greatest demand for that hotel. That tends to depend, in turn, on whether the hotel is more popular for business events or for social events. In fact, one Holiday Inn refused to accept an advanced meeting-room reservation for a seminar because, they told me, they might get a wedding or other social affair, which would be far more profitable for them than a seminar would be.

Usually, a hotel in a downtown location will charge higher rates for meeting rooms than will one located in a suburb, because of many considerations, such as higher costs generally for downtown enterprises and facilities. But, again, there are certain advantages in using a downtown location:

- Downtown locations are far more convenient, normally, for attendees coming from out of town.

- Downtown locations are more central, usually more readily accessible, and therefore more convenient for even those attendees from the local area, since so many work and live in suburban areas circumferential to the downtown area.

- Downtown areas tend to be more prestigious, in many ways, thus adding something to their appeal.

There are, of course, some disadvantages, too, principally that of cost and that of some inconvenience for those who would prefer to drive but who find it impracticable to drive to a crowded downtown area. If you expect to draw most of your attendance from the local area or at least from within convenient driving distance, you may want to consider this factor in choosing a location.

One of the more difficult matters, especially when you have had little or no experience with your seminar, is estimating the size of the room you will need. Some seminars draw as few as 10 or 15 attendees, while others draw 50, 100, and even more. To some degree, you can estimate this by certain assumptions, which are entirely arbitrary but give you at least something on which to base rough estimates. Assume that unless you ran a great deal of advertising or made extraordinarily large mailings, you will draw between 20 and 40 attendees, which is probably the bracket in which most seminars fall as far as typical attendance is concerned. And that assumes that you mailed out several thousand pieces of sales literature and/or ran several modest advertisements in some medium. The typical meeting room in a hotel is likely to be suitable for a group of about that size. You will probably not go far astray arranging for a room to hold about 35 people. Sometimes it is possible to change to a larger room before the seminar takes place if you find yourself more successful than you anticipated. (Results are usually not especially predictable, and many mailouts and advertisements produce surprises.)

The alternative is to refuse registrants once you have reached the limits of whatever room you have reserved. That is a distasteful alternative, of course, so you are well advised to plan on the optimistic side. The difference in cost is usually insignificant.

Refreshments

Most seminar producers provide coffee and some kind of sweet in the morning at the start of the seminar, and many have coffee available all day. Some provide cold drinks also, for the comfort of the attendees. Most hotels will provide such services from their kitchens and will bar you from bringing in your own from the outside. In most cases, the costs are not unreasonable, although they do vary. (Ironically, I have often found that those hotels who charge the lowest rates for their rooms charge the highest rates for the refreshments, and vice versa.)

If you choose to serve your attendees lunch, it may increase your attendance. (It appeared to me that those seminars which included a luncheon drew a better response, but without actual testing, there is no evidence that this is so.) Should you serve lunch, you will probably be provided with a room for the luncheon. Most hotels will also arrange for a cash bar, so that your attendees may have a drink before lunch if they wish. An included luncheon is also an excellent occasion for a guest speaker, and a good speaker adds substantially to the overall success of your seminar.

Obviously, all of this must be resolved before you do your advertising and order your printing. It is important, even, to decide what your handouts will be, although they need not be written yet. But whatever materials you are including—reference manual, hardcover book, or other useful materials—you'll want to describe them in your advertising.

Fees and Registration

You will have to announce your fee requirement, of course, so you must settle that in advance, as part of your planning. What you charge and how you arrive at your price is up to you, of course; there are no good guidelines for this because every set of circumstances is unique or at least totally individual. However, there are some basic approaches to setting registration fees that are practiced frequently, and you should know what they are.

The simplest way is a flat fee for each registrant, but there are many seminar producers who charge some discounted rate for each additional registrant from the same organization if all registrations are

REGISTRATION FORM DETACH AND MAIL **UNITED BUSINESS INSTITUTE**
Oxon Hill Center, Box 10448, Oxon Hill, MD 20745
(202) 822-3100

Proposals for Government Contracts
How to Develop Winning Proposals

To ensure participation in this exclusive seminar we urge you to register in advance. You may reserve your space(s) by telephone and confirm by returning the form below. List your name and other data in the space below and enclose remittance now or call 822-3100 for reservations. Late payment may be made at the door with firm reservations.

NAME _____   *Additional Registrants from same organization:
COMPANY/ORGANIZATION _____
ADDRESS _____   NAME _____
CITY _____ STATE _____   NAME _____
ZIP _____ PHONE _____   NAME _____
Remittance: $125.00 per person; $95.00 for each additional person.
☐ Check   ☐ Money Order   ☐ VISA   ☐ MasterCard
Card No. _____ Expiration Date _____
Planned Date of Attendance: _____   *Discount: additional registrants pay only $95.00.

FIGURE 8-4   Seminar registration form included in brochure

made at the same time—for example, $175 for the first registrant and $150 for each additional one.

As a variant on this, some charge a registration fee for the organization and an individual fee for each registrant—perhaps $50 for the organization and $150 for each individual registered.

Many charge less for advance registration than for registration at the door. There are, of course, advantages in getting registrations (and payment) in advance.

To facilitate and encourage advance registration, it is a good idea to provide a registration form of some kind with your brochure. Figure 8-4 is an example of such a form. Note in this form that a reduced rate is offered for additional registrations, and space is provided to list additional attendees, to further suggest and stimulate the idea.

Phase I: Advance Planning

The actual presentation of a seminar is quite simple in comparison with all the work that must be done before it can be presented. In fact, that preliminary work has three phases, the first of which is the advance planning and identification of options and alternatives which we have been examining here. Phase I, that is, consists primarily of planning all aspects of the seminar and making all the decisions necessary to carry out that planning.

Phase II: Coordination

Once all these matters have been settled and a definite agreement reached on a meeting-room reservation, copy can be finalized, printing ordered, news releases and advertising written, and many other details attended to so as to implement and coordinate all the activities necessary to producing and staging the seminar. (Some of these matters, such as the writing of news releases, are discussed in Chapter 9.)

Phase III: Marketing

Chapter 9 is devoted to marketing generally, to include the marketing of seminars. In line with what we have been considering here, marketing will include mailing out literature, sending out news releases, placing advertising, and other such activities.

CHAPTER 9

THE MARKETING
of Advice

Nothing happens until somebody sells something.
—Author unknown

SALES VERSUS MARKETING

Entrepreneurial success does not result from waiting for customers to seek you out—not even if you have built a better mousetrap. It is you who must seek out the customer if you want the sale. That is selling.

But there is another aspect to the business of finding or creating customers, and that is called *marketing*. Marketing also has to do with finding or creating customers but it is a far more subtle matter than the function we call *selling*. Putting it into the proverbial nutshell, selling is getting orders, but marketing is determining what orders to get. But that is greatly—grossly—oversimplified, in that it falls short of determining everything that marketing is—or should be. To get a true understanding of what marketing is, we have to consider the entire venture:

1 What you propose to sell
2 To whom you propose to sell
3 How you propose to sell

These three matters are closely related, of course, perhaps even more closely than you may appreciate at first. Let's have a closer look.

WHAT, TO WHOM, HOW

You can conceive and launch a venture starting with or from any of these matters, as a point of origin. Suppose, for example, you are an expert in public housing and can save those less experienced a great deal of travail and waste of money. Before you can sell your expertise, you have to decide who the prospects are to be. Obviously, they are not average citizens. But who are they? You might answer that by telling yourself that they are the public officials of the various communities and governments—perhaps even at all levels, federal, state, and local. And they are not just any officials, of course, but the officials responsible for public housing.

Having worked this out, you need to decide how you will reach these officials—the right prospects—with an appeal and offer of help. Will you make personal calls? Send out literature? Hire representatives? Speak at relevant gatherings? Use political contacts?

But wait a minute: Are these the only possible prospects? Let's think about this: How about large management consultant organizations who get involved in contracting for services for public housing projects—and even some of those who are not so large? How about construction companies who perhaps could use some help in winning some of the construction business that results from public housing projects? And how about some of the national associations of individuals and organizations who are involved, directly or indirectly, in public housing?

As you can see, a little thought (and research, of course) may triple and quadruple the size of the potential market. But there are other concerns: Can you use the same marketing/sales methods to reach all the prospects, or will you require different methods for different classes/groups of prospects? That is an important question. What you must do is divide your prospects into the various groups, on some basis, and analyze each group.

Of course, you do not necessarily start from what you propose to sell, although probably most people begin from that point—it appears the most logical place to begin. But successful enterprises have been launched from other bases, such as the circumstance of having access to some class or group of prospects not easily reached. Former Secretary of State Henry Kissinger, for example, is in that position: He has almost unique access to heads of state and other highly placed officials of many nations. It was therefore not surprising that he associated himself with other former diplomatic officials and set up a high-level international consulting service in Washington, D.C. For somewhat similar reasons, many former legislators and former government officials have also set up shop in Washington as consultants, on the basis of their "contacts."

Or you might start from the third point: Perhaps you have a brilliant idea for dramatizing an offer or appeal—perhaps you have some unusual publicity stunt in mind which you are sure you can pull off. The problem is to answer the other two questions: What will you sell, and to whom, based on this wonderful idea? We have the example of the late Joe Karbo, who sold a book title—a book he had not yet written—based on an idea he had and on his superb marketing ability. His idea was to sell a little book he would call *The Lazy Man's Way to Riches,* via full-page advertisements in national publications. But he had not even begun the book when he began to run his advertisements, the headline for which was the proposed book title, offering the book for $10. But he did not sell the book: He sold the promise to reveal how he had made a great deal of money, despite being broke and in debt a few years earlier. Only when his advertisements began to produce orders at an acceptable rate of return did he write the little book (he had the raw material ready and knew that he could write it almost literally overnight and get it printed up in paperback quickly) and fill orders. The basic messages and ideas in the book were not new or different from those already published in many other books, although they were in Karbo's own inimitable style, but the marketing was carried out brilliantly, and the project was a great success and is still carried on by his successors.

The three items sum up marketing. Marketing, in as simple a set of terms as it is possible to express it and yet define it, is the process of deciding what to sell, to whom, and how—how to reach those prospects, that is; getting the specific orders is selling.

Of course, the two—marketing and sales—are not unrelated. In fact, it would not be a distortion to consider sales part of marketing—the last act of marketing—were it not for the fact that too often people believe the two to be identical and interchangeable terms. For that reason, it is wiser to keep the two terms entirely separate from each other, and consider that marketing is what makes sales possible. That is, sales success depends on how well the marketing has been done—on whether the identification of prospects has been accurate; on whether the method for reaching those prospects does, in fact, work out successfully; and on the effectiveness of the sales strategies (which should be developed in the marketing activity, at least in principle), as well as on how effectively the sales function itself has been carried out.

THE SALES FUNCTION

Selling is the act of persuading a prospect to trade dollars for the goods or services you offer. Your success in doing that is based on one simple question: Does the prospect perceive, accept, and want the promised benefits of whatever you offer? For in the final analysis, you cannot sell something to someone who really does not want it. The art of selling is the art of persuading a prospect to want what you offer. That, in turn, comes about only when and if your presentation includes a promise of some benefit that the prospect finds appealing enough. A brochure from Verbatim, a manufacturer of storage disks for computers, advises retailers of its products that "People don't want products. They want benefits." And it goes on to assure the reader that people do not buy any given brand for its advertised or evident features, only for the benefits delivered by those features.

That is sound advice, and one can go even further in the analysis and point out that in most cases people are not even buying the benefits per se, only the *promise* of benefits. And that promise is rarely easy to sell, even when the prospect wants to buy, for even then the prospect usually wants to be convinced. Convinced of what? Convinced that the promised benefit is really worth what it will cost (that it is worth trading precious dollars for), and that you (what you are selling) really can and will make good on the promise and deliver the benefit.

But even that does not explain it entirely or establish the linkage to those items listed here as the essence of marketing. There is this, too: Your success in making your promise appealing enough depends on how well you have marketed—have matched up the item offered, with the prospect, and with the method for presenting the offer.

To illustrate this, let's assume that you decide to market an investment newsletter. Obviously, the right kind of prospect is someone with surplus funds to invest. But that is an extremely broad qualification or definition and could include almost anyone who is well above the poverty level. To be useful, for marketing purposes, you have to narrow that down a bit—unless you are prepared to try to sell your newsletter to buyers of penny stocks, mutual funds, and occasional stock purchases, as well as those who are serious investors, if not absolute plungers. But you cannot reach this diverse a group of prospects with the same appeal, ordinarily. Those who invest heavily, for example, will probably have no interest at all in penny stocks, and those whose investment is limited to a few dollars every week or every month are rarely prospects for an investment newsletter that covers the market broadly.

It is essential that all elements be *matched:* the right product, the right prospect, and the right promise. There are entrepreneurs selling advice to those who will gamble in a Las Vegas casino but would not invest five cents in stocks or bonds. But the reverse is true, also: Some of those plungers who gamble heavily in the stock market are not interested in gambling on roulette wheels or cards.

That brings us almost full circle, in a sense: If you start with an idea of something to sell, you must find the right prospects for what you want to sell—and that includes the ability to reach those prospects with your offer or sales appeal (promise)—and the right promise—the one that will appeal to those prospects. If you start with a class of prospects, you must match them with something suitable to sell and the right promise. And if you start with a marketing or sales-promotional inspiration, you must find the other two ingredients to match. We could, in fact, make a triad of this to help you remember the need for these matches (Figure 9-1); or even an algorithm:

$$\begin{matrix} \text{SOMETHING} \\ \text{TO SELL} \end{matrix} + \begin{matrix} \text{SOMEBODY TO} \\ \text{SELL IT TO} \end{matrix} + \begin{matrix} \text{A WAY TO} \\ \text{SELL IT} \end{matrix} = \text{MARKETING} = \begin{matrix} \text{SALES} \\ \text{SUCCESS} \end{matrix}$$

Does this seem too obvious a truth to belabor? In fact, it is not. The well-known marketing expert and consultant/author Peter Drucker has observed that if he discovers that he has told a client something the client never knew before, he is both surprised and disappointed. He believes that his job is primarily to remind clients of what they know or ought to know already, in a kind of, "You know what you should be

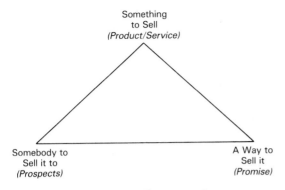

Something
to Sell
(Product/Service)

Somebody to
Sell it to
(Prospects)

A Way to
Sell it
(Promise)

FIGURE 9-1 The marketing triad

doing. Why haven't you been doing it?" It is Drucker's way of pointing out to all of us that we tend to forget what we know and to overlook the obvious all too often. But that is not the only problem. There is also the common problem of vanity and self-esteem. It happens that occasionally one comes up with an idea that seems exceptionally promising, so the originator of the idea "goes to bat" for it and begins to promote it. But if the idea does not work out—for whatever reason, which is often impossible to determine—the originator may tend stubbornly to insist on wasting money and effort on the idea because of some idea that his or her personal prestige hangs in the balance—that to admit defeat is to admit having been wrong in the first place. It is unfortunate, but true, that we find it possible to persuade ourselves to believe what we want to believe. Again and again, the backers of an unsuccessful idea keep attacking the market and pursuing success with the idea. Occasionally, something new is slow to catch on, but does eventually and becomes a success. More often, however, the energy and the effort is wasted, and the idea that did not quite make it never does make it, until the backer is finally forced—reluctantly—to put it mercifully to death.

We have lots of examples of this. Ford's Edsel automobile was one about which a great many jokes have been made because it was such a famous example. The loss on this was a quarter-billion dollars (when $250 million was a great deal more than it is today) before Ford Motor Company admitted defeat. And it was probably the timing that was wrong—it was a bad year to introduce a new automobile—and the car might have been successful at another time. Timing is important, critically so in many cases. (The automobile industry generally has been stubborn about recognizing the need for change, and this has been a disastrous mistake more than once.)

The example of Joe Karbo's book is one at the opposite extreme: Karbo pursued the conservative and sagacious method of *testing* the market before committing his time and money. Had his advertisements not produced enough response to encourage him in his idea, he would have written off the test expense and gone on to another idea.

With apologies to whomever it is that I am paraphrasing here about the achievement of greatness, it is apparent to anyone who makes a serious study of marketing that everything marketed successfully falls into one of these three classes: Some are "born" successful, some achieve success, and some have success thrust upon them. That is, some items appear to be such "naturals" that they are instantly accepted by the buying public and require little promotion and advertising to become profitable. Video-game computers, for example, may be said to have been born successful, since they were embraced instantly by the public, and perhaps personal computers had success thrust upon them by an eager public. But most items offered for sale are not seized that eagerly, but must be sold. The items that do not have to be sold are the exceptions, not the rule, and even those are soon confronted with ample competition, and their sellers must begin selling hard if they are even to survive against the competition, let alone lead the field. IBM, for example, did not introduce the computer to the commercial market, but they soon overtook the firm that did and became the undisputed leader in that field (and at least one other field: the electric typewriter). So in the end, even if you have had some remarkable good fortune in the beginning, survival and long-term success depend heavily on marketing and sales success.

REACHING PROSPECTS WITH YOUR OFFER

There are three basic ways to reach your prospects so as to make your sales appeal. (I prefer to think of it as an offer—an offer to trade some benefit or set of benefits for a stipulated number of dollars. It is a far more positive way of approaching the market.) These are the ways: through personal and direct presentation in some kind of point-of-sale situation, such as a retail store, fair, house-to-house canvass, or similar face-to-face contact; through paid advertising—in print, on radio and TV, by direct mail, and/or other means; and through special promotions, such as publicity campaigns, contests, tie-ins with others, and other events, some of which cost as much as paid advertising (although they offer certain advantages) and some of which are relatively free (cost little money).

Each method has its advantages and disadvantages, but even those are relative to what it is you want to sell. If you are selling advice— a newsletter, perhaps—it is difficult, if not impossible, to market it through a retail outlet or, for that matter, through any kind of personal presentation. Theoretically, you can sell newsletter subscriptions through paid advertising in print media—periodicals—and on radio and TV. In practice, according to all accounts from those who have published newsletters, direct mail generally proves to be the most practicable way of selling newsletter subscriptions and, from all accounts, the only way that is economically feasible.

On the other hand, some information items—magazines and newspapers, for example—are sold successfully by both mail (and telephone) and retail outlets. But some items can only be sold by retail outlets because they are perishable or for some other reason unsuited to sale by any other means. One very special information item—the personal computer—is particularly germane: Despite the fact that there are many mail-order houses offering computers by mail, computers are simply not sold that way—not to any large extent, at least. Relatively few buyers will buy an item of that magnitude (price, that is) without shopping for it personally. And the problem is not only that of understandable customer resistance to spending thousands of dollars with an unknown seller for a sight-unseen product: Many, if not most, computer manufacturers object to having their systems offered by mail, understandably. So those who advertise computers by mail order generally succeed in selling accessories and supplies by mail far more than they succeed in selling computers that way.

So the choice of *how* you will present your offer to prospects is not entirely arbitrary, nor should it be. To at least some extent it is dictated by several circumstances: what you are selling, to whom you are selling, the price tag, the nature of the market, the competition, and your own marketing strategy. All of these enter into decisions you make about how to get your offer in front of your prospects and how you attempt to persuade your prospects to take you up on your offer.

MARKETING STRATEGY

Successful marketing is based on successful strategy, a term that is difficult to define precisely. In general terms, it applies to the entire marketing plan. In more specific terms, and in the most common conception of its meaning, it refers to whatever special key to sales you have devised, such as a premium offer, sample giveaways at some convocation, a national contest, or something else upon which the whole marketing effort—its success, that is—hinges.

The implication of the word is that strategy is something special, something *different*. It need not be. It can be and most often is a perfectly conventional and well-known method, such as a normal direct-mail campaign, making personal calls on prospects, exhibiting at trade shows, or giving free (promotional) seminars.

The main point to be made about marketing strategy is not that it must be special or different, but that there must be a marketing strategy. Probably marketing failure is due less often to poor strategy than it is to no strategy—to the total lack of a marketing strategy. So often the entrepreneur launches a venture with no clear-cut ideas about marketing, but instead improvises spontaneously and makes no real marketing effort at all, at least not an organized and consistent one. As one of my readers who was twice unsuccessful in his efforts to launch an independent consulting practice wrote me: "The trap that you can get into is to think that you're so good that people will just call you automatically." He goes on to observe that one cannot just sit in the office waiting for the telephone to ring, but must do something positive and aggressive (in the marketing sense) about winning clients. Belatedly, he has come to this realization that successful marketing is rarely improvised effort, but must be planned, coherent, and carried out consistently over a long enough period of time to enable it to work. (Remember that most marketing successes must be achieved, and that this usually requires an unremitting effort applied over a period of time.)

EVOLVING STRATEGIES

There are many strategies possible, virtually an infinite number, in fact, depending entirely on your ingenuity. However, there are some practical considerations that should limit, or at least influence, the approaches you consider. For example, remembering that conventional wisdom about marketing newsletters dictates using direct mail rather than media advertising, you would not be well advised to make a major investment in or commit yourself to media advertising to market your newsletter. At most, you might test the conventional wisdom with a small investment in media advertising. Conventional wisdom is not always right, especially not for any given case, and yours may be the exception, but some caution is certainly advisable. So at least tentatively, until and unless proved otherwise, media advertising is ruled out as a newsletter-marketing strategy. And for the reasons already cited, strategies under consideration should be based on and compatible with the direct-mail marketing approach *or its equivalent.* And that latter suggestion is the key: If you can rationalize the reasons direct mail works (is practicable) for newsletter marketing, where media advertising does not, you may be able to devise an equivalent method—perhaps telephone solicitation—that embodies the essential mechanism and yet is new and largely untried; it may work better than the conventional method.

You need also to consider what is required to make a strategy succeed. If you launch a campaign to develop leads that must be followed up by personal calls, you have to be sure that you are prepared to make those calls with reasonable promptness after you get the leads. In fact, for many ventures, the nature of the enterprise dictates that all marketing be directed to developing leads to be followed up. That is because for many ventures it is nearly impossible to win orders directly, or even to close sales on the first follow-up call. These are often referred to by salespeople, in fact, as "not one-call sales" or one-call businesses. This, too, is something you must consider in devising your marketing strategy: You cannot fly in the face of some natural principle, such as this, and hope to succeed. In planning your marketing, you must recognize the basic and inherent nature of the venture.

In connection with the latter point and to clarify it a bit more, bear in mind that the total effort required to close a sale in any kind of business depends on the risk perceived by the prospect. The last phrase—*risk perceived by the prospect*—is the important one, for all depends always on the prospect's perception of things.

THE RISK FACTOR

One measure of risk is money. Most of us will spend a few dollars casually and not be greatly upset if the $5 calculator does not hold up for more than a few months' service. In fact, we hardly expected that it would, but perhaps it was worth $5 to find out.

A $25 calculator is another matter. We will probably want to look over a number of calculators and compare their features, reputation of the manufacturer, and perhaps the guarantee before spending what is a fairly large price for a small calculator.

A $100 calculator will definitely give us pause. We want to be sure that it will be everything we want a calculator to be, and we certainly want to do some comparison shopping first. We may even want to make more than one visit to the store before reaching a decision about it.

On the other hand, the busy proprietor of a small business might spend $200 or $300 for a super-duper calculator and not spend more than a few minutes on the purchase, especially if it is from a known supplier. Buying for a business enterprise is a much different matter psychologically than buying for personal use.

Nevertheless, even the busy executive will not act hastily when thousands of dollars are involved. That amount of risk justifies spending a little more time on the matter.

But money per se is not the only risk, although it is probably the one most commonly considered. Most of us have many other concerns —concerns about our health, happiness, comfort, security, reputation, and many other things. It is necessary to view the situation from the customer's perspective when assessing the risk factor, to determine not only the relative amount of risk the customer perceives, but the nature of the risk as the customer perceives it. And the amount of risk the customer perceives is at least one major determinant of how much selling you have to do before you close the sale.

THE PRICE FACTOR

There is no doubt that price is, of itself, a major consideration. Yet it is often not the major factor in a buying decision, and unfortunately many sellers leap to the mistaken conclusion that it is necessary to cut prices to make sales or that they lose sales because of price. Obviously, you must be "competitive," which means, simply, that you cannot be completely out of the ballpark, but must ask prices which are reasonably representative of what others ask for similar products and services. Yet you do not necessarily have to be lower priced than your competitors. In fact, being low priced may be a strategic error in itself, for there are at least two cost strategies: Keeping prices low has the obvious bargain appeal, but keeping prices relatively high has a strategic value, too, in that it implies a higher quality. The fact is that when customers have no other standard by which to measure quality, they tend to equate it with price, even though the lower-priced item may actually be of better quality than the high-priced one.

PRICE VERSUS VALUE

It is easy to identify and to quantify a price, because price is itself a quantity on an absolute scale. Not so with value. Value is an elusive idea, a subjective factor that can only be judged, in most cases. Moreover, it is almost always a *relative* factor, so that if one seminar costs $175 to attend, whereas another seemingly similar seminar costs $225 to attend, the first one may appear to be a better value. So it becomes the task of the seller of the $225 seminar to convince prospects that the latter is so good that it offers greater value at $225 than similar seminars offer at lower registration fees. And, of course, the other tries to demonstrate that the $175 seminar is at least as good as higher-priced seminars, if not better.

That, in a nutshell, is the typical problem of setting and using strategies based on prices—or price strategies as part of the appeal overall. But there are other kinds of price strategies or "twists" on the basic price-strategy idea, including at least these:

1. Retailers often offer loss leaders. These are items advertised at

such low prices that they represent a loss or virtual loss to the seller. But they bring customers to the establishment, seeking the bargains, and—the retailer assumes—the customers will do enough other shopping to offset the loss represented by the loss leaders. In any case, whatever those loss-leader bargains cost the seller must be marked up as marketing cost. Newsletter and magazine publishers who offer free books, extra months free, and other such inducements are turning the same idea to their own marketing needs. And those who offer a free seminar and use that occasion to sell the attendees something are using the free seminar as a loss leader. There are, no doubt, numerous other ways to utilize this idea in marketing advice.

2. Sometimes it is possible to appear to be lower priced than you are by putting the best possible "face" on your prices. There are a number of ways to do this, depending on individual circumstances. One way some have used is to offer an apparently modest price, but write carefully designed constraints on what goods/services are covered by those prices, leaving the door ajar for renegotiation. A kindred strategy is to offer an apparently low price in the main body of your presentation but add some "minor" items as footnotes or afterthoughts, which will add substantially to the price overall. For example, a consultant might charge extra for typing up and duplicating reports, and even for minor local expenses, or might use some kind of surcharge.

3. Quantify what you do or offer to do. If your strategy is to sell value and not price, you must take some positive action to do so. You cannot expect the customer to do an analysis to find out which is really the better value, yours or someone else's. It is possible that some customers might do this, but most will not. If you want to persuade a customer that yours is the better value, you must be aggressive and prove your case—assume, that is, that the customer will say to you: "Explain to me why I should buy from you when you cost more than brand X." Somehow, you must demonstrate how much "bang for a buck"—result per dollar of cost—you will deliver. In doing this, you must also explain how you arrive at your figures for at least two reasons:

(a) You must prove your case by showing the customer the rationale for it and make it convincing.

(b) You must give the customer your yardstick so that he or she can measure your competitors' prices by that same yardstick and make a fair comparison.

There are many other appeals, of course, and we will look at some of them as we review specific marketing "packages." One, in fact, arrived in my morning mail only today from the publisher of a newsletter about computers.

PREMIUM OFFERS

The package I received today—and actually it was all contained in a single business-size envelope, so the term "package" is not to be taken literally—consisted of the following elements:

- A letter
- A brochure
- An order form
- A postage-paid return envelope

This is a fairly typical direct-mail package, although some are more elaborate and some less so. The letter was two pages, typed, in two colors (the company logo, the signature, and one other line were in red ink, the rest in black). It opened with "Dear Colleague," and went on in a chatty manner to explain to me why it was in my interest to read this newsletter every week. It included a postscript which promised me, as a premium, a digital travel alarm clock.

The brochure was printed in full process color—expensive—had five panels printed on both sides, and folded down to fit easily into the envelope. It explained that I would get some other benefits, such as several special reports during the year. It also included, as one of the panels, another order form, although there was also a separate order form enclosed.

The order form was a letter-size sheet, also in two colors, that stressed the bonus alarm clock premium, and included a little questionnaire (you can bet they are going to make use of this in renting their mailing lists!).

It is an attractive package, and it ought to work reasonably well. I confess, however, that I personally do not like it. Why not? Because I somehow find it objectionable whenever someone sells the premium rather than the product. It strikes me as just a bit dishonest and even hypocritical. If the product is really worthy, it should not even be necessary to offer a premium, much less concentrate most of the selling effort on it. To me it suggests that the seller lacks confidence in the product. It also suggests to me that the seller has no confidence in his or her own selling abilities but must resort to bribery, just as do salespeople who rely entirely on cutting prices to make sales.

It is my belief that the marketer must truly believe in the product and must sell the product by finding legitimate sales arguments. Using premiums, cut-rate prices, and other bribes—and calling them "inducements" or "premiums" does not change the fact that they are offered as bribes—is marketing weakness and cannot *keep* the product sold.

Let us look at the sales arguments offered in the letter, for that is where the main sales argument is made:

1 The publisher *implies*, but does not specifically *state*, a circulation of over 100,000 readers. Maybe. But that is probably based on the assumption of several readers for each copy sold, or the publishers would have talked about *paid subscriptions*. Deceit. Maybe it will not be detected because most people will not analyze it, but still deceit (in all probability).

2 Bad writing. For example, platitudes and clichés, such as "information-packed" and "cutting edge." Makes your eyelids heavy.

3 No message: With it all, the entire two pages rarely gets specific but focuses on trying to promise all things to all possible readers. (You cannot possibly keep a focus when you try to reach everyone at the same time, and without focus, there is no message.)

The best part of the letter is the promise of three other publications or special reports. Although there are also vague scatterings of hyperbole and more platitudes and clichés, such as an admonition to "do your homework," they are at least focused on specific segments of computerdom, such as communications, office automation, and buying guides. These almost persuaded me to order—I admit that I was tempted because I am interested in some of this kind of coverage—but I drew back because I am biased against buying anything that I do not fully understand. I did not succeed in overcoming my instinctive antipathy to huckstering, as this strikes me as being.

The premise that one must keep up is itself a weak one because many readers will reject it. Some think that they do already keep up and may even resent the suggestion that they do not; others will believe that in their positions, they really do not need to work that hard at keeping up. Thus the letter fails, for these people at least, to prove either the premise—that one must keep up—or the promise—that the newsletter will enable them to keep up. There are claims, but no proof, and certainly no evidence that the advertiser can make good on his promise.

One contributing factor here is that the package attempts to appeal to everyone—engineers, managers, executives, decision makers, systems planners, and chief executives—and talks about responsibilities for planning, purchasing, implementing, and/or interfacing with various systems. It does not miss many targets, but that is one of its key weaknesses: It is difficult to find any premise that is valid for all, except a most general one, and that is the kind of premise that is least effective as a basis for a sales appeal.

It is far more sensible to identify each kind of target prospect and design a sharply focused direct-mail package for each. Better a 3 percent response from 10,000 prospects than 0.1 percent from 100,000.

THE TYPICAL DIRECT-MAIL PACKAGE

The direct-mail package just described is reasonably typical. Conventional wisdom in this field dictates an introductory letter, a brochure, an order form, and a return envelope. Many claim that there is a difference in response between the package that includes a return envelope and one that does not; the return envelope supposedly increases the rate of response. Moreover, the rate of response is supposedly increased further if the return envelope is the postage-paid type.

The basis for this and other provisions that are claimed to increase the effectiveness of a direct-mail package is the premise that the easier it is for the reader to respond, the more likely it is that the reader will respond. Entirely logical and true. But the second premise, that these various provisions make it more convenient or easier for the reader to respond—to order, that is—are not necessarily true. For one thing, the executive in an office finds it no more convenient to use a postage-paid return envelope than to hand the matter over to a secretary, with instructions to fill out the forms and place the order. So what is true for the individual consumer is not necessarily true for other kinds of prospects. Always weigh the benefit against the kind of prospect you are addressing. Remember that there are two general types or classes of prospects for whatever you wish to sell—the individual consumer, buying for personal use as an individual consumer; and the businessperson, buying for use in and of the business environment. You cannot assume that the same features and sales motivators work equally for both.

Many direct-mail packages include various novelty items—some marketers have included in their mailings a plastic card, with the respondent's name embossed on it in gold. It resembles a credit card or a membership card and is expected to warm the prospect's heart immediately.

Another device that has seen a good bit of use in recent years is the little folder that says on its outside, often in handwriting, something such as this: "Don't read this unless you have decided not to buy [order]_____." Of course, the advertiser wants you to read it, and expects your curiosity about this apparently negative message to compel you to read it, whereas you may not have read any of the other enclosures.

Still another device is what some have called "envelope copy" or "teaser copy," which is copy on the outside of the envelope. The premise here is that since it is difficult to conceal from addressees the fact that the envelope contains advertising matter—"junk mail"—you should take the opposite tack: Proclaim it as advertising matter, and put a message on the outside, which may help induce the respondent to open and read the package.

Of course, some also use small premiums, such as calendars, memo pads, key rings, and other such items. Some use contests, with various tricky gimmicks, such as seals and rub-out surprinting to reveal "lucky numbers."

SOME OTHER BASICS OF DIRECT-MAIL

People who specialize in direct-mail marketing tend to evaluate the results of their mailing campaigns in terms of response rates—percentages of mailings that produce orders. The conventional wisdom is that responses on the order of 2 to 5 percent are to be expected from successful mailings. Anything better than 5 percent is outstandingly good, and anything less than 2 percent is, conversely, unacceptably bad. Unfortunately, it is a meaningless measure. Here's why:

A typical mailing will cost you on the order of $250 to $350 per 1000 pieces mailed. It is difficult to get much below $250 per 1000, for even the most efficient and economical effort, and it is quite easy to get well above the $350 figure. But let's take $250 as a good average number.

A response of from 2 to 5 percent means that orders cost you from a high of $12.50 to a low of $5 each to get. The order—sale—must therefore recover that amount, plus the cost of the merchandise, plus the cost of filling the order, plus the overhead cost, before it returns a profit.

If you sell a $20 book or product that costs you $10 and get only a 2 or 3 percent response, you cannot turn a profit on the proposition. Even with a 5 percent response it is a tight fit.

On the other hand, if you sell newsletter subscriptions at $48 and get even a 2 percent response, you will manage quite well. In fact, there are many campaigns where a 1 or even 0.5 percent response pays out well.

The rate of response has no meaning of itself, therefore. The only meaningful measure is ROI—return on investment. But there are some other measures that help you in your planning. Even though they are not something you "can take to the bank," they do give you some worst-case guidelines. One is the admonition that in direct mail it can easily cost you as much as one-half the selling price to make the sale—to get the order.

Another is that the absolute minimum of cost to selling price must be 1 to 3—the item that cost you $1 must bring you $3. But that is an absolute minimum and carries a great deal of risk with it. It is far better to increase that ratio, and most successful direct-mail campaigns are run at a more favorable ratio than that.

What this means in practice is not that you must find a way to get at least three times what you paid for the item, but that you must deal in items that afford you the margin you need. That is one reason that newsletters, reports, and other publications are so well suited to direct-mail marketing: They are inherently of that high cost-to-selling-price ratio. Yet even that does not tell the whole story, for there are exceptions to these "rules."

TURNING A PROFIT AFTER LOSING MONEY

You may be led to believe, after reading this, that anyone operating a successful mail-order business must be getting at least a 3-to-1 markup on whatever he or she is selling. Moreover, you may find it hard to believe that there is that much markup in many items sold by mail, such as vitamins, printing, office supplies, computer supplies, and camera equipment. And you are right; these items cannot be bought for one-third of their selling price or less. How, then, do mail-order dealers sell these kinds of items and remain in business unless they are getting impossibly high response rates on their mailings?

The fact is that it is quite common for many of these merchants to lose money on orders—to incur a much greater expense in getting the order than the profit on the order—for the first order from a customer, that is. Such merchandise is of a nature that it entails repeat business. These mail-order dealers are not pursuing sales; they are pursuing customers. The money they lose in getting the first order from prospects is a marketing expense; it is the cost of gaining a new customer. Getting future business from the customer will not cost money, and the profits will come from future business.

This, too, is a factor to consider when selling by direct mail. Decide whether you wish to pursue sales or customers—and, of course, whether what you sell is compatible with the idea of making customers and getting repeat business.

In the case of newsletters, for example, many newsletter publishers make their profits out of the ancillary reports, books, and even other items, and so may postpone profit taking and be willing to lose money to get the subscription, which is the key to other, added sales.

WRITING ADVERTISING COPY

Copywriting—the writing of advertising copy—is not exactly an art form, but there are those writers who specialize in and have special talents for this kind of writing. Writing skills per se are only part of the knowledge that copywriters employ in their field; knowledge of and even instinct for marketing and, especially, for marketing strategy are at least as important as writing skills are. Yet that does not mean that copywriting cannot be learned, for there are some rules—or, at least, some principles—to guide you in this.

One of these is *focus.* Have only *one* major point, one major objective, one major strategy for your copy. Do not try to promise everything to everybody. Decide who your prospect is and what your main premise is and stick to them. Let's "look" at some well-known TV commercials to illustrate the point:

"Ring around the collar." Aimed directly at all housewives, as prime target. Strategy: fear . . . fear of embarrassment. (Secondary target: husbands, with the same motivation—fear of embarrassment.) "Proof": visual demonstrations of cure for problem. (Remember, "proof" is not what would stand up in court, but whatever the prospect will *accept* as proof.) Note the focus: always on collars. The product specializes in collars, although it is probably not better or worse than any other detergent at doing the laundry generally. Good example of specializing and focusing. And that is the marketing strategy, of course: specializing where no competitor does. (What competitor would dare to, and be put in a "me, too" position?)

Almost any beer commercial. Almost without exception beer commercials imply a promise of fun—good times laughing it up on the beach and at the friendly corner tavern. That is the strategy for most—emotional appeal to everyone's love of fun. (Of course, all effective sales appeals, like the "ring around the collar," are emotional ones.) Some overlay the appeal with a strong implication of being the drink for "real men"—the macho image. More emotion. Few advertisers make any great effort to prove their beer is any better than anyone else's.

"Plop-plop, fizz-fizz." This renowned Alka-Seltzer commercial is light, semihumorous. The promise: relief when you drink or eat unwisely. Always that focus. For other uses and promised benefits—such as relief from cold symptoms—Alka-Seltzer wisely uses a somewhat different version of their basic product. The main product keeps its focus on stomach relief.

The *". . . so you can sleep medicine."* There is a definite strategy and focus in this commercial, although it is not as obvious as some other advertisers' strategies. Despite the long string of adjectives placed before the name, the key is the last phrase: ". . . so you can sleep medicine." That's the main appeal, main promise, main strategy, and it has powerful emotional appeal.

"*. . . relieves 12 cold symptoms.*" This product claims to relieve 12 cold symptoms whereas others relieve only six. That's the promise, and the strategy for the claim to superiority. Proof? There is none; only claims. But it is presented in such a way and repeated over and over so that a great many people finally accept it as proof. And that is the strategy for convincing the prospect.

"*Don't leave home without it.*" A well-known commercial using well-known figures as the proof of their claims. Would all these successful and prominent people use this service if it were not the best? But the main strategy is strongly emotional: promised security. Very close, in principle, to that other famous insurance company symbolized by a pair of cupped hands, and another, symbolized by the Rock of Gibraltar.

Each of these has a distinct focus, as well as a clear promise, explicit or implied, and a clear strategy—or two.

HOW TO "PROVE" YOUR PROMISE

Actually, there are at least two distinct strategies required to make advertising work: You need a strategy of appeal—the promise that will capture a prospect's attention and arouse interest or desire for the promised benefit. But you need also some strategy to prove your claim, to convince the prospect that you will deliver the benefit. Here are some strategies used commonly, which you will recognize readily:

Testimonials: Testimonials can be delivered by well-known public heroes and heroines—movie stars are a prime choice because their faces are usually as well known as their names, and their mere appearance in a commercial has some entertainment value.

Sports stars are slightly less well known—at least their faces are not as well known—but are also good for endorsing products, as are a few other popular figures, such as well-known sports announcers.

Authority figures can be used. They can be professional actors, but dressed in white laboratory coats, or otherwise dressed for an appropriate role, they are taken as authority figures.

Tests: Advertisers frequently run what appear to be unbiased tests and surveys, presenting ordinary citizens in a special form of testimonial. But professional announcers and narrators also offer test results, which may or may not be truly relevant to the claims made. (For example, the tobacco stain on the handkerchief, "proving" that tobacco will stain your teeth and that the toothpaste advertised will overcome the problem.)

Logic: Arguments that are supposed to be logical are offered, to "prove" through sound reasoning that the claims are valid. You witness a great deal of sophistry and logical absurdity in these efforts.

Statistics: If you have sold enough of the product, you can cite as evidence the number of "satisfied users," or the number of years you have been in business, or other impressive numbers which may or may not have any bearing on your claims.

Reputation: Old, large, well-established, and well-known corporations often use that image as the keystone of their advertising. The strategy, overall, is that the prospect can have complete confidence in this fine old company, which has been serving the public faithfully for so many moons. But the age of the company is not the only means for trading on reputation or image; one can build an image in a relatively short time. Many do that by presenting advertising that tends to demonstrate solid reliability, integrity, and other sterling qualities.

The point is, again, that the proof is whatever the prospect will accept as proof.

POSITIONING

Advertising people use the term *positioning* a good bit today. It is considered to be a rather sophisticated idea and is concerned with the image that advertisers present of themselves or their products. Advertising professionals explain that positioning is "what you do to the prospect's mind." In fact, two advertising professionals who wrote a rather widely read book on the subject billed positioning as the *battle* for one's mind.

Perhaps it is that dramatic in some of its applications. But we can see the idea illustrated in the foregoing examples. One product referred to here is positioned as the product to keep collars clean and avoid that embarrassing "ring around the collar." The advertiser is clearly intent on creating that image or "position" for the product.

In the case of automobiles, certain makes or models achieve an image or position of being "in," in the sense of stylish or faddish, whereas another achieves the position of being the luxury car that denotes the successful person, and still another is the practical car for the practical person.

Individuals and organizations position themselves similarly. One investment firm might build an image as a high flyer—innovative, daring, imaginative, and brilliantly successful—whereas another might strive for and achieve the image of being staid, sedate, conservative, and totally safe.

Of course, sometimes an advertiser achieves a position as a consequence of various circumstances, rather than through deliberate image building. But today's advertising professional is conscious of the need to *achieve* some position for what one sells and is, and not leave that to chance.

In short, you and whatever you sell in the marketplace are whatever the prospect thinks you and what you sell are. That is reality, as far as your marketing is concerned, because it is the prospect's reality, and that is the only reality that counts in the marketplace.

That means that you must think out what you wish yourself and/or whatever you sell to appear to be. Of course, it may be that it does not matter what you appear to be, or it may be that it does not matter what you sell appears to be. In some cases, what you sell is independent of what you appear to be; in other cases, the reverse is true. If you are a consultant, for example, your personal image is of overwhelming importance because it is you, in fact, that you are trying to sell to the prospects.

But we can and should look at positioning in another light. Choosing the position you wish to occupy in the customer's mind is not an arbitrary matter—or shouldn't be. Quite the contrary, it is dictated to you by other considerations, primarily the answers to the following two questions:

1 Who is your prospect?
2 What is the principal motivation to which you intend to appeal?

Without these definitions positioning does not make a great deal of sense. You must match your positioning decision to these two basic marketing decisions defining your customer-prospects and their motivation in responding to your appeals. The "ring around the collar" people are obviously appealing primarily to all housewives who do the laundry at home and whose husbands are "white collar" careerists. They will reach some other people, too, of course, but the former are obviously the prime targets. The motivation has already been covered, and it is a powerful one: fear—the fear of embarrassment—and the desire to avoid that embarrassment.

Obviously, too, those who do not do laundry at home—or at least, those who do not do shirts at home—and those for whom shirts are generally of the "blue shirt" category will not find the message as appealing. That's the other side of the coin when you specialize: Your message becomes so selective that you inevitably lose some of the population to which you might have appealed, so you must be sure when you decide to become sharply focused and specialized in your marketing/sales appeals that you have selected a market segment that is large enough for your purposes. That is the trade-off (there is always a trade-off in all things): vertical market penetration (sharp focus and specialization) versus broader coverage (more general focus and less specialization).

WRITING THE SALES LETTER

One problem that appears to trouble all writers of the obligatory sales letter in the direct-mail package is the salutation. Shall it be "Dear Sir or Madam? Dear friend? Dear colleague? Dear housewife? Dear consumer?"

Somehow, everyone appears to believe that the letter must have a salutation to Dear somebody. And the brouhaha about "male chauvinism" has aggravated the problem further: How do you address the letter so that you do not give offense to women who are already offended by the traditional male dominance in our society? (Even the term "ladies" has become anathema to many women today, as I have learned, painfully.)

One solution has been to turn to the computerized mailing list and have the computer address each letter individually to the name on the mailing list. That method is rather expensive unless you have your own computer, and even then it is somewhat laborious and time consuming. But worse, it has certain hazards. I often get envelopes addressed to "Herman Holtz Publications" with letters that begin, "Dear Mr. Publications." Or, even worse, "Dear Mr. and Mrs. Publications."

A better solution is to avoid the transparent device of making the letter appear to be a personal one. Only the most naive individual would be deceived or even flattered by having the letter addressed personally; the hand of the computer in this is well known by now. The fact is that it is simply not necessary to have a salutation at all. Compare the two methods shown in Figure 9-2. Instead of that patently contrived congeniality of the vague salutation, consider the alternative shown—a businesslike presentation, with no effort to make it appear a personal salutation. It begins with a headline or a blurb (the second example combines the two ideas), which is a brief statement that summarizes the main point of the letter. This lets the reader know what the thing is essentially about, with information intended to capture interest immediately.

Headlines have become common in direct-mail sales literature, often appearing above the salutation because one can hardly follow a "Dear somebody" with a headline. As Maxwell Sackheim, an acknowledged expert in direct-mail copy, and others have pointed out, if you do not manage to capture that interest in the headline—to "sell it in the headline," in fact, as they tend to put it—you probably will not sell it at all. Even the strongest body copy—the text following the headline—is not likely to salvage a bad start. It is extremely important to start right.

In today's busy world, with so much competing for everyone's attention—books, magazines, newspapers, radio, TV, and other media—it is difficult enough to capture anyone's attention for even a moment, let alone hold anyone's interest long enough to do a job of persuasion. You probably have only seconds in which to do this, in most cases,

HRH COMMUNICATIONS, INC.
P.O. Box 6067
Silver Spring, MD 20906
(301) 460-1506

January 14, 1984

Dear friend:

Not long ago I helped a client--a small company--develop a proposal to design and write a training program in connection with a Department of Energy project at a western government facility. I treasure the postcard I received from my client a few weeks later:

Idaho Falls is beautiful this time of year, and thanks to your help I'm here to enjoy it and get paid at the same time. Our proposal rated far ahead of the other six (some of which were from very "heavy" firms . . . . . .Thanks for your help.

(a)

HRH COMMUNICATIONS, INC.
P.O. Box 6067
Silver Spring, MD 20906
(301) 460-1506

MY CONSISTENT SUCCESS AT HELPING OTHERS WIN GOVERNMENT CONTRACTS--OVER $160 MILLION WORTH, TO DATE--SURPRISES EVERYONE BUT ME. I'M USED TO IT. I'VE BEEN DOING IT FOR OVER 20 YEARS.

Not long ago I helped a client--a small company--develop a proposal to design and write a training program in connection with a Department of Energy project at a western government facility. I treasure the postcard I received from my client a few weeks later:

Idaho Falls is beautiful this time of year, and thanks to your help I'm here to enjoy it and get paid at the same time. Our proposal rated far ahead of the other six (some of which were from very "heavy" firms . . . . . .Thanks for your help.

(b)

FIGURE 9-2 Alternatives in sales-letter format

especially when the prospect is all too aware that what is offered is advertising matter.

The automatic, almost instinctive resistance to advertising is primarily defensive. The prospect immediately senses that the two of you are in adversary positions: You are trying to take something—money— from him or her, and he or she must resist this attack on the pocketbook. Anything in your message that reinforces this idea only solidifies the reaction into actual hostility and hastens the ultimate defense: withdrawal—abandonment of further reading.

If you want to avoid this withdrawal, however, you must do more than merely refrain from focusing attention on what you want and go to the other extreme: focus immediately on what the prospect wants. Advertising people speak of featuring and stressing benefits in advertising copy, which amounts to the same thing, except that it is necessary to establish and keep that sharp focus, at least initially. Decide which is the *chief* benefit—the most important one. That—the most important— means the one the prospect will most urgently want. If there are other benefits to stress, save them for later. Do not dilute the effect of your opening barrage with the distraction of secondary and less important benefits.

Referring to Figure 9-2 as an example of a successful sales letter, note that in the first opening, it took a little while to get to the point of the letter. In fact, it is not until later in the letter, beyond the opening shown here, that the real sales appeal begins. Until then the sales appeal is only implied. The success of this version of the sales letter depends on whether the reader grasps where the message is headed—the implications of the opening—and is willing to read on.

The second version approaches the entire problem differently. Instead of a simple headline, which would be a vast improvement in itself, it goes further and offers more than the "teaser" many headlines offer. It actually sums up the entire appeal, in a brief paragraph: the main message—helping others win government contracts—and a brief summation of the offeror's qualifications. It has both elements, you'll notice: the promise—help in winning government contracts—and the "proof"— with figures (quantification always makes a claim far more credible). Will this now persuade the reader that it is worthwhile to spend a few more minutes seeing what the writer of this letter has to offer? If the reader is the right prospect—someone who is responsible for or desirous of winning government contracts, such as a sales/marketing manager, proposal manager, or proprietor of a business suitable for substantial sales to government agencies—there is now an excellent chance that the reader will go on.

Some Facts about Headlines and How to Write Them

A certain amount of nonsense—mythology—appears to spring up around every field. In the case of advertising, there is the curious idea of some that advertising with lots of "white space" is superior to advertising that contains a great deal of text which fills all or nearly all the space the advertisement occupies. And this is further extrapolated as meaning that short copy—brief sales messages—are more effective than long ones are.

That this is sheer nonsense is testified to by the fact that many full-page, "set solid" (all textual copy) advertisements have been highly successful. The Joe Karbo advertisement referred to earlier was one of these. The simple fact is this: If the copy attracts and holds attention—is of interest to the reader—it can be of any length and readers will read it to the very last word. If the reader finds the copy boring, thinks it banal, or otherwise reacts to it adversely, even short copy will not hold reader interest to the end. The ultimate sin in advertising, as in show business, is boring the audience.

This applies as much to headlines as it does to any other part of the advertising or sales message. Headlines do not have to be short to be effective; they have to get and hold attention—to be interesting in what they say. They need to embody, somehow, the basic essential elements of effective advertising/sales messages, as already noted, but there are some other considerations. Here are a few things to bear in mind about headlines and headline writing:

- The headline should include the chief motivator (benefit), clearly expressed (preferably explicit, but at least plainly implied), and the proof (evidence) that makes the promise credible, at least on a tentative basis, such that it induces the reader to read on.

- The headline should be kept as short as it can be, *consistent with getting the message across.* This means that you eliminate all words that do not contribute to the message—use a telegraphic style. But never shorten it at the expense of sacrificing or compromising the basic message and those two basic elements of promise and proof.

- Use punchy, action words as much as possible, and use them in the active voice. Example: Not "benefits derive from my services," but "I produce results."

This is not a place for subtleties. Marketing requires that you be as explicit as possible. Nor is it a place to be clever. Many otherwise good advertising ideas are destroyed by copywriters who cannot resist the temptation to be clever, often with such horrors as clumsy and obvious puns in the headlines. Example: The print advertisement for a chain of motels urged readers to "turn in" at their motels, insteading of using that critically important headline to *make an offer*—an offer to *do* something for the reader (provide a benefit). Forget cleverness, as well as subtlety. Think out your main message and say it as plainly as you can.

PROMISE VERSUS OFFER

You may have noted the use of the word "offer" where you might have expected to see the word "promise." The substitution was deliberate, to make a point. In fact, the promise *is* an offer. A good advertisement or sales presentation is an offer. There may be some slight differences in the way offers are made, but the real distinction is in the mental set of the presenter/advertiser. It is helpful to some to think of the promise as an offer, for there is a subtle difference between the promise and the offer, and it is just this: The promise is part of a solicitation, rather than an offer to do something for the prospect. Somehow, that mental set often makes itself felt in a presentation, but more important, it helps the advertiser psychologically. If you come across in your copy defensively, or as a supplicant, your copy will be far less appealing. So it is often helpful to think of your proposition as an offer and to prepare your copy with that mental set.

CLOSING

One strange phenomenon that has been noted by advertising and sales specialists is that even the most sophisticated, intelligent, and educated customers will generally fail to act if not prompted. It is possible to persuade a prospect to buy something and then lose the sale because you do not shove the order form under the customer's nose and hand him a pen. That is figurative language, of course, because it also afflicts small, point-of-sale contacts, where the salesperson waits fruitlessly for the prospect to say, "I'll take it." It is what sales experts mean by the word "close"—not *get* the order, but *ask* for the order. But "ask for the order" is itself allegorical and is actually implemented in various ways, such as actually telling the customer what to do—"Fill in your name on the enclosed form" or "Simply call in and use your credit card."

In the case of selling big-tag sales and services—consultation or other costly technological services, such as computer programming, for example—closing is quite a different proposition. Such ventures are not one-call businesses, of course, but require multistep marketing and sales effort to identify prospects in general, then to identify specific prospects—get leads—and then follow up the leads with enough sales effort to make sales. Making initial contacts and getting leads is the primary objective in sending out literature or otherwise making an initial contact. But when using direct mail for the purpose, the methods used to sell vitamins or office supplies by mail will not work here. The obvious and incorrect thing to do, however, is to invite readers to call or write for more information about your services. This kind of appeal may produce a few inquiries, but is nevertheless a rather weak way of identifying prospects and is not likely to bring very substantial results. To get an adequate response, it is usually necessary to offer some kind of special inducement. And it is getting that response that represents the close—"asking for the order"—in this case.

For example, you might offer a free item, perhaps a brochure with useful information relevant to what you do professionally (e.g., "10 Tips for Reducing Your Taxes" if you are an accountant or tax specialist). "Selling" that brochure, that is, your efforts to persuade the recipient to respond by calling or writing for the brochure, is the close in this case. Getting that request gives you a lead. It identifies someone interested enough in tax savings to go to the trouble of writing or calling, possibly even someone with specific tax problems.

"QUALIFYING" LEADS

Your purpose in giving away your tax-tips brochure—which costs you money—is to identify individuals who are good prospects as clients for your services. These are people who have large enough businesses and/or tax obligations to make it worthwhile to pay your fees for your help. It is a waste of your time to try to sell your services to a working person who has only the ordinary tax obligations of most working people. However, unless you impose certain requirements, you have only limited control over who sends for your brochure, and you may very well get requests from people who could not possibly become clients, even from schoolchildren and shut-ins who like to receive mail. If you are to avoid wasting your time trying to sell such prospects—and you can waste a great deal of time in such pursuits before you discover that you are wasting your time and money—you must "qualify" each prospect or lead. That means, simply, taking some steps to establish that each is a fair prospect, that it is at least *possible* to do business with that prospect.

There are several ways to do this, but they fall into one of two broad categories: qualifying the prospect beforehand by placing some kind of restriction or screening measure into effect, and qualifying the lead after getting it but before spending time and money pursuing it.

Prescreening Methods for Qualifying Leads

Qualifying leads in advance means narrowing the number of responses you get while, presumably, raising the quality of the responses. If, for example, you perceive that only those in established businesses or professions are likely to be suitable prospects for you, you might screen responses by requiring some evidence that the inquirer is a businessperson or a professional. One way to do this is require that all requests for the free brochure be made on a company letterhead or be accompanied by the requestor's business card. Theoretically, this should screen out requests from those who are not suitable prospects for you, without jeopardizing responses from those who are good prospects—good leads. This means trading off quantity for quality—at least it should mean that.

Unfortunately, it does not work out precisely this way, because in your effort to prequalify responses, any restrictions that you place on requests tend to reduce the number of responses you would like to have, as well as those you do not want. It is an unfortunate truth, but you have to decide which response mode is in your best interests.

I had an example of this when I was in the business of advising individuals and small businesses about selling to the government, and managed to get a write-up in a nationally syndicated newspaper column. To maximize the response and turn the item to advantage—in fact, to make the notice attractive to the columnist—I offered a free information brochure to anyone who would send me a self-addressed, stamped envelope. The result was some 3000 such requests, which I filled at some expense for printing and labor, despite the fact that most did comply with my request for that stamped envelope. But very little business resulted from it because the majority of the requests were from people who were not truly good sales leads for me. I succeeded only too well in encouraging a great many responses, but I did nothing to prescreen them.

You can avoid that mistake of being so general in how you describe your offer that you invite inquiries from the wrong kinds of prospects. You can make the copy itself do the prescreening by being much more specific about who should inquire. For example, that hypothetical brochure on tips for reducing taxes is likely to appeal to everyone, including people for whom the information in the brochure is totally inappropriate. If you qualify the brochure further by explaining that it offers tax-reducing tips for businesses only, deals with tax shelters only, or otherwise has a narrow focus, that itself will reduce the number of requests from the wrong kinds of prospects. (Note how important it is that you know precisely what kinds of prospects you seek.)

Qualifying Leads after Getting Inquiries

It is not at all uncommon for inexperienced salespeople to invest many hours of their time and effort in making presentations to a prospect, only to learn, belatedly, that the prospect is not in a position to buy under any circumstances. Nor is that preliminary qualification achieved through prescreening a guarantee that the lead is a fully qualified one, for even that prospect may not have the authority to buy, may only be "window-shopping" without an intention of buying, or for some other reason may represent no chance for closing a sale successfully. Therefore, even if you have done some prequalification—and especially, if you have not—you have to do whatever is necessary to fully qualify your leads. These are the kinds of questions you seek answers for:

- *Can* the prospect buy (has the money, authority, or can get the approval)?
- Is the prospect *genuinely* interested, or merely too polite to cut you short? (Or only window shopping out of idle curiosity or a vague idea that may or may not result in a sale in the distant future?)
- Will you be seriously considered as a source/supplier, or are you being *used* (exploited) by the prospect?

Getting answers to these and related questions is really not that difficult if you ask diplomatically, or ask other questions that answer similar questions indirectly. Here are some ways that have worked well in the past.

Ability/Authority to Buy.   At some point, after you perceive that the interest is or appears to be genuine, you can simply ask quietly, "Are you funded [budgeted] yet for this, or will you have to get budget approval first?" Other relevant questions are: "Who in your company must approve this kind of purchase [or budget] normally?" or "What is your normal budgeting procedure for projects of this kind?"

Sincerity of Interest.   Answers to questions about funding may be good indicators of the sincerity of the prospect's interest. However, you might also politely inquire into probable start dates, whether a project has been approved in principle yet (i.e., whether the company is committed to getting someone in to do the job or provide the product), and whether the company made a firm decision to "go outside" for this rather than handle the need in-house. Getting answers to these questions can be revealing, as can evasions when you seek these answers.

Are You Being Used/Exploited? Unfortunately, calling in specialists to pick their brains and even to write formal proposals is not unknown; it has happened to many of us. The reasons some people (and companies) sometimes do this are (1) to appropriate the information and ideas of experts so that they can generate their own internal proposals and plans (ambitious and unscrupulous people sometimes make "heroes" of themselves in their companies in this manner), (2) to pick the brains of experts so that they can write a report or statement of work to be included in a request for proposals or bids, and (3) to falsify an appearance of honest competition when they have decided in advance to buy from someone else. (I have had the unhappy experience of being so used on two occasions.)

Admittedly, and happily, such occurrences are the exception rather than the rule; not many companies are this venal. Still, it is a hazard, and there is always the danger that someone will do this while concealing it from his or her own employer. (That is far more likely to occur.) It is wise to become and remain conscious of the hazard and take whatever steps you can to combat it:

- Release information discreetly—enough to demonstrate that you are the expert you are supposed to be and to prove that you can do the job, but not enough to educate the prospect completely. But be sure that the prospect knows that there is far more detail necessary. (Explain that this is only general information and that the subject requires study to develop full details.)

- Be especially careful about releasing information even discreetly when the prospect has asked for a written proposal. Be sure to ask the questions about whether the project is funded, whether the proposal is exploratory, or whether there is a firm commitment to go ahead with the project. Be doubly sure to include in your proposal a notice of copyright and of proprietary information. If you have any doubts or suspicions, it may help to send a copy of your letter of transmittal to an appropriate company officer to establish this.

USING PUBLICITY TO GET FREE ADVERTISING

Publicity, or PR (for "public relations"), is a time-honored way of getting free advertising. Not only does it offer the boon of being free advertising, but it is also often more effective than paid advertising because it appears to be objective, whereas one expects you to laud yourself in space or presentations that you have paid for; therefore, it is more credible.

The mainstay of PR is that staple, the release, also called a press release, news release, information release, or publicity release. Figure 9-3 is a reasonably typical release, one issued by a federal government agency, the GSA (General Services Administration). Note that it carries a serial number (because the GSA issues a great many releases and so needs to have file numbers for them), has a modest headline to summarize what the release is all about, is dated, and says "more" at the bottom to tell the reader that there is more copy on at least one additional page. If the item ended here, the GSA would use # # #, instead of (More), to signify the end of the copy. Most releases use "more" to signify additional copy on succeeding pages, but the end of the item is indicated in various ways, such as "END" and "-30-."

Note that the copy is double-spaced, as though it were a manuscript, for that is what it is intended to be. Editors who wish to use the release will probably not use it precisely as written, but will edit it to suit their own styles and space availability. The editor who gets a single-spaced release will probably discard it immediately because (1) the single-spacing is the mark of a tyro, and the editor therefore has little hope that the release is worth reading, and (2) the copy is too much trouble to work with when it is not double-spaced.

On the other hand, the editor may find the item intriguing or that it ties in with something else of interest, and therefore may wish to call the author of the release with a request for photos or more information. In the case of this release, the editor can cite the serial/file number but is likely to run into trouble trying to find the author of the release or even the office that originated it. That alone may kill it. Far more useful is the "contact" name and number shown in the example of Figure 9-4, which is far more indicative of journalistic professionalism in writing releases. Note some features here:

1 The contact name includes a telephone number. Busy editors are far more likely to want to use the telephone than a letter in following up a story lead such as that which a good release may represent.

2 There is a dateline—Washington, D.C.—even though the release carries the address of the organization issuing the release. The dateline is a useful, pro-

News Release

GSA Simplifies Teleprocessing Services Acquisition

Simplified procurement, lower costs and increased competition in providing computer services to federal agencies are expected to result from revisions in teleprocessing services acquisition procedures adopted by the U.S. General Services Administration (GSA).

The revisions are incorporated in the teleprocessing services multiple award schedule (TSP/MAS), which GSA has negotiated with private vendors. Federal agencies use this procurement method to acquire computer resources from vendors, utilizing vendor-owned networks at prices substantially lower than those offered to large commercial users.

Federal use of vendor computers and such related services as training and technical support totaled more than $160,000,000 in fiscal 1983 through both the TSP/MAS and individual requirement contracts under the TSP.

Frank Carr, GSA assistant administrator for Information Resources Management, said the recent changes should be attractive to large federal users because they will result in more economical procurement. Small users, too, will find the schedule simpler and more flexible.

In the past, agencies often issued individual procurements for large teleprocessing service requirements, a lengthy, complicated process. Carr said

(More)

U.S. General Services Administration, Washington, DC 20405 (202) 566-1231

FIGURE 9-3   One sample of a news release

fessional addition, even if the organization is in the same city as that of the dateline.

3   It authorizes immediate release. In some cases, releases are "embargoed" until a given date (e.g., "Release date 3/25/84"). This advises the editor that the information should not be released until that date. That might be the case when the release contains advance copy of a speech not yet delivered, for example.

HRH COMMUNICATIONS, INC.
P.O. Box 6067
Silver Spring, MD 20906
(301) 460-1506

NEWS-FOR IMMEDIATE RELEASE

                                        Contact:
                                        Jim Green
                                        (301) 555-1212

                    HELP FOR WORD-PROCESSOR USERS

    Washington, DC. Jan 21, 1985 - Martin Tannenbaum, President of HRH

Communications, Inc., announced the marketing of a new computer-information

service today. The new service, explained Tannenbaum, will be a hybrid

magazine and newsletter, issued weekly and devoted entirely to news and

information about word processing software and hardware for business

applications.

    "There is a superabundance of software for word processing," said

Tannenbaum, "but that is the problem: trying to find out what is best suited

to your needs is almost totally baffling because it is impossible for the

average individual to survey all the software and hardware available. Our new

publication, "Word Processing News," will do that every week, but will also

offer subscribers a consulting service when and if they find that necessary."

    More detailed information is available from the company's Public

Information office at (301) 555-1212.

                                                          ###

FIGURE 9-4   News release with more conventional features

4 An effort is made to present a bolder headline. Not all releases carry head-lines, but they are useful because they help the busy editor to grasp quickly the overall content. In the case of the GSA release in Figure 9-3, the author chose to summarize the release as an announcement of a simplified procedure for selling teleprocessing services to GSA. Equally useful and perhaps even more meaningful to readers might have been a headline announcing multiple-award schedules for teleprocessing services. ("Multiple-award schedules" is far more specific than "simplified procedures," thus more informative and there-fore preferable.)

There are at least two things to remember about releases:

1 The content must be "newsworthy."
2 The editor must be able to get the main message quickly.

Let's discuss these points and see what they mean.

What Is "Newsworthy"?

You have probably heard the old bromide that when a dog bites a man that isn't news, but when a man bites a dog that is news. But events and information need not always be bizarre or even novel to be newsworthy. Almost any information that captures readers' interest is newsworthy. Editors are motivated entirely by what will interest their readers: If it appears to be something that will appeal to readers, it will appeal to the editor.

Matching information and readers is a double-sided coin. Given a release, you can seek out the proper readership for it. The release of Figure 9-4, for example, would not find a home at *Popular Mechanics* magazine but might be welcomed at *Money* magazine or at any of those many computer magazines on the newsstands today, at least those that address the business use of word processors.

On the other hand, if you sent it out to newspapers and news magazines, and perhaps some other general-interest publications, you would most likely get some consideration from the financial/business-pages editor but probably would not fare as well with the city editor.

You might also go at this problem from the opposite viewpoint. Instead of seeking out the right readers for your release, write the release to appeal to the kinds of readers you want to reach. Again using the example in Figure 9-4, suppose that what Tannenbaum really wanted was consulting work, helping business-office users or prospective business-office users of word processing to design and select total systems of hardware and software for word processing, with subscriptions to his new periodical more of a marketing ploy than an objective in itself. In that case, his release is all wrong, for it stresses the new periodical and mentions the consulting only briefly. As the release now stands, editors are likely to sigh over yet another computer periodical to add to the many (estimates run as high as 200) computer periodicals already in existence. In short, even though specialized, emergence of a new periodical is simply not news; it is too commonplace an event.

On the other hand, a consulting service that specializes in word processing is not an earthshaking innovation, but it is not one of 200 such services, either, and with a proper headline might capture some interest. The following might be a suitable lead:

> *SPECIAL CONSULTING HELP AVAILABLE*
> *FOR WORD-PROCESSOR BUYERS*
> *With word processing the most popular and fastest-growing application of microcomputers today, matched by an equally fast-growing and confusing array of word processing hardware and software, HRH Communications, Inc., has decided to gallop to the rescue of business offices with consulting help to ease the agony of too many choices.*

After a brief elaboration of that lead, the release would mention the new periodical and advise the reader of where and how to get more information—probably a free brochure or newsletter would serve well here to draw inquiries and thus generate leads. One of the best ways to get attention is to highlight a common problem and suggest a solution to it, as the proposed lead here does. (Note that the original version mentioned the word *help,* but in a vague and general way rather than in relation to a specific problem.)

There are, in fact, several kinds of material used in newspapers, and understanding these is an effective way of understanding what "newsworthy" really means, at least as the term is used here. Basically, the items in any newspaper fall into two categories:

1 Straight news
2 Features

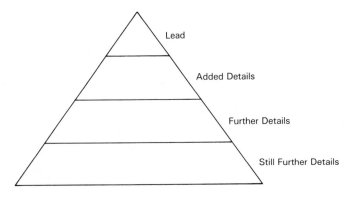

FIGURE 9-5 The journalistic pyramid

Straight news is just that—information about something new, and if what you are offering in your release is indeed straight news, it ought to be written in the traditional journalistic style, sometimes called the pyramid, because it begins with a brief account—who, what, when, where, why, and how, and then goes on to add detail steadily. But the story is summed up in the first sentence, or at least in the first paragraph, and if the editor wishes to cut it anywhere, what remains will still be a coherent story. That is the point of the "pyramid" (see Figure 9-5).

Features are different. Sometimes they are time sensitive, as when they are sidebars to a news story. For example, interviews with witnesses might furnish sidebar stories to a news item. But many features can be run any time, and they can be humorous, of general interest, novelties, or just about anything that might interest readers. If some of them do not fit the daily newspaper very well, they might easily be suitable for one of the Sunday supplements, which carry all kinds of stories not found in the daily paper.

Of course, newspapers are not the only periodicals, however, and you might slant your release to the type of coverage some magazines are fond of.

How to Make It Easy for the Editor

The busy editor will not dwell over your release, trying to decipher what it is all about. You probably have only a few seconds to "sell" your release to the editor. That is one reason for the headline; it is intended for the editor as much as it is for readers. (The editor is likely to change it, anyway.) Some PR professionals advocate not using a headline for that reason. Their idea is that since editors are fond of writing their own headlines, they may resent your trying to foist your headline on them. I happen to think that is nonsense, but use your own judgment.

Using a good headline, then, helps the editor grasp the main thrust of the release immediately, and writing in journalistic style enables the editor to cut the story to fit available space. Straight news stories are easy to cut when they are written in pyramidal style, but feature stories do not always fit that style readily. However, you can always write "tightly"—sticking to the point and avoiding excursions into interesting but not directly relevant byways. Editors generally appreciate that style because it, too, helps them fit the story.

Newsletters and Publicity

Whether you publish a newsletter for profit or marketing purposes, your newsletter is always useful as a publicity medium. Aside from the obvious method of circulating it to anyone interested, there are other methods for using your newsletter in the direct interest of publicity.

Many newsletters carry a notice that any material in it may be reprinted or republished without express permission (the notice is a blanket permission), as long as the source is credited. This, of course, helps to circulate your newsletter and your name through other people's publications.

An easy way to do this is to identify other newsletters and periodicals that reach the audience you want to reach, and add the publishers to your "comp" (complimentary subscription) list, even without making a special arrangement. Usually, the other publisher will reciprocate, but even if he or she does not, you are still offering your material freely for the PR you can get out of it.

Add others to your comp list, anyone you think can be helpful in furthering your publicity objectives. Public officials might wish to quote you in some of their speeches, for example, and organizations such as businessmen's clubs may be interested in circulating your newsletter by putting copies in the racks of their reading rooms and lounges. Send complimentary copies to public libraries if you want to reach those who visit those establishments. See that copies get into whatever reading rooms and lounges you believe are frequented by those you would like to reach. In general, if you are using your newsletter for publicity rather than for direct profit, treat it as though it were a brochure or direct-mail piece (for it is acting as such) and give it the widest possible circulation by whatever means you can think of.

Writing for Others

You can add to the publicity you get through your own releases and newsletter by contributing to other publications. Do as many articles as you can, without charge, for other periodicals, and do not neglect the "letters to the editor" type of piece. For many publications, this is an important feature—subscribers are generally highly enthusiastic about this section—and your letters can draw a great deal of attention. (One man I know had a letter published in a major business magazine and drew a response from a large publishing house, inquiring whether he would be interested in writing an entire book on the subject of his letter.)

Be Active

Belong to as many professional groups or business associations as you can manage and be as active in them as you can. Serve on committees, speak at meetings and conventions, write for their newsletters. You do not have to confine your activities to the groups of which you are a member, either. There are many other groups and associations who would welcome your articles and speeches. Seek them out and offer to write and speak for them. Just *being* in the public eye—being *known*—itself contributes heavily to your success.

A great many seminars are held every year throughout the United States, on a wide variety of topics. (It is a rare week that my own mailbox fails to produce fewer than a half-dozen brochures inviting me to attend seminars.) Some of these are produced by large organizations, some by individuals. Some are delivered by an entire staff of speakers and presenters, whereas some are presented entirely by a single person. Most, however, welcome outside speakers who speak without charge or, at most, for an honorarium, which is usually rather nominal.

Many speakers provide free or nearly free services because they believe that the publicity is worth it. Usually, you are not only introduced in whatever terms you wish—you can usually write your own introduction—but you are usually also able to distribute your business cards, brochures, newsletters, or other literature. In most cases, there is a "literature table" on which you can deposit a supply of your literature for the benefit of all. You can also circulate among the audience during breaks and after the seminar, which is itself often directly productive of business.

METHODS VARY AS DO MARKETS

Inevitably, marketing methods must vary, according to what you are trying to market and, even more significantly, whom you are trying to reach and persuade in your marketing approaches, as well as according to the price tag on whatever you sell. There are no universally effective methods, of course, although there are some more or less "traditional" methods for selling various kinds of goods and services. Some of these have been covered before, but here are at least three major categories of "advice" ventures and how they have usually been marketed successfully:

1 *Newsletter and magazine subscriptions, books, and reports:* It has become conventional wisdom that periodical subscriptions and other specialized publications can be sold effectively—or, at least, affordably—only by direct mail.

2 *Seminar registrations:* Usually, direct mail—most often large brochures, mailed flat, in great quantities, and without envelopes—when soliciting organizations to send their employees; and newspaper advertisements when appealing to individuals to attend.

3 *Consulting and related personal services:* Often the most difficult to sell because the client's confidence must be gained first, and so usually sold on the strength of a personal image, built through prestigious professional activities—writing, speaking, making many appearances, and being written about.

MUTUAL MARKETING SUPPORT
AMONG PRODUCTS AND SERVICES

One of the most effective and too often neglected marketing approaches is to structure everything you do to support everything else. If you publish a newsletter, whether for promotion or profit, use it to promote whatever else you offer: seminars, consulting services, reports, books, or other. If you run seminars, be sure that everyone in attendance gets literature explaining other products or services you offer. Your books and reports should include appended information on whatever else you have to offer.

Although this may sound too obvious to require pointing out, experience reveals quite clearly the necessity for *stressing* your other offerings. Here are a couple of anecdotes to reveal the truth of that.

The Educational Science Division of U.S. Industries manufactured and marketed a "teaching machine," called AutoTutor, which used a reel of 35mm film to present the material to students. The company wrote the programs that were recorded on film, and they wrote both proprietary programs in academic subjects (algebra, history, etc.) and in common vocational subjects (electronics, automotive repair, etc.) and custom programs for client companies that wished to train their employees in a special subject. But the company also undertook custom work to prepare "paper" programs—training materials in printed formats.

Again and again, the company found that a client for film programs had gone to other suppliers for printed training programs. Because the company did not make adequate efforts to educate their clients, many clients simply *assumed* that the company did not do anything other than the film programs for their teaching machines.

In another case, a supplier of custom training materials developed texts for a client, repeatedly pointing out that they also had a large and complete graphic arts department ready to serve. Despite this, they nearly lost the graphic arts work because the client said, "Oh, I didn't know that you did that kind of work, too." Only by being constantly vigilant did the supplier manage to win this work.

The reason for this kind of problem is that it is a human tendency to label everyone and everything. Whether you wish it or not, the clients will themselves decide that you are a specialist of one sort or another. Once the client has decided what your label is, you must work at changing that image. It is for this reason that even tiny businesses sometimes decide to create "departments" or "divisions," each with its own distinctive label, in the hope of overcoming this problem.

Chapter 10

The Economics of the Advice Business

In the end it always comes down to dollars income versus dollars outgo.

THE COST OF GETTING STARTED

All business ventures require investment. Unfortunately, most people in our society think of investment only as money—in terms of dollars only. But money is not the only thing you can or should invest in a business venture: There is also *you*—your knowledge, skills, and experience. And there is something others have called "sweat investment" or "sweat equity," referring to your personal labor, usually representing the dedication of long hours, with little or no time for personal pursuits and pleasures.

Never assume, therefore, that the investment is small because a great deal of money is not required. Quite often money is the "cheapest" and easiest investment required of you. At the same time, you cannot put that kind of investment on the books as part of your equity, nor, ordinarily, can you borrow against it. Despite all the sweat equity and other noncash assets, the enterprise needs at least some cash investment.

THE COST OF EDUCATION

Although it is necessary to have a positive outlook, if you are to succeed in any venture, it is also necessary to be a realist. While some entrepreneurs meet with immediate success, whether through brilliance or fortune, the odds against this happening are heavy. It is far more likely that you will struggle, make your share of costly mistakes, and grow to a position of profitability and relative security only slowly.

You probably will make those mistakes; most of us do; and they will cost you something, which you may regard as losses. But you should not regard them as losses; regard them as the cost of your education, and do make sure that they are part of your education.

Be sure to recognize, too, that $50 lessons are just as useful in your education as $500 lessons. That is, if you are properly conservative in the beginning and do not venture sums any larger than absolutely necessary, you will get the same education as if you had ventured larger sums, but the education will cost you far less.

The time to plunge is when you are sure that you know what you are doing because you have done it successfully before. In the beginning, when you are still getting your education, be as conservative as you can.

Fortunately, many of the kinds of ventures we have discussed here as part of the advice business can be launched with modest amounts of cash—with virtually none, in some cases, especially when they begin on a part-time basis, operated from your home, and with no requirement that the venture furnish income immediately. For example, anyone may decide to be a consultant, and at least in some cases, you can establish your office in your own home, the chief requirements being business cards and stationery, access to a decent typewriter, and a means for soliciting your first account. But even if you decide to have a product, such as a newsletter or report of some kind, the up-front cash required is not great if you are willing to start modestly and grow gradually. Let's look at a few typical ventures of these and other kinds and see what kinds of "numbers" are involved.

A CONSULTING VENTURE

The chief asset of a consultancy is you, your knowledge and skills. Those are, essentially, your stock in trade, what you can sell. The chief investment in establishing a consulting practice is for the physical assets required and for marketing your service, and the physical assets vary with the nature of the consultancy or the kinds of services involved.

For example, if your work is such that all or nearly all of it is performed on the client's premises—interior decorating, office-procedures design, or technical writing, for example—you probably do not need a great deal in the way of an office of your own. Probably a desk and chair and a typewriter will suffice, possibly with the addition of a filing cabinet and a bookcase. If you are producing newsletters and reports, however, you will need a few other fixtures and pieces of equipment (unless you are willing to stand the expense of contracting it all out), such as a light table and some other production equipment, and perhaps some mailing equipment.

Working at home not only reduces your investment and operating costs, but pays off in another way: You can write off some of your home expense—the prorated portion of whatever part of your home is dedicated to business use and part of your telephone and automobile expense on the same basis.

Working at home, however, assumes that you will not have clients visiting you, except perhaps on occasion. If your venture requires a stream of people visiting you in your own office, you will probably have to face the reality of an office in a commercial location, and such facilities are quite expensive. In modern office buildings in many cities, office rents run as much as $25 per square foot and more. That means that a modest little office only 12 by 15 feet can easily cost you $375 per month. To that you must add the cost of an office telephone and probably some extras, which are written into most leases today, such as an increase in taxes. (This can easily represent an extra month's rent each year.)

There is also the cost of parking your automobile or riding public transportation (which itself may not be an economy), expensive lunches, and other items, all of which can easily bring your monthly obligation to well over $500, whether you do any business or not. There are alternatives, however, even if you require an office away from your home. You can opt for a location in which the rents are not exorbitant and which is not far from your home, you can seek out one of the older office buildings, where the rents are modest (or relatively so, in any case), or you can share office space, for the best possible financial arrangement. There are at least three ways to manage that:

1   There are many other people who need a business office but want to keep the costs down. You can run a small classified advertisement, seeking out one or

more people who want to share office space, and also watch the advertisements for such opportunities. You might even turn this to your advantage by representing yourselves as associates, as long as you are not directly competitive with each other.

2   There are many established small firms who find they have more space than they need for themselves and are willing to sublet a small room in their own suite. (I once rented a suitable small room from an employment agency for only $100 per month.)

3   There are offices designed especially for people who require a business address but not much more than a desk and chair and access to some amenities —a conference room, a copier, and secretarial services. You can get such facilities quite inexpensively, sometimes for as little as $50 or $75 a month, although you will, of course, pay extra for use of the copier and for secretarial services. (Frequently, those services are provided by a public stenographer, who also rents space in the establishment.) Generally, the monthly fee includes telephone-answering service and the use of the conference room, and the desk and chair are furnished as part of the basic service.

   This arrangement is useful for those who are not in the office all day— for those who spend relatively little time in the office, in fact—and require a business address, a mailing address, and a telephone-answering service. If your venture is such that you must spend a great deal of time in your office, this will probably not be a good arrangement for you. On the other hand, you may want to start this way and "trade up" to more splendid facilities after you have established yourself and feel ready for something better.

Whether you do or do not start this way, it is wise to keep your initial cash investment as small as possible in all ways. Some beginners invest far more than is necessary in elaborate stationery and brochures, for example, in the mistaken notion that this will add to their image and appeal. In fact, in many ways the most prestigious and "classiest" stationery is that on a good grade of plain white bond, printed simply in black ink. True "class" is never ostentatious. Overly elaborate stationery and other obvious efforts to "put up a front" weaken your image because they suggest how conscious you are of the need for image. On the other hand, being quietly businesslike suggests that you have adequate confidence in yourself and have no driving need to impress anyone. That is a far better image to project.

Do not order stationery in large quantities, since it is highly likely that you will make changes within the first year or two that will make your stationery obsolete. You are likely to want to change your stationery, anyway, after you have had a year or two experience with your venture.

If you must buy new office furniture, use some seasoned judgment about the investment. You can buy what some call an "engineer's" desk for as little as $150, but you can also spend $2000 on a desk quite easily, and the same goes for other office furniture and fixtures.

A word processor (which is actually a microcomputer with a word-processor program installed in it) is most useful today in almost any business, but is not a must for everyone; an amazingly large number of microcomputers are idly gathering dust in the closets and back rooms of buyers who could not find a good use for them after succumbing to the fever to buy one. Wait until you have a clear idea of your needs before spending several thousand dollars on a computer. A good type-writer will serve your needs quite well while you are getting started.

The same considerations apply to marketing costs in general and advertising costs in particular. An advertisement in the Yellow Pages of the telephone book is a firm commitment for a year; the cost shows up in your telephone bill every month. If it is only $50 per month, the total commitment is $600. That is almost the cost of a good typewriter or several pieces of office furniture. There are probably more effective ways to use $600 to get clients, since conventional advertising rarely works well for consulting ventures.

Printing costs money, and you can spend a small fortune on a bro-chure if you use several colors of ink, costly papers, die cutting, and other budget-busting gimmicks that do not usually add proportionately to the effectiveness of the brochure. Use the same philosophy as that advocated for stationery: the good taste of *not* being ostentatious. Remember, too, that you will pay for all the fancy touches.

ACCOUNTING AND THE COST
OF DOING BUSINESS GENERALLY

Most of what has been pointed out already in this chapter applies gen-erally to any venture. But there is more, a great deal more, to be said about the cost of doing business generally. And unfortunately, accoun-tants, like most technical and professional specialists, tend to shroud their work in mysterious jargon and technical idiom that obscures basic principles and has the effect of making the simple appear complicated.

The fact is that accounting is basically a quite simple proposition once a few fundamental truths are clearly established. Here are some you should know, whether you do your own books or have an accountant do them for you:

- There are only two kinds of dollars in business, no matter how accountants disguise them with other names: those coming in and those going out (or those you can keep and those you must pay out, if that is an easier idea to accommodate). Those coming in are called *income*, while those going out are disguised under such euphemisms as *overhead, direct costs*, and *fringe benefits*, among others.

- There must be more of the first kind (those coming in or those you can keep) than of the second kind (those you must pay out) if your venture is to survive.

- The main purpose of accounting is to feed back to the manager (you) information about how the venture is doing so that the manager can make intelligent decisions about what to do and what not to do. (Requirements to keep records for tax and other legal purposes are relatively recent developments and are not the main purpose of accounting, necessary though they are.)

- Accounting reports are *management* information and are absolutely essential to decision making. The sooner you get the information, the sooner you can take appropriate action to stop doing whatever is not working well and to step up doing whatever is working well. For the small business, you need the information *now*, while it is happening, not three months from now.

- Dollars can assume another form, such as *inventory, furniture*, and *fixtures, but they are still dollars, although now called investment.*

It is partly the practice of giving dollars all those other names that makes accounting so mysterious for most people. In accounting, as in many professions, words mean what the practitioners want them to mean, no matter what the rest of the world wants them to mean. For example, if you do business on what they call a "cash basis," you might think that means that you sell for cash only and pay by cash as well. Not so, not at all. It means, generally, a system wherein you count dollars in and out when received, not when due or "receivable." Perhaps you think of "sales" as getting orders from buyers. Again, that's not what the word means to your accountant. To him the word refers to income, as in the case of a little retail store, counting up cash received at the end of the day. It probably stems from an earlier time, when most trade was on that basis. Perhaps you think that "cost of sales" (another euphemism for dollars paid out) is the cost of getting the orders. But in actuality it is the total cost of filling the order. So even when the accountants are using what appears to be plain English, they are still using their own argot.

The way to cut through the curtain that surrounds accounting is to remember always to count dollars as one of two kinds—in or out. However, if you are to maximize the first and minimize the second (which is the basic goal of all business, all modern platitudes to the contrary notwithstanding), it is necessary to understand where and why each dollar comes in and goes out. Let's have a look at some accounting basics, which we will discuss in plain English.

Direct versus Indirect Costs

The biggest problem in business is almost always costs and controlling them, and that which is called *cost accounting* appears to be regarded as among the more important accounting activities. Generally, there are more concepts, records, reports, terms, and efforts associated with costs than with any other facet of accounting; in fact, cost accounting is probably 90 percent of accounting generally.

Types of costs or "cost centers" vary widely according to the types of businesses, so the discussions here must necessarily be rather general. However, there are some basic similarities, or at least characteristics, that are common to all or most business ventures, and we can certainly point these out. One is that all or nearly all businesses have both *direct* and *indirect* costs, although these vary in their nature from one type of business to another. But first let's look at some basic definitions.

Direct costs are those that can be assigned directly and specifically to each sale, costs that would not have been incurred at all if the sale had not been made. For example, if you win a contract to advise someone regarding decorating his or her home, the hours you spend actually doing this are direct costs, as are any long-distance calls you make, travel you do, or other expenses incurred to satisfy your obligation to that client. If you sell a product, such as a newsletter or style guide, as your venture or part of your venture, the cost of that item is also part of direct costs.

Indirect costs include virtually all other kinds of cost: the costs of being in business but which cannot be assigned to specific sales or jobs, such as general telephone, heat, light, rent, taxes, insurance, advertising, depreciation, interest, and other general overhead costs. They are the costs of keeping your doors open, costs not assignable to a particular sale or project, costs you incur whether you do a great deal of business or only a little, although they will normally be in some rough proportion to the amount of business you do—a consideration that has a significance all its own, as will soon become apparent.

Some costs can be either direct or indirect, according to your own arbitrary decision or according to circumstances. For example, you may choose to make all telephone costs indirect, even though some charges are for long-distance calls made in behalf of specific clients and specific contracts. Or you may make your basic telephone service and local calls an indirect cost, while making the toll calls direct charges to projects. Of course, to do that you must keep a telephone log or otherwise keep track of all costs incurred for each project. Similar considerations may apply to printing, postage, and other costs, which can be both direct and indirect.

On the other hand, some costs are inherently indirect because it is extremely difficult—totally impractical—to assign them to specific clients and projects. That would be the case for rent, heat, light, advertising, and many other items. Yet these are legitimate costs of doing business, and they must be recovered somehow if the business is to survive. To recover them, it is necessary to know what they are, in terms of units of sale. That is, you cannot price whatever you sell properly if you do not know what it costs you. So one of the major functions of accounting is to keep you *accurately* informed of what things cost you, so that you can price effectively. If accounting does nothing else for you, it must do that.

Suppose that you sell a newsletter, for example, and it costs you 35 cents per copy for each issue for printing and postage. That is the direct cost, or at least the principal direct cost. But there are other costs, which you can choose to make direct or indirect. There are, for example, the costs of writing the copy, typing or typesetting it, and mailing it (the labor required to mail it, that is, not the postage). If you keep track of all that cost and prorate it according to the number of copies you mail out (in the same manner that you determined the per copy printing and postage costs), you can also count those costs as direct.

But you still have not accounted for all the costs. How much of your rent, heat, light, and other indirect costs should be charged to the newsletter business and recovered in pricing the newsletter? Determining that is another major function of accounting. Just as you determined the direct cost of writing, typing, and mailing labor chargeable to the newsletter, so you determine the right portion of your indirect costs to charge to the newsletter; you establish an overhead or indirect *rate*—a percentage to charge.

The basis for establishing that percentage—what it is a percentage of—varies from one business to another and from one case to another. The important thing is that the rate be on a basis that enables you to set your prices realistically, so that you can recover all those costs. The rate is usually set as a percentage of whatever your major direct cost is, as a markup of that cost. For example, let us suppose that the newsletter is your sole enterprise and that your direct costs for producing it during the entire year (counting your own labor for writing it and other labor for typing and other functions) total $42,000. You find that your indirect costs are $29,000. Your overhead rate (counting all indirect costs as overhead, although some businesses do not do this) is $29,000/$42,000, which equals 0.69. The percentage is 0.69 × 100 or 69 percent. If you have 3000 subscribers, your direct cost per subscription is $14 and your indirect cost per subscription is therefore $14 + (0.69 × 14), which comes to $23.66. That is your actual cost per subscription. If you charge subscribers $23.66, you are only recovering your own costs, not turning a profit. That is, you are only earning whatever salary you pay yourself. (Your salary is, of course, part of the cost of doing business, not part of the profit.) Your gross profit is the amount over $23.66 that you charge subscribers. (That is profit before taxes, of course.)

The Variability of Overhead

You can see that if you sell a great many more subscriptions, your per subscription cost will come down because it will not cost you any more for writing and typing or typesetting, but those costs will be spread over more subscriptions—over a larger base. Of course, much of your indirect cost will also be spread over the larger base, so that the rate or per unit allocation will also be smaller.

That is an important point. Overhead—the rate, that is, not the total overhead dollars—generally comes down as the direct-cost base or sales volume increases, so that you generally have lower per unit costs. That is because some kinds of costs are *fixed*—they do not change with increases of volume (or do not change with increases to some limit, at least)—whereas others are *variable*. These are two accounting terms that are, mercifully, in English and that mean what they appear to mean.

Capital Items and Depreciation

Some items of cost are constant—telephone service and insurance, for example—as well as fixed. Some are virtually constant—office supplies and printing, for example—but vary in amount, according to business conditions. And some costs are occasional because they are for items that are not consumed, as services and materials are, but are *capital* items, or investments, such as furniture, fixtures, machines, vehicles, equipment, and other items that have relatively long lives and are not consumed.

Each business has some policy about what items are carried as capital items rather than as "expensed" items (the significance of this will be clear shortly), generally based on price. A capital item is generally one that has a useful life of more than one year and costs some sum stipulated by the organization's policy, perhaps $500. However, there is the constraint of the IRS, which has the presumption and the force of law to dictate some policies. Currently, the IRS has dictated that any capital item costing over $5000 must be put on a depreciation schedule rather than "expensed out" (written off) in the year of purchase. Let's see what this means and why the IRS thinks that it is their right and in their interest to dictate this policy.

Any item that is totally "expensed" or written off as an overhead item in the year of its purchase represents total cost in that year and is deductible as cost. Otherwise, the item is put on a depreciation schedule and costed out over its presumed life. For example, if you buy a computer for $5000 and depreciate it over five years, you can deduct only $1000 each year for five years, even if you paid cash for it. That means that you will be paying taxes on the other $4000, in effect, because you cannot deduct the total cost in the year that you paid it out. So it would appear to be in your interest to "expense" the item entirely in the year of its purchase and get the full deduction. To offset this problem, somewhat, the IRS currently allows a special tax deduction for investment—an "investment tax credit," in IRS language. For capital items up to $5000 in cost, you can choose which you prefer. But for items over $5000, the IRS insists that you "capitalize" them on depreciation schedules, take your investment tax credit, and recover the rest of your cost slowly over the five or ten years of depreciation allowed.

Obviously you do not want to capitalize and depreciate small items, even if they have long useful lives—staplers and $10 calculators, for example. That is the whole point of setting price limits, to make practical policy on what to capitalize (depreciate over several years) and what to charge off entirely when purchased, insofar as IRS tax codes permit, of course.

Do not make the mistake of allowing your accountant to make this decision for you. In this and other matters pertaining to the conduct of your enterprise, your accountant may advise and should do so, but it is you, not the accountant, who must make the decisions. Your accountant, like your lawyer and any other advisor, should give you all the facts on both sides of the question, and may offer an opinion. But ordinarily, neither your accountant nor your lawyer really knows as well as you do what is the best policy for your business.

The Cost of Your Own Labor

Labor costs money. In many enterprises it is the most expensive item of cost, particularly in those ventures in which relatively little money is required for initial investment because the venture is concerned primarily with selling services or a product that is created almost entirely by human labor. Periodicals, such as newsletters and magazines, for example, are generally in that category. Such ventures are known as "labor intensive," as distinct from ventures that require large sums of investment capital, which are known as "capital intensive."

Some people make the naive assumption that since they are self-employed in one-person enterprises and work from their own homes, they have little or no overhead, and their labor is free. This is a dangerous assumption as well as an incorrect one. Here are some basic principles of which you should always be highly conscious:

- You must always consider and treat your business venture as a separate entity, even if it is not incorporated, which employs you on a salary or other basis of compensation.

- *Every* business venture has overhead. If you work out of your home, you must arrange matters so that your venture is charged rent, heat, light, telephone, and whatever other resources of yours it uses.

- The salary you pay yourself—the income from your business—is not profit; it is cost, the cost of doing business, and should be charged against the business.

- Any time you spend doing things that do not produce income—marketing, working on your books, or whatever—is overhead. The business is paying you for that time, although it produces no income for the business and is therefore indirect cost.

Profit

Profit, to put it as simply as possible, is what is left, if anything, after you have cleared all expenses, including your own salary. If there is nothing left, or if you consume all gross profit by taking everything left after expenses are paid, the business is operating without a profit. That is not a healthy situation. Businesses need profit. It is on profit that the business is enabled to grow, to become not only larger, but better. To ensure a profit, it is wise to keep your personal salary or drawdown to the minimum with which you can manage, permitting the business to accumulate some profits as capital for growth.

A while ago we looked at direct and indirect costs. Let's have another look at those costs and how we arrange pricing to produce a profit. You may remember that we were discussing a hypothetical newsletter with 3000 subscribers, produced at a total cost of $23.66 per subscription or approximately $71,000. That figure includes your salary as well as all other cost items, but it does not include profit. You must charge the subscriber something in excess of $23.66 to produce a profit.

Let us suppose that you are charging the modest sum of $28 for each subscription. That produces a gross profit of $4.34 per subscription, which represents about 18 percent of cost or 15 percent of selling price, which is the way some businesses calculate profit margins. For some businesses that would be a comfortable margin, even as a pretax profit (which this is). But percentage of cost or selling price is only one standard against which to measure or estimate a proper selling price, and is certainly not the only one.

PRICING YOUR PRODUCTS/SERVICES

Perhaps $28 is a fair price for your newsletter. But it may also be far too high a price. Or even far too low a price. The reason it may be so at variance with what it ought to be has nothing to do with percentages, margins, or markups; it has to do with something called "the market," a euphemism for what such items are bringing at the time. For example, the market for any automobile 10 years ago was considerably different from the market for that automobile today. In fact, some cars bring more as used cars today than they cost originally as new cars.

Everything has a market, in that sense. Newsletters, as one case, fall into groups or classes, each of which occupies a different cost environment. The investment advisory newsletter, for example, is normally priced far higher than is a newsletter for philatelists, stamp collectors. Should you try to get $200 a year for the latter newsletter you would get mighty few subscribers, quite possibly none at all. On the other hand, you would be foolish to offer an investment advisory newsletter at $18 a year, and might very well also get no subscribers because those who would normally subscribe to such a newsletter would have little faith in one costing so little.

So you must price your product or service in keeping with whatever is a fair market price, and you must do whatever you have to do to research the market and determine what that price is.

PRICE VERSUS VALUE

But even this is not the whole story. The market—all your competitors collectively—influences your prices but does not set them, finally. You do not permit competitors to determine what your own products and services are worth. The marketplace is full of products and services that buck the tide and swim upstream successfully. The final arbiter of price is *value,* and value is only partially what the market says it is; it is also what the customer says it is. If a dozen newsletters similar to yours are selling for $36 a year, you may yet be able to get $48, $78, or even more for yours if you are successful in convincing customers that your newsletter is worth that much.

On the other hand, you may decide that it is in your interest to meet the $36 competition with a $24 newsletter, expecting to get enough volume to make the venture profitable at that price. In that case, your task is to convince the customer either that your competitors' newsletters are overpriced at $36 and that yours is at least as good as theirs, despite its lower price, or offer some other convincing rationale for your lower price so that customers do not interpret it to mean a product of lesser quality. Even price is dependent on marketing, to a large extent.

SHOULD YOU INCORPORATE?

A great many beginners in business are convinced immediately that they should incorporate—*must* incorporate. Some believe that they are more prestigious with an "Inc." or "Corporation" in their business name. Some believe that they are better protected by being incorporated. And some, perhaps the majority, are persuaded by their accountants or lawyers that incorporation is desirable if not an absolute necessity. (Perversely enough, my own accountant was against my incorporating myself.) Let's look at some pros and cons regarding this.

Prestige. It is questionable whether being incorporated really gives you added prestige.

Protection Against Personal Liability. One reason for incorporating is to protect yourself and your family against personal liability for debts, damages, and/or other liabilities resulting from your business venture. The corporation is a separate legal entity, and with a few notable exceptions, such as fraud, you are not liable for obligations of the corporation. In the case of bankruptcy or lawsuit, no one can attach your personal property.

Credit. Your creditworthiness—your ability to borrow capital and/or to get "trade credit" from suppliers—is usually no greater when you incorporate and may even be lessened because you are now protected against personal liability, making you an even greater risk if the corporation does not have any tangible assets.

Cost.   Being incorporated costs money. The cost of incorporation itself is small; in most states you can do it yourself by filing a simple document and paying perhaps $40 or $50. But there are many other costs that you now encounter: more bookkeeping, various other taxes, and in some cases special licenses. On the other hand, there are some benefits in sheltering income. For one thing, the corporate tax rate is generally lower than the personal tax rate. Too, as a corporation you can bestow various employee benefits on yourself that have the effect of sheltering income. This is perhaps the greatest benefit, for most people, of incorporating their ventures. However, be sure to explore all aspects thoroughly before making your decision, and do not make that decision until you not only *know* all the facts, but have also *projected* all of them into specific advantages and disadvantages to you. Note that—not the general advantages and disadvantages, but what they will mean specifically in your own individual case. *That* is the bottom line.

TYPICAL PRICES

Despite wide variations in the market for the many products and services that we have been discussing here, there are many examples that are typical of the markets for these things. Although you are certainly free to establish your own markets for what you sell—and you certainly should try to do so—insights into typical prices will help you, at least in the beginning, while you are feeling your way. The following should not be taken as firm mandates, therefore, but only as the most general of indicators.

Newsletters

We have discussed newsletters frequently in these pages because they are relatively easy to launch and are quite popular. Subscription prices vary quite enormously, along three parameters or according to three influences:

1 *Frequency of publication:* Obviously, you would charge more for a daily or weekly newsletter than for one that appears only at monthly or quarterly intervals.

2 *Size:* Again, a 16- or 32-page newsletter is going to bring a greater subscription price, normally, than one of four or eight pages.

3 *Exclusivity:* Some newsletters carry highly exclusive information, perhaps "insider" information or any other information which is not readily available elsewhere. That kind of information is often worth a great deal to subscribers (and may cost a great deal of money to collect, as well), and they are charged accordingly.

There are some other factors that affect price. The reputation of the publisher or editor may affect the price. A newsletter published by some well-known or celebrated person who is an acknowledged authority will bring a good price for that reason alone. The publisher may subsidize the newsletter, as noted several times already, because it is useful as a marketing tool or because it is included in some "package deal." Or the newsletter may simply have built a reputation over the years, and thus be able to command a large price.

Newsletters, then, vary from as little as $5 per year to as much as several hundred dollars per year (occasionally, well over $1000 per year).

Consulting Services

Consulting fees also vary widely. There are consultants who work for as little as $200 per day (probably the low figure), and there are some who charge as much as $5000 per day. (This does not consider the unusual case of the well-known authority or celebrity who may collect even more per day for services.) Again, the factors are these, generally:

1 *Exclusivity of the service or expertise required:* A computer consultant whose knowledge ranges to the most sophisticated of today's "supercomputers" will certainly command far more per day than will the expert whose knowledge is confined to the popular microcomputers, for example. It is relatively easy to find consultants of the latter class, rather difficult to find those of the first type.

2 *Personal reputation of the consultant:* Some consultants have built a reputation and come highly recommended, whereas others are unknown or relatively unknown. This affects the fee, of course.

3 *Track record of the consultant:* Even though unknown or relatively so, some consultants can produce an impressive track record of accomplishments and

furnish good professional references. This enables them to command better fees than if they were still rather new and not yet able to point to a track record.

4 *Other credentials:* Some consultants can produce other credentials than track record per se, such as remarkable educational or professional accomplishments. Some clients are impressed by the possession of a doctorate, for example, or by a background as an executive or professional of some sort, and will pay good fees for that alone.

5 *Effective marketing:* Some consultants simply do a better job of marketing themselves than do others—a better job, that is, of creating a good image for themselves and convincing clients that they are worth what they ask.

6 *Value:* Some services are simply worth more to clients than others. The consultant who can help a client produce better technical manuals cannot ordinarily claim as much as the consultant who can help a client win contracts or increase sales, simply because the latter services have far greater payoff value to the client.

If we were to set a general ballpark figure for consulting fees in today's economy, we would say that the lower range is approximately $300 to $500 per day, the midrange $500 to $800 per day, and the upper range $800 to $1500 per day. That can be translated into hourly rates, of course, and some consultants prefer to calculate fees on an hourly basis, or in some cases, the hourly basis is more practicable for them than is the daily basis.

Seminars

The general costs of seminars and fees have been covered in an earlier chapter. The range of charges for "open registration" seminars runs generally from about $60 to $150, for the lowest-priced ones, and those are the ones running not more than one day and produced on a modest scale, usually by small organizations or individual entrepreneurs, often as an adjunct to newsletter publication or other enterprises. The more ambitious efforts tend to something on the order of $200 to $250 per day per registrant.

In terms of costs, the lower-priced ones are generally produced on modest budgets of less than $1000 and in single, local sessions, whereas the others entail much larger budgets, with huge mailings and rather costly brochures. Moreover, the latter seminars are generally produced on a tour basis, with a number of sessions announced in the brochure and nationwide mailings, so as to spread and justify the large front-end marketing cost as well as the cost of travel and subsistence. Results vary widely, as might be surmised, but often the modest, low-budget, low-priced seminar is more profitable than is the more ambitious effort. Assuming a front-end (primarily marketing) cost of $1000, producing and presentation costs of perhaps $500, and an attendance of 30 people at a median price of $100, the entrepreneur can net a pretax income of approximately $1500 from each session.

Public Speaking

Many people speak publicly for fees as their main occupation, although a great many of them also write and publish books (often selling their own books in "back of the room" sales sessions when they speak) and/or offer consulting services. Fees for public speaking vary even more widely than do fees for consulting. "Stars"—celebrities and other well-known people—get several thousand dollars for an appearance, even for only an hour, and some can earn as much as $25,000 for each speech.

In terms of speaking fees, agents for speakers and speakers' bureaus are rarely willing to handle any speaker who cannot command at least $500 for a speech, so we may regard that figure, $500, as the minimum for a professional speaker. In general, however, a fair market for a good speaker who is not well known would be $1000 to $2000.

It is not easy to persuade speakers' agents and bureaus to handle you until you have established a following of some sort. In general, agents and bureaus tend to pursue the celebrity speakers first, the less well known but still professional speakers second, and generally to ignore and brush off the hopefuls who are not yet established as speakers. Perhaps this is understandable, since the bureaus work on the commissions they can command—these range generally from about 25 to 40 percent—and do not normally get exclusive rights to book the speaker. (Most speakers who make a full-time or nearly full-time activity of public speaking tend to be their own agents, to a large extent.) Of course, as in the case of consulting, these fees are exclusive of travel and subsistence costs which clients must pay the speakers.

Custom Seminars and Training

There is a special class of public speaking, which is really in the training field and consists, most commonly, of presenting seminar training sessions to audiences on a custom and, usually, in-house basis. If, for example, you present seminars of such a nature as to attract companies to send employees to your sessions, you have the basis for offering these seminars as custom presentations to companies with staffs of people to train.

The point is that it will usually cost a company less to train 10 or more people in this manner than to send only two or three off to another city to attend an open-registration seminar. Many sales seminars are presented in this manner by sales professionals who are also sales trainers. Others are by speakers who teach "positive thinking" and similar psychological ego or self-confidence reinforcement, but there are many such seminars on managing time effectively, reducing or handling stress, effective writing, and numerous other subjects that employers are likely to find useful for training their staffs.

Even if your seminar is of the type that attracts individuals to attend as individuals, you may be able to offer your seminar on a custom basis to associations to which the individuals belong—clubs, professional societies, and others.

The presentation can be a "canned" one, one that you have given many times but which is appropriate to a great many organizations as is or with only modest changes to customize it, or you may tailor each one to the organization if you can manage to do so without raising the price to an unacceptable level. I personally do some of these kinds of seminars in proposal writing, and I found it necessary to find inexpensive ways to customize the presentation before I met with success in marketing it. In my personal experience, I found price to be a major factor in marketing this idea.

I have observed that some seminar presenters who do these kinds of custom seminars make a charge for each attendee, with a guaranteed minimum. Some make a flat charge, allowing some number of attendees, and charge per person for any over that number. Some make an additional charge for handouts or seminar manuals.

Of course, you need to test and discover what works best for you. In my own case, after much experimentation, I found that overall, what works best for me is to charge a flat fee, plus expenses (unless it is a local assignment) for the day, and to provide a master copy of a seminar manual, with permission to duplicate enough copies for handouts. In the beginning I charged clients a simple day's consulting fee, but I soon learned that I was undercharging my clients and I raised the fee to a more equitable level. I learned, too, that many clients are of the opinion that any in-house seminar or other training session that costs them less than $1000 cannot be very good! Let that also be one of your guides.

SHOULD YOU "DO IT YOURSELF" TO MINIMIZE COSTS?

In all these activities it is possible to do a great many things yourself and so keep costs to a minimum. You can make transparencies—"view graphs" for overhead projection—on any good office copier. You can write your own handouts and seminar manuals using a good typewriter or word processor and have them duplicated at a local copy shop. You can prepare and mail your own brochures, sales letters, and other marketing materials. If you check with your local art-supply and stationery houses, you will be surprised at how many types of products are available to help you do a professional job of developing many kinds of materials.

Whether it pays you to do these things is another matter. True, you will save the costs of having others, professionals at the game, do them for you. But there are two things to consider in making your decision:

1 Is doing all this the most effective and most profitable use of your own time, or could you be doing things more important and more profitable to you?

2 Will you do as effective a job on these things, or will the specialists turn out products that are so much more effective as to more than offset the costs of having it done for you? (Example: Are you a good enough copywriter to turn out effective direct-mail packages that will bring in enough business to be worthwhile?)

"Do it yourself" is a splendid way to save money if you have nothing more important to do with your time and if you can do a really good job. It is a false economy—in fact, no economy at all—if you could be doing more beneficial things with your time and if outside contractors can produce markedly better results for you than you can produce for yourself.

In the next and final chapter, you will find some listings and guidelines directing you to other sources of information, ideas, and other kinds of help should you decide that you are better off getting experts to help you design, develop, and operate a successful venture.

Chapter 11

A Reference File

Sources for additional information, ideas, and help.

At least part of success in any venture lies in the availability of resources, and one of the important resources is information: knowing where to turn for ideas, guidance, and help of various kinds. This final chapter is intended to provide at least part of that resource by providing a number of checklists for your use and at least some beginning lists of agencies and specialists who can help you in a variety of ways. There is no special order in the way in which these items are listed and presented.

PUBLIC SPEAKING AND LECTURE AGENTS

There are many individuals and organizations who act as agents for public speakers. Some of the individuals are themselves speakers, who also act as agents for others. Some are full-time lecture bureaus and list themselves as such. There are those who offer services as booking agencies for entertainers; others who offer training development and

training services, including seminars; and still others who are conference and convention arrangers, booking speakers and other kinds of
talent for such convocations. Only a partial listing is offered here, but
this is representative of a much larger number of such individuals and
organizations.

Following the list is information about a widely read periodical
for those who speak publicly for fees and profit, published by a well-
known figure in this field, Dottie Walters, of Glendora, California. (You
will also find her listed as a lecture bureau.)

CALIFORNIA

Professional Speakers Bureau
P.O. Box 20007
Buellton, CA 93427

Jane Lee Hawkins
Full Service Speakers Bureau
  and Advertising Agency
2001 East First Street
Santa Ana, CA 92705

Marj Horn
California Speakers Bureau
1517 Andreas Avenue
San Jose, CA 95118

SRI International
333 Ravenswood Avenue
Menlo Park, CA 94025

Dottie Walters
600 West Foothill Boulevard
Glendora, CA 91740

Stan Jacobi Star Productions
4000 Mission Boulevard, Suite 3
San Diego, CA 92109

COLORADO

International Speakers Bureau
100 Everett Street
Lakewood, CO 80226

Colorado Convention and Reservations
1665 Grant Street, Suite 9
Denver, CO 80203

CONNECTICUT

Conference Mangement Corp.
17 Washington Street
Norwalk, CT 06854

Conference and Exposition
  Management Co., Inc.
Box 844
Greenwich, CT 06830

WASHINGTON, D.C. (AREA)

Potomac Speakers, Inc.
3001 Veazey Terrace NW, No. 1625
Washington, DC 20008

American Society of Association
  Executives
1101 16th Street, NW
Washington, DC 20036

Washington Speakers Bureau, Inc.
201 North Fairfax Street, No. 11
Alexandria, VA 22314

Conference Speakers International,
  Inc.
1055 Thomas Jefferson Street, NW,
  Suite 300
Washington, DC 20007

FLORIDA

Adele Cox Convention Service
  and Consultants
321 NW 186th Street
Miami, FL 33169

Bureau of Speakers and Seminars
P.O. Box 37
Maitland, FL 32751

GEORGIA

Jordan Enterprises
Success Leaders Speakers Service
Lenox Square, Box 18737
Atlanta, GA 30326

Convention Consultants of Savannah
  Delta, Inc.
117 West Perry
Savannah, GA 31401

ILLINOIS

Programs Unlimited
515 North Main Street
Glen Ellyn, IL 60136

Convention Entertainment
  Productions
1645 River Road, Suite 12
Des Plaines, IL 60018

National Speakers Bureau, Inc.
222 Wisconsin Avenue, Suite 309
Lake Forest, IL 60045

Burns Sports Celebrity Service, Inc.
230 North Michigan Avenue
Chicago, IL 60601

KANSAS

National Association of Sales
  Education
P.O. Box 12222
Overland Park, KS 66212

LOUISIANA

Custom Conventions
1739 Julia Street
New Orleans, LA 70113

MASSACHUSETTS

American Program Bureau
850 Boylston Street
Chestnut Hill, MA 02167

Sherman Exposition Management
1330 Boylston Street, Suite 209
Chestnut Hill, MA 02167

Universal Speakers Agency
235 Bear Hill Road, Suite 203
Waltham, MA 02154

Lordly & Dame, Inc.
51 Church Street
Boston, MA 02116

MICHIGAN

Alternatives in Motivation
10031 Handel Street
Portage, MI 49081

Convention Services International
494 Lake Shore Lane
Grosse Pointe, MI 48236

MINNESOTA

Key Seminars
5912 Newton Avenue
Minneapolis, MN 55419

Midwest Speakers Bureau
6440 Flying Cloud Drive, Suite 205
Minneapolis, MN 55344

NEW JERSEY

Leigh Bureau
49–51 State Road
Princeton, NJ 07070

Unconventional Conventions
8 Park Road
Paterson, NJ 07514

NEW YORK

Harry Walker Agency
Empire State Building, Suite 3616
350 5th Avenue
New York, NY 10018

Thalheim Expositions, Inc.
98 Cutter Mill Road
Great Neck, NY 11021

Program Corporation of America
595 West Hartsdale Avenue
White Plains, NY 10607

Royce Carlton, Inc.
866 United Nations Plaza
New York, NY 10017

National Expositions Co., Inc.
14 West 40th Street
New York, NY 10018

Marketing Concepts, Inc.
Two Pennsylvania Plaza
New York, NY 10001

OHIO

Bestconventions, Inc.
24118 Woodway Road
Cleveland, OH 44122

Tourcrafters, Inc.
3 East 4th Street
Cincinnati, OH 45202

OKLAHOMA

Greater Life Rallies
2907 East 51st Street South, Suite G
Tulsa, OK 74135

OREGON

People Potential Speakers Bureau
3560 Lancaster Drive, NE
Salem, OR 97303

PENNSYLVANIA

Eastern U.S. Show Productions
121 Chestnut Street
Philadelphia, PA 19106

Shea Management, Inc.
1326 Freeport Road
Pittsburgh, PA 15238

TENNESSEE

Meeting Services and Convention
Consultants
4515 Harding Road, Suite 110
Nashville, TN 37205

Candace Barr
Celebrity Speakers Bureau
50 Music Square West
Nashville, TN 37203

TEXAS

SCL Group and Convention Service
10521 South Post Oak, Suite 101
Houston, TX 77035

Joan Frank Productions
9550 Forest Lane, Suite 101
Dallas, TX 75243

PERIODICALS FOR SPEAKERS

There are not a great many periodicals for speakers, although from time to time various periodicals carry articles on speaking. The most popular periodical directed entirely to those who speak for fees and profit is probably the bimonthly publication of Dottie Walters, *Sharing Ideas,* usually about 24 pages of editorial matter, with some advertising, and many useful and interesting letters and articles from readers, most of whom are professional speakers. You can write for details to Dottie Walters at 18825 Hicrest Road, P.O. Box 1120, Glendora, CA 91740, or call (818) 335-8069.

Another, somewhat more specialized periodical, is the monthly *The Toastmaster,* the official publication for members of International Toastmasters, Inc., Box 10400, Santa Ana, CA 92711, (714) 542-6793.

Another, of less direct interest because it is addressed largely to hotel and resort interests, is the monthly *Meeting News,* of Gralla Publications, 1501 Broadway, New York, NY 10036, (212) 869-1300.

NATIONAL SPEAKERS ASSOCIATION

Not surprisingly, there is also a National Speakers Association, which has a number of chapters, with headquarters at 5201 North 7th Street, Suite 200, Phoenix, AZ 85014, (602) 265-1001. That office should be able to direct you to the nearest local chapter of the association.

DIRECT-RESPONSE MARKETING
AND COPYWRITING HELP

There are a great many people in the mail-order and related direct-response fields, ranging from millions of the greenest beginners in the field to almost literally a corporals' guard of true experts. (Interestingly enough, and probably revealingly enough, it is the true experts who freely admit that no one really *knows* what will work without testing each proposition and each piece of copy. Only the 90-day wonders *know* all the answers.) In any case, there are a number of experienced people who know more than most do about the field and who can help initiates in a number of ways. The ones listed in this chapter are by no means all those who are capable of providing expert help, but they are all true professionals in this field, and they may all be trusted to provide reliable services. Among them, they cover the field rather well.

THE "MAIL ORDER CONNECTION"

Few businesses have captured as much interest and enthusiasm as has mail order. Something about the notion of working in the warmth and comfort of your own home, as many beginning mail-order dealers do, and opening a bag of mail each morning to extract checks and money orders, quickly captures the imagination. There are probably few businesses that have as wide a range of ventures in types and sizes as does the mail-order field. The well-known "biggies" in the field are Montgomery Ward and Sears, Roebuck, but there are many other rather large, if somewhat less well known firms in this field—Spiegel and Fingerhut, for example. And there are thousands upon thousands of enterprising individuals earning a living by getting orders through the morning mail and filling them through the evening mail.

Mail Order Connection is a monthly newsletter addressed to this field, published by Stilson & Stilson (Galen and Jean Stilson). Galen is a copywriter/consultant headquartered at Tarpon Springs, Florida. As one should expect from a true expert, Stilson points out that there are no absolute rules—all have many exceptions—although he counsels the less expert copywriter to depart from the "rules" only under exceptional circumstances. In fact, Stilson offers 15 guidelines which he advocates considering very carefully in writing copy and which are reproduced here exactly as he wrote them, by his permission.

STILSON'S 15 GUIDELINES

1 *Should have a big idea* . . . Before you begin writing, decide what it is you are trying to accomplish. Make it specific. Limit to one theme.

2 *Do not clutter* . . . A cluttered ad or sales letter makes it look difficult to read and will cause the prospect to skip it.

3 *Make the headline stress a benefit* . . . Take the most appealing benefit your product or service has to offer and develop a headline from it.

4 *Fire your biggest gun first* . . . Don't hide your biggest benefit . . . put it right up front. If you don't, the prospect may never get to it.

5 *Make the first sentence a powerful one* . . . If you're lucky enough to have a prospect start reading, don't chance losing him with your first sentence. Hit him with some "up front sizzle."

6 *Be "you" oriented* . . . You need to get the reader involved. The easiest way to do that is to put him/her into the copy. Say "you will realize . . . ," "you will receive . . . ," "you will want . . . ," etc.

7 *Use short sentences and paragraphs* . . . Short sentences are easier to read and understand. Short paragraphs make the copy look easy to read. Both are important.

8 *Make it flow* . . . One of the difficult tricks of copywriting is tying together the total copy. The easiest way to handle this is the use of sub-headlines when making a transition to a different thought. Plus, you should learn and use "transition" phrases, such as, "In addition to . . ."

9 *Use "action" words* . . . To make the copy seem more alive, more stirring, more motivational.

10 *Make it believable* . . . Be cautious with overstating the benefits. Consumers are somewhat cynical of advertising claims.

11 *Underline or capitalize for emphasis, but don't overdo* . . . Selective use of underlining and capitalizing important points can be effective. It loses its effect when over-used.

12 *Forget humor* . . . Unless you are skilled at writing humor, don't use it. You'll lose more sales than you will gain.

13 *Ask for the order* . . . Don't forget to ask for the sale. Many prospects need prompting.

14 *Explain how to order* . . . Don't take a chance. Tell your prospects exactly how to order . . . don't make it confusing.

15 *Spell out guarantee* . . . Be specific. Don't try to hide anything.

Stilson stresses that his newsletter is designed to serve the needs of the established small and not-so-small mail-order companies, not the beginners or the large mail-order corporations. Each issue carries a number of articles by various experts in the field, many of whom are listed on the cover of the newsletter (see Figure 11-1). Note that they represent various kinds of mail-order skills and experience, and they do not all limit themselves to the mail-order field but will apply their skills to other marketing arenas.

Rene Gnam, for example, conducts many seminars on the techniques of developing effective copy and also offers consulting services in that field, as do several others listed. At least two conduct mail-order enterprises of their own in addition to offering counseling and other services for writing copy, developing complete mail-order packages, finding the right mailing lists, placing advertising, and otherwise placing their skills and knowledge in the service of others. Ed Burnett, for example, not only rents mailing lists but gives seminars and

Volume 2   Number 12   January, 1984

MAIL ORDER CONNECTION

published by:
STILSON & STILSON
P.O. Box 1075
Tarpon Springs, FL 34286-1075

THIS ISSUE:
Marketing Plans ... Questions & Answers ... What To Do Next Month ... Copywriting ... Formats ... Viewpoint ... Postage Savings ... Etc.

MANAGING EDITOR

GALEN STILSON
Copywriter/Consultant
P.O. Box 1075
Tarpon Springs, FL 34286

ASSOCIATE EDITOR

JEAN STILSON
P.O. Box 1075
Tarpon Springs, FL 34286

CONSULTING EDITORS

RENE GNAM, President
Rene Gnam Consultation Corp.
Consultant/Copywriter
P.O. Box 6435
Clearwater, FL 33518

LUTHER BROCK, Ph.D.
"The Letter Doctor"
Consultant/Copywriter
2911 Nottingham
Denton, TX 76201

ED BURNETT, President
Ed Burnett Consultants, Inc.
Consultant/List Management
2 Park Avenue
New York, NY 10016

CRAIG HUEY, President
Infomat, Inc.
List Consultant/Full Service
25550 Hawthorne Blvd., Ste. 304
Torrence, CA 90505

ANDREW S. LINICK, Ph.D.
The Copyologist®, President
L.K. Advertising Agency
Seven Putter Building
Middle Island, NY 11953

WILLIAM COHEN, Ph.D.
Professor of Marketing
California State Univ., L.A.
5151 State University Drive
Los Angeles, CA 90032

PAUL ALEXANDER
Paul Alexander & Associates
Small Business Consultant
14504 Lanica Circle
Chantilly, VA 22021

>> SOMETHING TO THINK ABOUT ...

"Your prospect should never -- but never -- have to re-read a single line of your copy. The words in that line should be so clear that he understands them at once, at the first reading. And the presentation of those words on the paper by the artists should also be so clear that the words move effortlessly through his eyes into his brain. Because once he gets stuck, once he's confused, you have a 50-50 chance of losing him.

And if you confuse him twice on the same page, then he's simply going to crumple up your direct-mail piece and throw it in the wastebasket -- where I absolutely agree it belongs."

-- Eugene M. Schwartz --
(from his book, MAIL ORDER!)

>> BUILD "CONFIDENCE FACTOR" INTO YOUR AD ...

Consumer cynicism with ad claims is understandable. For years they have been bombarded with "Get Rich Overnight," "Lose Weight While Eating More," etc.

In addition, they have ordered from product photographs which have not accurately depicted size and appearance ... they have waited for weeks to receive a mail order ... they have been exposed to media-hype of isolated mail fraud ... and, they have struggled to get guarantee satisfaction.

You and I both know that those exaggerated claims and problems of customer satisfaction are applicable to only a small percentage of marketers. But the consumer doesn't.

Therefore, it's important for you to incorporate a "confidence factor" in your ads.

Use testimonials not only for your product but also for your attention to customer satisfaction ... strengthen your guarantee ... if you say "free," give it free ... give the names of professional references or guarantors ... provide specifics, not generalities ... be honest.

################################

"MAIL ORDER CONNECTION"...the professional mail marketer's newsletter of effective response/profit techniques... is published monthly by Stilson & Stilson, P.O. Box 1075, Tarpon Springs, FL 34286-1075 [Phone: (813) 938-1555]. Your subscription investment is only $64 per year. Quotes with complete attribution are permitted...Reprints require written permission...Reproduction is prohibited. News releases & short articles/briefs of direct interest to mail marketers are invited. Comments from subscribers are welcome.

FIGURE 11-1 *Mail Order Connection* and consulting editors

consults with clients on the subject of list selection and writes many articles on the subject of mailing lists. In fact, his firm, Ed Burnett Consultants, Inc., proudly lays claim to *inventing* list management. Burnett invites customers to "Lean on me. I *like* to help."

Dr. Luther Brock, who likes to call himself "The Letter Doctor" (possibly inspired by the time before modern office copiers, offset printing, and other such do-it-yourself conveniences, when there were such businesses as "letter shops," which created direct-mail packages for customers), is a consultant and typewriter for hire. He was a professor teaching business communications at a Texas state university before he decided to set up his own shop.

Andrew Linick runs his own successful mail-order enterprise, as an advertising agency and consultant analyst to others. (He refers to himself as The Copyologist.) Among the principles he advocates for "tight, snappy copy" are the following (copyright by *Mail Order Connection* and abstracted from that publication by permission).

- Use short words instead of long ones.
- Toss out anything that borders on gobbledygook.
- Guard against the clichés that often slip in.
- Use similes or metaphors to show comparisons.
- Analogies also put zip in a manuscript.
- Appeal to the reader's senses.
- Use the active voice.
- Be specific.

Dr. William Cohen teaches marketing at California State University at Los Angeles, writes books on marketing, mail order, and related subjects, and was once a contracting official with the federal government (Department of Defense). Somehow, Cohen also manages to find time to engage in other, "outside" marketing activities.

Paul Alexander is what one might call an old timer in mail order, well known to a great many people who operate modest at-home mail-order enterprises, and although he conducts his own full-time mail-order business and writes regular columns on the subject, he manages to find time to help others too, acting as a consultant.

MAILING LISTS AND LIST MANAGEMENT

Initiates to direct-mail have some difficulty understanding just how to get mailing lists and how the mailing-list business functions. There are, in fact, three main points to be made about this subject:

1   Ordinarily, you *rent,* you do not buy mailing lists, and you pay rent for *each individual use* of the list, not for a period of time. (There are exceptions, but this is the general rule.)

2   Most lists are marketed by "list managers" and "list brokers," not by the owners of the lists. (Again, there are exceptions, as in the case of Dun & Brad-street, but that is a special case of one corporation owning a large number of companies, including the one that does most of the list marketing.)

3   Your own mailing lists, made up of customers and inquirers, should be care-fully built and maintained, as a valuable property, until they are voluminous enough to interest a special list manager/broker, who will market them for you, to your profit.

If you were to read such publications as *DM News* (19 West 21st Street, New York, NY 10010), a tabloid of the direct-marketing industry, you would find literally dozens of firms advertising their services as list managers. What this means is that such firms will accept the lists of owners and market them, for commissions. This means doing a great deal of work in computerizing them, arranging them so that they can be compiled in any of many kinds of order or selectively by categories, and keeping them up to date with necessary additions and deletions.

All sorts of companies who amass long lists of buyers and inquirers —especially buyers—turn these lists over to manager companies. The latter, in turn, broker—rent for commissions—lists of magazine subscribers, buyers from large mail-order houses, and many other lists to those who use them. In many cases, their clients are renting each others' lists!

As Craig Huey, head of Infomat, a list consultant, and consulting editor to *Mail Order Connection,* puts it in an issue of that publication, "Consider list rental income as a new source of untapped revenue readily available to you." Also: "List owners who opt for self-management often find their lists go without proper promotion."

Here are a few other sources for lists, a small sampling, in no particular order (position of a listing has no significance):

Ed Burnett Consultants, Inc.
2 Park Avenue
New York, NY 10016

Craig Huey, Infomat
25550 Hawthorne Boulevard
Torrance, CA 90505

List Services Corporation
890 Ethan Allen Highway
P.O. Box 2014
Ridgefield, CT 06877

Woodruff-Stevens & Associates, Inc.
40 East 34th Street
New York, NY 10016

NCR List Management
30 East 42nd Street
New York, NY 10017

American List Counsel, Inc.
88 Orchard Road
Princeton, NJ 08540

Names & Addresses, Inc.
3065 Woodhead Drive,
    Suite 101
Northbrook, IL 60062

JAMI List Management, Inc.
275 Forest Avenue
Paramus, NJ 07652

The Direct Media Group
90 South Ridge Street
Port Chester, NY 10573

Market Data Retrieval
Box 2630, Room 21
Westport, CT 06880

The Direct Response Corp.
601 Skokie Boulevard
Northbrook, IL 60062

Dunhill International List Co., Inc.
2430 West Oakland Park Boulevard
Fort Lauderdale, FL 33311

Edith Roman Associates, Inc.
875 Avenue of the Americas
New York, NY 10001

Dun's Marketing Services
3 Century Drive
Parsippany, NJ 07054

W. S. Ponton, Inc.
5149 Butler Street
Pittsburgh, PA 15201

Cahners Direct Marketing Service
1350 East Touhy Avenue
Des Plaines, IL 60018

DSI List Management
325 Hudson Street
New York, NY 10013

Zeller & Lettica, Inc.
15 East 26th Street
New York, NY 10010

One reason for so many list managers and brokers is that many tend to specialize in certain types of lists, while others generalize. There is one list broker, for example, who specializes in "outdoors" lists—lists of those who buy outdoors equipment. If you search hard enough—and reading *DM News* or other such publications helps—you can search out those who are strongest in whatever kinds of lists interest you: investors, entrepreneurs, professionals of various kinds, or whatever.

You may wish to find the managers or brokers for one or more specific lists, such as the list of subscribers to some periodical, if you believe that subscribers to that periodical are exactly the right prospects for you. You can, of course, write to the periodical itself, but you may also find your answers by reading such trade publications as *DM News.*

OTHER SERVICES

Not surprisingly, there are many other services available to those who wish to do business by mail. There are, for example, mailing houses who will do all or any part of your job for you, even to the extent of handling the printing of your newsletter or reports. Unless you are mailing on too small a scale to make it worthwhile for a large mailing house to handle your account, you can turn the whole job over to such an establishment.

The size, facilities available, and scope of services offered by such firms varies considerably, as you will soon discover if you check under the general heading of "Mailing" in your Yellow Pages directory. Some offer mailing only, some will handle printing and list rentals for you, and some have all these facilities—printing plant, mailing equipment, and list-management organization—in-house. That is, the mailing house may also be a list manager/broker or, vice versa; the organization that is primarily a list manager may also have a mailing service.

Advertising Agencies

The major advertising agencies work with the major advertisers—large corporations and other organizations that advertise heavily. The reason for this is quite simple: These agencies work on a discount, normally 15 percent, granted them when they buy space in publications and time on radio and TV. When the client is a heavy advertiser—buys a great deal of space and/or time—the discounts add up to enough dollars to enable the agency to provide the free services and yet turn a profit.

Of course, advertising agencies cannot afford to provide free services to small accounts because the total amount of space or time bought by small accounts simply is not large enough. The discounts just do not add up to enough dollars to make the account profitable. Small clients must therefore pay directly for any services they get, and there are some agencies who will work for fees from small clients; some *specialize* in so doing, in fact. In general, these will be the smaller agencies, often a one-room graphic arts shop. Those special consultants listed earlier can help you, probably, in finding such an agency, and some will themselves act as agencies for you. You can also usually find a large number of advertising agencies listed under the heading of *Advertising* in the Yellow Pages directory of any metropolitan area, many of them specializing in one way or another. (Many small agencies list themselves as advertising "counselors," suggesting that they are primarily consultants.)

Public Relations Services

There are a great many PR firms that, like advertising agencies and consultant firms, range in size from one person to large organizations. In fact, sometimes the same firm acts as both advertising agency and public relations agent or "counselor."

Again, the combination of the two basic services, advertising and PR, tends to appear more in the small to medium-sized firm than in the large firm. For public relations work, firms tend to charge time-based fees, so much per hour or day. However, there are some who will charge flat rates or fixed prices for specific tasks, such as writing releases and brochures.

Writing and Editing Support

In most metropolitan areas today you will find professional writers and editors listed under those headings in the Yellow Pages of the telephone directory. Again, these range in size from the self-employed person to the large organization. The former tend to the small jobs, not surprisingly, whereas the latter tend to the large projects, such as turning out technical manuals for major equipment systems.

Freelance writers who do custom work tend to generalize, and more than a few turn to PR work because a large portion of it is writing releases, brochures, newsletters, direct-mail packages, and other printed material. Some regard themselves as consultants, who will either advise you or will do the work, so you have a wide range of choices, especially with the small independent, who tends to be more flexible than the large organization.

COMPUTERS AND THE ADVICE BUSINESS

Personal computers—"personal" simply means that the computer is small enough and inexpensive enough to rest on one's desk or side table and be as much reserved to one's personal use as is a typewriter or dictating machine—are rapidly becoming an indispensable part of business life, if not of individual existence. As they grow in popularity they grow also in versatility; the number of things that a human being can do more efficiently than a computer is shrinking rather rapidly. This is as true for most advice-business ventures as it is for any other, and even more true for some ventures, such as any that produce a great deal of "paper" (proposals, bids, manuals, newsletters, etc.) or depend to a large extent on organizing, storing (filing), and retrieving data.

Computers have two types of application in advice businesses. On the one hand, computer systems can be used to perform the direct work of the business, such as preparing printed products which are sold (newsletters, manuals, and training programs, for example). Computers are also useful in performing the indirect or "overhead" work of administration and management, such as preparing proposals, maintaining mailing lists, and doing the accounting work.

Sometimes it is difficult to segregate the two classes of computer functions, as in the case of preparing materials used for both satisfying customer needs and operating the business—preparing newsletters, for example, which are used both for earning income directly and for marketing. However, the computer should be considered to be basically an overhead or indirect cost, both in its acquisition costs and in its operating and maintenance costs.

A FEW THINGS YOU SHOULD KNOW
ABOUT COMPUTERS

Most reports agree that word processing is by far the most popular use of personal computers, especially for small business offices and by self-employed professionals. That has led a great many manufacturers and dealers to offer their systems as word processors, and it has also led to a great misunderstanding of just what a word processor is. For one thing, it is not a machine. Although there is such a thing as a "dedicated" word processor, a computer designed to function primarily as a word processor, a word processor is, in literal terms, a software program, designed to be installed in a general-purpose computer. Said computer, however, can also accommodate a great many other programs, designed to do a great many other things: accounting, payrolls, inventory control, spreadsheet projections, mailing list maintenance, and literally thousands of other applications.

It is therefore not usually a wise plan to buy a system for one use only, since the same system, with other software, can do a great many other things for you. Just about everyone who is knowledgeable about computers and their applications agrees that when buying a computer, you must first decide on software and then buy the hardware that will accommodate the software you want. (That conventional wisdom is, however, beginning to change.)

The reason for this is that software is always written for specific kinds of hardware systems, because the computer industry enjoys relatively little standardization. For one thing, each computer must have an *operating system,* and the software programs must be written to be compatible with the operating system. So a program written for one operating system will not work in a computer using another kind of operating system. For example, Radio Shack TRS-80 computers use Radio Shack's TRS-DOS (Tandy/Radio Shack-Disk Operating System), and the Morrow Micro Decisions MD3 computer on which these words are written uses a CP/M (Control Program for Microcomputers) operating system.

STEPS IN SELECTING A SYSTEM

Considering all this, you should give some serious thought to your needs and the typical problems when buying a computer. (It will represent a sizable investment for even the most basic system bought for "serious" use.) In fact, these are the three main steps in deciding on a system to buy:

1 Decide what kinds of functions you want/need the system for: word processing, accounting, inventory, mailing, etc.
2 Research, survey, and decide on the software programs you will want/need to carry out these functions.
3 Select the hardware system that will accommodate all these programs.

At this time, CP/M is the most popular operating system for personal computers, even for some of the larger, "mainframe" computers, other than the three best known "names": Apple, Radio Shack, and IBM, which have their own operating systems. However, because they are so well known and so widely sold, an abundance of software has been developed for these computers, offering you an ample assortment from which to select the programs you want. On the other hand, if you are buying one of the lesser known brands (such as the Morrow, for example), you will be well advised to study the compatible software offered and make sure that you can satisfy all your needs from the supply.

That is a good argument for selecting a system using CP/M if you are not buying one of "the big three" of personal computers: CP/M normally offers you the widest choice of software (however PC-DOS and MS-DOS are catching up rapidly).

HOW TO RESEARCH/LEARN
ABOUT PERSONAL COMPUTERS

Many stories have already been told about how difficult it is to get effective help from retailers of computers. Unfortunately, a great many store salespeople either know little about computers in general, or can only cite the technical characteristics of each, without being able to translate these into terms of your own needs and concerns. I can confirm that from personal experience. I originally had some interest in the Radio Shack models, which appeared to me to be a good investment, but I got little help from any of the salespeople in any of the Radio Shack stores I visited, so I soon began to research the field by reading a number of articles intended for the average person, appearing in popular periodicals, such as *Money* magazine, *Popular Computing,* and *Personal Computing.* (These are by no means all; there are other popular publications about computers that do not require technical knowledge to understand.)

In addition to reading everything you can find on the subject—and even if some of it tends to be confusing or you think it "over your head" in the beginning, you will soon begin to understand a good bit of it—visit the stores and permit salespeople to demonstrate the models to you. (Again, you may be a bit confused, but just persevere and you will soon begin to grasp even that which at first seemed incomprehensible.) If you watch the advertising, you will probably learn of free seminars, which many dealers offer to help people begin to understand personal computers.

WHAT TO WATCH FOR AND CONSIDER

There are on the order of 150 manufacturers of computers (although many manufacture only one component and are really assemblers of computers from available off-the-shelf components) and probably well over 200 computer models. They vary widely in many ways. In externals, the chief variants to consider are the "soft" display and the keyboard. Most personal computers intended for serious business applications have CRT (cathode-ray tube) screens, similar to the picture tubes in TV sets. A few have black-and-white screens, but most have black and green (green phosphor), and a few have blue or amber phosphors. Many are available in full color—"RGB" (red-green-blue) tubes. Except for color, and green appears to be the most popular, the chief difference is size, with 12-inch screens (measured diagonally) the most popular, although there are 9-inch screens on many of the popular transportable types.

Do not be confused about that adjective "transportable." With the advent of so-called "pocket" computers, "notebook" computers, and other hand-held personal computers, it became necessary to distinguish between full-sized computers that were portable and those that were transportable. Hand-held computers are not considered here.

The keyboard is usually patterned after the standard typewriter keyboard, with the addition of a number of special function keys, although many also have what is referred to as a "numeric keypad." This is in addition to the number keys that appear at the top of the keyboard and are included as a convenience in using the system for mathematical work. (The numeric keypad is a redundant set of number keys laid out in the style of a calculator or adding machine keyboard.)

Keyboards vary widely in their "touch." Some are quite close to typewriters in their touch, whereas others are so different as to make their users feel somewhat uncomfortable. It is a good idea to actually try out the system you are considering to see whether you are satisfied with how the keyboard feels to you in actual use.

One final point about the externals of keyboards and computers. Some systems are monolithic—contained entirely in a single cabinet—whereas others are made up of several separate components as in some stereo systems. But even the monolithic systems often tend to have a detachable keyboard, and many people find this an indispensable convenience. In fact, probably the majority of personal computers today offer a separate or separable keyboard.

There is, finally, one more point to be made, an important one. Computer memory is like money: No matter how much you have, it is never enough; you always wish you had a bit more. There are two kinds of computer memory: the internal memory: RAM (random access memory) and storage, usually disks, most often 5¼-inch disks. You would probably be well advised to settle for nothing less than 64K RAM (that is approximately 64,000 *bytes,* each equivalent to a numeral or alphabetic character), since you can get that in many popularly priced systems today. Storage varies according to the number of disk drives and types of disks, but you should have two drives and the maximum disk capacity that you can get. Disks come in the following configurations:

- Single side, single density
- Single side, double density

- Double side, single density
- Double side, double density

The last-named offers the most storage capacity, as the adjectives suggest, and is preferred if you can get that kind of disk storage.

Today, you will find some computers offering 128K RAM and even more. (The next size is 256K.) However, if you have ample disk storage, several hundred K, at least, you can usually get along pretty well with 64K of RAM. But one more point: Some systems are expandable, and although they have 64K RAM, provide the means for increasing it. That is a good feature, too, if you can get it without sacrificing something else you want.

Among the most popular personal computers suitable for serious business use and relatively modest in cost are these:

- Tandy Corporation/Radio Shack TRS-80: various models
- IBM PC (and now the controversial PC*jr*)
- Apple (numerous models, including the recent Lisa and Macintosh)
- Kaypro (a portable)
- Texas Instruments

All of these have good reputations and appear to be solidly backed by stable companies who will be around to support their products with spare parts and maintenance facilities. There are a number of very inexpensive computers offered also, some of which require that you use your TV set or a terminal you purchase separately for a display. These are marginal, at best, for the work a small business will require of them and are not advanced much beyond the stage of being expensive toys, hardly suitable for serious business or professional applications. They will probably not stand up to the types of demands you will make of them.

Today a market in used computers is springing up, and there may be a dealer in used computers near you. Some of these are still relatively new and are machines traded in by users who were "trading up," buying larger systems. You may be able to save a good bit of money by exploring this possibility, or get a great deal more computer capacity than you otherwise might have been able to afford.

Index